POLITICAL PHILOSOPHY NOW

Political Philosophy Now is a series which deals with authors, topics and periods in political philosophy from the perspective of their relevance to current debates. The series presents a spread of subjects and points of view from various traditions which include European and New World debates in political philosophy.

For other titles in this series, please see the University of Wales Press website: *www.uwp.co.uk*

POLITICAL PHILOSOPHY NOW

Politics and Metaphysics in Kant

Edited by Sorin Baiasu, Sami Pihlström and Howard Williams

UNIVERSITY OF WALES PRESS • CARDIFF • 2011

www.uwp.co.uk

British Library Cataloguing-in-Publication Data
A catalogue record for this book is available from the British Library.

ISBN 978-0-7083-2377-9
e-ISBN 978-0-7083-2378-6

Printed by CPI Antony Rowe, Chippenham, Wiltshire

Contents

Abbreviations and References to Kant's Works

The following abbreviations for Kant's works are used throughout this book:

AA	Akademie-Ausgabe
Anth	Anthropologie in pragmatischer Hinsicht (*AA* 07)
GMS	Grundlegung zur Metaphysik der Sitten (*AA* 04)
IaG	Idee zu einer allgemeinen Geschichte in weltbürgerlicher Absicht (*AA* 08)
KpV	Kritik der praktischen Vernunft (*AA* 05)
KrV	Kritik der reinen Vernunft
KU	Kritik der Urteilskraft (*AA* 05)
Log	Logik (*AA* 09)
MpVT	Über das Mißlingen aller philosophischen Versuche in der Theodicee (*AA* 08)
MS	Die Metaphysik der Sitten (*AA* 06)
Prol	Prolegomena zu einer jeden künftigen Metaphysik (*AA* 04)
Refl	Reflexion (*AA* 14–19)
RGV	Die Religion innerhalb der Grenzen der bloßen Vernunft (*AA* 06)
TP	Über den Gemeinspruch: Das mag in der Theorie richtig sein, taugt aber nicht für die Praxis (*AA* 08)
V-Eth/Vigil	Vorlesungen über Ethik Vigilantius (*AA* 27)
V-MP/Dohna	Kant Metaphysik Dohna (*AA* 28)
V-MP-L2/Pölitz	Kant Metaphysik L2 (Pölitz, Original) (*AA* 28)
VRML	Über ein vermeintes Recht, aus Menschenliebe zu lügen (*AA* 08)
ZeF	Zum ewigen Frieden (*AA* 08)

In references, abbreviations will be followed by the volume and page number from Kant's *Gesammelte Schriften* (Berlin: vols

1–22, Preussische Akademie der Wissenschaften; vol. 23, Deutsche Akademie der Wissenschaften zu Berlin; vols 24–, Akademie der Wissenschaften zu Göttingen, 1900–). Translations used are listed under 'References' for each paper. References to the *Critique of Pure Reason* will follow the A (first edition), B (second edition) convention.

1 • Metaphysics and Politics in the Wake of Kant: The Project of a Critical Practical Philosophy

Sorin Baiasu, Sami Pihlström and Howard Williams

> Hence human reason, ever since it has been thinking or – rather – meditating, has never been able to dispense with a metaphysics, yet has nonetheless been unable to expound one that was sufficiently purified of everything extraneous. The idea of such a science is just as old as speculative human reason; and what reason is there that does not speculate, whether such a speculation be done in a scholastic or in a popular manner? (*KrV* A842/B870)

1. Historical contexts

The past three decades have witnessed the emergence, at the forefront of political thought, of several Kantian theories. Both the critical reaction to consequentialism inspired by Rawlsian constructivism and the universalism of more recent theories informed by Habermasian discourse ethics, for instance, trace their main sources of inspiration back to Kant's writings. Yet much of what is Kantian in contemporary theory is formulated with more or less strict caveats concerning Kant's metaphysics. These range from radical claims that theories of justice must be political, not metaphysical, to more cautious calls for replacing Kant's metaphysics with a less demanding ontology, such as one informed, for instance, by the relatively recent linguistic turn in philosophy.

What motivates such a reluctant attitude towards metaphysics among Kantian scholars? To begin with, the very meaning of metaphysics is deeply contested: depending on whether the word 'metaphysics' is used critically, approvingly or merely descriptively, and depending on what those who practise metaphysics take themselves to be doing, the word 'metaphysics' will refer to distinct and sometimes even contradictory areas of inquiry. Apart from the more technical difficulty of finding a definition of the term that would meet with at least general agreement, philosophers and especially political philosophers seem to have a reflex reaction of rejection and alarm at the very mention of the word 'metaphysics'.

For the wary amongst us, the term evokes fundamentalist conviction, obscurantist argumentation and deep complication. It is, therefore, no surprise that metaphysics has often not had a good press in moral and political philosophy and has not received entirely favourable treatment even amongst philosophers, such as Kant and Hegel, who have ended up espousing it. Amongst its critics, the name of metaphysics has conjured visions of abstract, over-complex and remote thinking that has lost touch with everyday reality.

The idea of metaphysics invites comparison with common sense. Metaphysics evokes a notion of thinking and meditating that is out of touch with the ordinary world and irrelevant to the active concerns of human life. Metaphysics is often seen as too close to religion and, in some instances, even identical to it. Many major metaphysicians such as Aquinas, Leibniz and Spinoza have presented systems that are coextensive with theology.

Metaphysics for these philosophers is a depiction of divine truth and reality. They have encouraged a view of metaphysics that is immense in its ambitions. At the same time as projecting a view of metaphysics that is coextensive with religion, they can sometimes be read as acquiescing in the aspiration of religious thinkers, in particular those belonging to the medieval tradition, to subordinate all philosophical reflection to religious conviction. This is an undesirable state of affairs, and in so far as metaphysics is understood as comprehending religious doctrine that ultimately relies on dogmatic pronouncements, it should be resisted.

However, we do not have to accept this image of metaphysics. It is legitimate for metaphysical reflection to include thinking about religious doctrine, but it need not be defined or limited by it. The problem is that historically, religion and metaphysics have overlapped considerably, and some have thought it appropriate that they should suffer the same fate in the modern period: decline.

The connection of metaphysics with religion can be traced back at least as far as Aristotle. It is usually suggested that the term 'metaphysics' was coined soon after Aristotle's death in 322 BC to describe 'a number of treatises' that 'were placed "immediately after the *Physics*"'.[1] These treatises contain inquiries of a fundamental kind, including a philosophical lexicon that seeks to define such terms as 'principle', 'cause', 'element' and 'nature'.

The treatises are speculative, adventurous and unfinished. They are immediately recognizable to us now as metaphysics, and they rest on a tripartite distinction which Aristotle makes between physics which 'studies mutable objects, and for the most part deals with essence as inseparable from matter', mathematics, as a similarly speculative science, and a speculative science, which is 'prior to both', deals with 'first causes' and 'must be eternal'. What is notable about this third speculative inquiry or 'the highest science' is that Aristotle depicts it as what is 'visible of the divine' or theology.[2] In Aristotle's description of metaphysics, then, there seems to be a marked overlap between the domain of philosophy and the domain of religion.

However, since Aristotle's first science or 'theology', which looks at concepts and being in general, is an open-ended inquiry in which no one true answer is claimed, it is arguably different from most religions which begin from what their adherents regard to be indubitable truths or articles of faith. The connection of religion with metaphysics is not necessarily one of identity. The subject matter of metaphysics and religion may in many respects be similar, but in Aristotle's schema religion can itself become the subject matter of metaphysics.

Aristotle opens up the possibility, on which Kant capitalizes, that metaphysics need not accord with conventional religion. Thus, although Aristotle gives an extraordinarily ambitious scope to metaphysics, inviting the most uninhibited speculation, he does not suggest that it should lead to dogmatism and zealotry: speculation must, to his mind, be guided by reason and argument. Indeed, his treatment of Plato's theory of Forms suggests an awareness of our epistemic limitations and proposes a methodology which takes these into account.[3]

Whatever our fears about the idea of metaphysics, anyone concerned with Kant's political philosophy – especially if we want to probe and understand what is most illuminating about this philosophy – has to attempt to come to grips with the idea of metaphysics and the hopes and limitations Kant associates with it.

An important point to make is that Kant himself had doubts about the desirability and feasibility of metaphysics as it was understood in his day. He does not give an indiscriminate stamp of approval to everything that is presented in the name of metaphysics. In his mature philosophical system he presents a critical metaphysics which is distinguished from a good deal of what had gone on in the name of metaphysics up to his time. Indeed, Kant regards what is innovative about his thinking as deriving from the new view of metaphysics that he has to propose.

For instance, Kant dramatically transforms Christian Wolff's account of knowledge and philosophy, an account that was quite influential in his time.[4] By introducing the distinction between the various faculties of mind, in particular between reason and the understanding, Kant relocates in the understanding the traditional concern with the identification of categories as the ultimate constituents of what exists. Wolff's general metaphysics thus becomes Kant's transcendental analytic.

Furthermore, Wolff's three branches of special metaphysics (which deal with the soul or mind, with the world as a whole and with God) are regarded by Kant as the province of reason and form the object of study of transcendental dialectic.[5] But Kant retains Wolff's view of the significance of practical philosophy and even regards practical reason as able to provide (moral) cognition of the soul, world and God, something which on Kant's account is impossible for theoretical philosophy.[6]

Hence Kant's new view of metaphysics is not a complete rejection of earlier systems, but derives rather from a debate and close engagement with those systems. Metaphysics he regards as necessary but complex and always potentially confusing. In undertaking the *Critique of Pure Reason* he was conscious that he had to clear away much of the rubble left by the decay of traditional metaphysics.

He depicts metaphysics in the opening pages of the work as the 'combat arena' of 'endless conflicts' aroused by the ambitions of pure reason. Reason faces its own defeat; where once metaphysics 'was called the *queen* of all the sciences', 'the tone in vogue in this era, however, has made it fashionable to treat her with total disdain' (*KrV* A: viii). Kant sees this defeat as deserved, even if for a while Locke's 'physiology of the human understanding' had seemed to provide a new confidence that her reputation might be saved.

There are two ever-present dangers that metaphysics faces: on the one hand it can transform itself into dogmatism, where one system claims to present all the answers to the problems raised by pure reason; on the other hand, it can transform itself into indifferentism, 'where all paths have been tried in vain' and the conclusion seems to be that there is no sure path for reason to follow. Kant regards these approaches as equally harmful. We should neither give in to sheer scepticism nor be blinded by the attractions of dogmatism. Thus at the very beginning of the *Critique of Pure Reason* he presents himself as an advocate of a revived but significantly more modest metaphysics. This metaphysics is empirically bound to appearances and gives in to the more ambitious demands of reason only in practical philosophy.

Kant, of course, was not alone in criticizing the assumptions of traditional metaphysics. A radical re-evaluation and critique of metaphysics has taken place over the last two centuries. This is noticeable not only in the empiricist tradition, from Hume to recent empiricists like Bas van Fraassen; it is visible also in the less unified direction initiated by Kant and continuing with Nietzsche and the classical pragmatists, among others, culminating in the downright scorn for metaphysics in logical positivism and ordinary language philosophy in the mid-twentieth century.

The debate over the role and status of metaphysics is, however, again highly relevant in contemporary philosophy. Especially in analytic philosophy, there seems to be growing interest in metaphysics, and the positivist declarations of the death of metaphysics can no longer be taken seriously. Leading thinkers have dedicated decades of work to metaphysics understood as a fundamental realm of philosophical inquiry, a 'category theory' largely in a realist, Aristotelian spirit.[7] These and other metaphysicians disagree, sometimes sharply, about what the basic ontological categories to be postulated *are* (for instance, whether there are universals, tropes, real modalities and so on), but they largely agree on what metaphysics is all about.

We have just said that the debate over the role and status of metaphysics is again highly relevant in contemporary philosophy. A qualification must, however, be made here. For metaphysics in this context is seen as an inquiry into the way the world is, independently of the mind of the inquirer and without any Kantian restrictions or worries about the unknowability of things in themselves. So there are indeed debates concerning the structure of the world understood, almost in a pre-Kantian sense, as what there is independently of human consciousness.[8] Unfortunately, however, this is usually taken to be an assumption, rather than a debatable claim in need of defence and with direct implications for the status and role of metaphysics.

The present-day 'Kantian' metaphysician, however, emphasizes our need to inquire into the ontological structure of the 'human world', of the world as it is for us, by contrast to an alleged noumenal, intelligible world of things 'in themselves'. The Kantian inquiry into the constitutive structure of the human world can, however, go beyond an account of how the world is. Thus, it is sometimes argued that when dealing with the world in any manner whatsoever (however theoretical), we always, at least implicitly, make ethical choices and engage in moral valuation.[9] For human reality is in fact constituted categorially from standpoints always already laden with ethical ideals and assumptions. Hence our human reality is itself deeply value-laden, as Hilary Putnam, among others, has suggested in his recent work attacking the fact/value dichotomy.[10]

The issue may go deeper than the uncontroversial idea that different metaphysical positions may have different ethical implications. The question may even be whether metaphysics, in the Kantian 'critical' sense, might not be *grounded* in ethical considerations, based on ethical premises. Metaphysics might not, then, even be *possible* without a tight connection to ethics. Accordingly, we cannot arrive at *any* understanding of reality as we humans experience it without paying due attention to the ways in which moral valuations and commitments are constituents of that same reality.

If these general questions concerning the relationships between metaphysics and ethics are raised in this way, then a similar investigation of the relationship between metaphysics and politics (and political philosophy in particular) becomes even more urgent.

2. Conceptual contexts

What kind of an angle should one then adopt in an investigation of this relationship? The question is difficult, since the various issues that the relationship between politics and metaphysics gives rise to are not easy to prioritize. As we have seen, the question of this relationship not only pertains directly to political issues of norm justification and legitimation but also raises various philosophical problems, from that concerning the very meaning of 'metaphysics' to that of the possibility of a metaphysics-free political philosophy.

In principle, in so far as practical – that is, ethical and political – philosophy is primarily concerned with the *justification* of normative standards of action, of rules about what we *ought* to do, philosophers are bound to rely on arguments which go beyond a mere description of what happens in the world: the focus is on (ethically and politically) *right* actions, actions which *ought* to be done, rather than on what *is* usually done or what *usually* happens. This implies that practical philosophers will have to advance arguments which are correct for all and, moreover, which go significantly beyond what we can describe on the basis of our sense experience.

While reliance on the rules of traditional logic may indeed provide validity without recourse to sense perception, the resulting arguments seem to be nothing more than formal claims, which can only clarify an issue and eliminate any implicit inconsistencies. To be sure, clarification is very important and helpful for evaluation of the rightness of the rules of action; yet such a process is not sufficient to justify the correctness of the rules concerning what we ought to do, since ethically or politically correct rules may be as semantically clear and logically consistent as those which are morally objectionable.

There seems to be nothing particularly unclear, as far as semantics is concerned, about, say, the political decisions of certain totalitarian communist regimes or of other undemocratic states. Yet at least some of these decisions are obviously wrong. Similarly, I may make sure that an accurate description of such decisions contains no logical contradiction, but this only guarantees that the description is not contradictory and can refer to some decision or action; it cannot guarantee that the action is not wrong.[11]

It is therefore doubtful that anything morally substantive can be discovered by following this method of clarification, which is confined to the tasks of making explicit and spelling out already existing content. Since metaphysics is the discipline which claims to be able to make substantive claims independently of sense experience, it is usually considered to be a discipline which relies on the dogmatic assertion of certain (unjustifiable) claims.

For instance, certain claims about how we ought to live our lives will be acceptable only to those who adopt the particular cultural perspective from which the claims are being made. But then, even within the same cultural tradition, the arguments concerning the validity of certain rules may seem little more than dogmatic pronouncements, at best accompanied by various 'metaphysical' justifications: religious, cultural-philosophical or mythological. Given the plurality of the views, perspectives and experiences that people in modern liberal democracies make manifest, the outcome will be an almost permanent conflict of normative claims. Moreover, the appeal to dogmatic adjudication through such a metaphysics cannot be a good basis for conflict resolution, for it is impossible to justify such an adjudication as *correct for all.*

We therefore face a dilemma: either we try to justify such rules as right on the basis of arguments which aim to be correct for all, or we try to explain them further by clarifying the cultural contexts in which such rules are in place. In the first case, we must go beyond simple description of how such rules have been put into practice, beyond the mere clarification of their meaning and beyond the 'argument' that they are the rules of tradition. Hence nothing but a dogmatic postulation of the rules seems to remain available.

In the second case, one perhaps avoids this kind of dogmatism, but one ends up instead with a description and clarification of the meaning of the rules and hence fails to explain why such clearly presented rules are right rather than wrong. This approach falls short of providing a *justification* for the rules;[12] unless a person already accepts these rules as right, there is nothing further which can decide her to accept them.[13]

It is for this reason that recent Kantian philosophers like John Rawls, Jürgen Habermas or Karl-Otto Apel have tried, each in his own distinctive way, to make explicit the relationship between practical philosophy and metaphysics. This is certainly a necessary move, which echoes Kant's distinction between dogmatic and critical metaphysics and his warning that dogmatic metaphysics makes speculative claims which go beyond our cognitive capacities.

Kant also suggested the possibility of a *sui generis* (transcendental) logical discipline, which would be able to provide substantive arguments without relying on sense experience. Since it is not simply the result of dogmatic adjudication, such a discipline seems able to resolve the dilemma presented above, in particular the problem of finding a standard of adjudication which would enable us to evaluate the rightness of conflicting claims; however, since Kant developed his view of a transcendental logic in his theoretical philosophy, it would also be necessary to identify a parallel approach in his practical philosophy.

The main assumption which is required to get the argument for a discipline like transcendental logic going is that not all our concepts should be completely reducible to experience; in other words, the empiricist claim that we derive all our concepts from experience by abstraction and generalization would have to be reduced in scope to allow also for some non-empirical concepts. Following Kant, general logic deals with the laws of thinking about objects in general without concern for the kind of objects to which judgements refer. The formal validity of a syllogism, for instance, will be determined irrespective of how the variables in the argument are realized (*KrV* A55/B79–A56/B80).

Take the following inference: 'All Xs are *a*; A is X; hence, A is *a*.' The validity of the argument does not vary with the content of the variables X, A and *a*. Whether we replace the set with (human beings, Socrates and mortal) or (planets, Venus and green) is not relevant for what Kant calls 'general logic' (*KrV* A52/B76). Hence, while general logic does assume a reference to objects of cognition, these objects are only specified as objects in general, their particular features being logically irrelevant.

By contrast, the idea of a transcendental logic is that of a discipline which studies the relationship between judgements in so far as these employ concepts which are not empirical (and hence derived from the experience of certain objects) but a priori and, hence, capable of referring a priori to objects of experience and capable of saying something correct about these objects. This means that transcendental logic will investigate laws which regulate relationships between our judgements, in so far as they can say something a priori about the world. These laws will be more substantive than the laws of general logic and, at the same time, have a necessary character.

The link with practical philosophy can be established, at least prima facie, relatively easily, since Kant talks about the a priori, non-empirical concepts and the object of (pure) practical reason.

Hence, the idea of a discipline which investigates the relationships between judgements which employ non-empirical practical concepts is precisely that of a transcendental logic in the practical domain, and the result should be more substantive than that of general logic while at the same time presenting the necessary character of the laws of general logic.

In fact, in the Preface to the *Groundwork*, Kant draws two distinctions that may help to illuminate our argument. The first is the distinction between universal practical philosophy and metaphysics of morals, and the second between general logic and transcendental philosophy. Kant claims that, just as general logic investigates the laws of thinking as such, universal practical philosophy explores the laws of willing as such. By contrast, just as transcendental philosophy investigates the laws of pure thinking or of the thinking whereby objects are known a priori, metaphysics of morals examines the laws of a will determined by a priori, non-empirical principles (*GMS* 4: 390–1). We can in this way draw an analogy between transcendental logic and metaphysics of morals. The former has the role of identifying the a priori laws which constitute experience and, hence, through which objects of experience can be known a priori. Analogically the latter can be seen as playing the role of a practical transcendental logic, which investigates those laws of a will which have a constitutive role in practical judgement and, hence, make practical cognition possible.

To be sure, more needs to be done to spell out this idea of a metaphysics of morals as a practical transcendental logic, but despite the ongoing nature of the endeavour, the analogy points clearly to a possible solution to the dilemma presented above. Recall the dilemma: either we try to justify rules as right on the basis of arguments which aim to be correct for all or we try to explain them further by clarifying the cultural contexts in which such rules are in place; the first alternative requires us to do more than the second allows and suggests that we need to have recourse to a dogmatic assertion of rules; the second alternative avoids such dogmatism, but falls short of providing a justification of the rules. Hence, the question is that of providing a substantive and necessary standard of action which is non-dogmatic. For recall the assumption which was needed for the notion of a transcendental logic to be possible: that the empiricist claim that all concepts are reducible to experience (together with activities of abstraction and generalization) be weakened in order to admit some concepts which are of a non-empirical origin.

Now, even if the plausibility of this assumption is not considered sufficient, and even if the objection that the notion of an a priori concept is dogmatic is again raised, one can still advance the following argument. Given the difference between theoretical and practical philosophy and, hence, given the normative character of practical rules, the notion of an a priori concept in practical philosophy is easier to justify than that of an a priori concept in theoretical philosophy, since justification in practical philosophy must go beyond what we can describe merely on the basis of sense experience or of the rules of general logic.

But can such a justification be genuinely non-dogmatic? Such a question points to a potentially rich area of further investigation. To be sure, transcendental idealism is metaphysical for Kant and the task is to identify the type of metaphysics it incorporates and the extent to which this is legitimate. In the context of current debates, the more problematic aspect is not simply the a priori, non-empirical character of the concepts of practical reason; rather, it is their constitutive character in the determination of the object of practical reason which must be defended as legitimate. Nonetheless, we think the discussion above offers at least some ammunition for the defender of the non-dogmatic character of such a transcendental or critical practical philosophy.

We regard the project of a critical philosophy as one concerned with transcendental idealism. The transcendental idealist character of critical philosophy refers to the attempt this project makes to steer a path between (and hence to avoid the traditional problems of) realism and idealism, as well as rationalism and empiricism. There are, of course, various accounts of transcendental idealism.[14] Distinguishing between those which are, in some sense, accurate (or correct or convincing) and those which are not would not be an easy task. One test should perhaps be accepted here, namely that an account which regards transcendental idealism as dogmatic cannot be seen as accurate (or correct or convincing) without further qualification and discussion, especially given the importance, for Kant, of justification as opposed to uncritical acceptance of existing norms and authorities.

3. Texts

The conceptual and philosophical character of the problems presented in the previous section in relation to Kant's project of a critical philosophy goes some way towards explaining the relevance of Kant's thought for current debates. Another important consideration has to do with the concrete political problems with which such an account of justification has the potential to deal. In the current context of pluralism and diversity, the main advantage of such a Kantian project is that, if successful, it can offer an account of moral objectivity and a corresponding strategy of adjudication on moral conflicts without a commitment to moral realism.[15]

Moreover, such an account would not simply reduce moral objectivity to intersubjectivity. As a result, apart from sidestepping problems of demandingness created by most versions of moral realism, this account would also avoid difficulties which are usually associated with conceptions of justification based on modus vivendi, status quo or other versions of agonal politics. At the same time, this account offers a view of justification which is also distinct from many current contractarian, constructivist and discourse ethics conceptions.

The discussion in the previous two sections foreshadows some of the arguments and debates that have to be explored in relation to the question of the relationship between metaphysics and politics in Kant. The essays in this volume focus precisely on these arguments and debates, and make in this way an important contribution to the literature in the area.[16] In fact, given that only very few studies have addressed this issue so far, this volume opens up an area of research which is not only philosophically intriguing, but which also has implications for highly concrete and urgent contemporary political issues.[17] Moreover, taken together, the papers in this volume can be seen as offering the sketch of a research programme on the nature of critical practical philosophy.

To begin with, on Kenneth Westphal's account, Kant adopts a constructivist philosophical method, which is based on core principles of rational justification. Such principles do not rely on the assumptions of transcendental idealism, and yet are able to fulfil their function: that of justifying practical (moral and political) claims. Thus, according to Westphal, Kant's justificatory strategy needs only to make appeal to a notion of justification, which requires that sufficient reasons be provided in order for all parties consistently to be able to adopt or follow the same principle in thought or action.

Such a notion of justification relies only on a view of reason as autonomous, a view which avoids naturalism (and hence is properly normative) and at the same time does not involve an appeal to transcendent or even transcendental authorities. While Kant's systematic approach may suggest that metaphysics is a necessary assumption for practical philosophy on Westphal's view, contemporary Kantians like Onora O'Neill can defend and implement constructivism without appeal to transcendental idealism.

Even though it represents one of the most distinctive and significant conceptions of justification in contemporary literature, Onora O'Neill's position is clearly influenced by John Rawls's. Yet, as Alyssa Bernstein argues in her contribution to the volume, while Rawls explicitly made claims for the exclusion of metaphysics from political theory, he only referred to a narrow sense of 'metaphysics'. Hence, while the Rawlsian constructivist method may well reject certain types of metaphysical claim, it does not reject metaphysics altogether and may even rely on some assumptions of a metaphysical nature. Thus Rawls's Kantian constructivism may be one way of sustaining an explicitly Kantian metaphysics in practical philosophy.

In his contribution, Sami Pihlström defends the thesis that ethics and (possibly) political philosophy are entangled with transcendental idealism, in a relationship which needs further elaboration but which cannot be ignored. Interestingly, the context of his discussion complements that of the previous papers. Thus, rather than focusing on debates sparked by the work of philosophers such as Rawls and O'Neill, he starts from the thought of Ludwig Wittgenstein and Emmanuel Levinas. He reads them as Kantian philosophers and explores the ways in which Kant's view on the metaphysical status of practical reason paved the way for the views of these two important twentieth-century philosophers.

It seems evident, given the nature of Kant's critical philosophy, that he thinks that his theoretical philosophy is linked in important respects to his moral or practical (ethical and political) philosophy. He sometimes elaborates at fair length on the differences between his theoretical and his practical philosophy (for instance, *KrV*

A795/B823–A831/B859; *KpV* 5:119–21 or 5:134–41). Yet many questions remain unanswered and unclear in this respect. In particular, it is unclear how his critical metaphysics will function in the context of ethics and political philosophy.

Perhaps the best way to develop this aspect of Kant's philosophy further is by trying to identify areas in his practical philosophy where significant similarities with theoretical philosophy can be identified. By examining how his critical philosophy is deployed in the theoretical context, an appropriate starting point for a similar practical account can be provided. Several chapters in this volume adopt this strategy.

According to Lucas Thorpe, for example, there is at least one strong connection we can draw between Kant's theoretical philosophy, ethics and political philosophy. Thus, he argues that Kant's ethical ideal of the kingdom of ends is essentially the same as both his political ideal of a community of individuals governed by juridical laws and his theoretical ideal of an intelligible world. Here Thorpe draws on the normative character of the ideals, which move beyond the simple description of the world towards the prescription of states of affairs to be realized.

Tatiana Patrone's chapter focuses more specifically on several similarities between Kant's key concepts of political theory and his ideas of reason in the theoretical philosophy, starting with their function as representations of the unconditional. The claim she defends is that a regulative function is performed not only by Kant's ideas of reason in the theoretical domain, but also by fundamental concepts of political philosophy in the practical domain. Specifically, she argues that just as ideas of theoretical reason unify cognitions formed through the contribution of the concepts of the understanding, concepts of the unconditional public right bring into systematic unity concepts of private right, thus making possible their coherent application to the world.

In her contribution, Lea Ypi also starts from Kant's *Critique of Pure Reason*; not, however, from the Dialectic chapter, but from the Methodology section, more precisely the 'Architectonic of Pure Reason'. This part of the first *Critique* deserves much more attention than Kantian scholars usually pay it, and Ypi tries to address this concern at least in part. Her assumption is that in the attempt to link the systematic unity in science with the imperative of promoting the complete good, as presented in the second

Critique, Kant relies on teleological principles. The way in which these principles are deduced in the first *Critique* leads to tensions in their use in the theoretical and practical domains, and the aim of the paper is to illuminate these tensions and, thus, reconstruct the background which made possible Kant's discussion of teleology in the third *Critique*.

Yet equally pertinently, Katerina Deligiorgi emphasizes the role of moral experience in practical philosophy, in particular in the application of practical principles. Her contribution to the volume explores the role of moral experience in Kant's ethics and practical philosophy more generally. This brings into discussion the analogy between practical philosophy and theoretical philosophy with particular reference to an aspect of the latter which seems to have no place in a practical theory, namely sensibility. Deligiorgi agrees that an appropriate account of the justification of practical principles along the Kantian lines will have to explain the link to moral law. But, once justified, these principles can be applied if some reference to specific, concrete circumstances is possible. Here, then, at least an analogy with experience in theoretical philosophy would be useful.

An identification of the nature and structure of Kant's practical philosophy will have to go beyond an exploration of the analogy with theoretical philosophy and focus also on what is specific to Kant's practical philosophy. Three of the chapters of this volume do precisely this. Thus, in his article, Sorin Baiasu focuses on the unconditional character of practical principles. He explores the way in which we can hope to be able to justify in a Kantian manner particular principles of action as unconditional. More exactly, the question he raises is how to justify these principles on the basis of the supreme principle of practical reason, the moral law.

On Baiasu's account, ethicists and political philosophers who would like to account for the unconditional character of practical principles would do well to acknowledge the ultimate irreducibility of these principles to principles of logic or empirical science, although, of course, such principles of logic and science have an important role to play in practical philosophy. An appropriate account, he claims, will have to devise a justification which preserves the specific, fundamentally practical nature of Kant's practical philosophy. Yet, he goes on to claim, there are sufficient resources in Kant for a reconstruction of such an account of practical justification, and he offers an outline of such an account.

Garrath Williams's argument centres on the issue of accounting for the specific normativity of practical philosophy and, in particular, philosophy of responsibility. More exactly, given that this type of normativity makes necessary arguments which go beyond a mere description based on sense perception, he calls normative practical principles 'intelligible facts'. He explores the nature of these facts, firstly by making explicit their conventional, constructed character, and secondly by examining their necessary, unconditional nature. This suggests that a distinction must be drawn between the conditional elements of moral or political principles and their unconditional aspects. Garrath Williams anchors the latter in the mutual critique that arises when we are regarded as authors of, and hence as responsible for, our thoughts and actions.

In his contribution, Howard Williams examines the specifically practical character of Kant's political philosophy by dint of a direct investigation of concrete and specific issues, such as property, the state and war. Williams's starting-point is still an analogy with Kant's theoretical philosophy; he focuses not only on the ideas of pure theoretical reason (whether or not mediated by principles of the faculty of judgement), but also on synthetic a priori propositions of practical reason. From this analogy, he moves on to an examination of the nature of the principles of Kant's political thought which regulate interpersonal relationships involved in issues of property, political statehood and war. He also aims to identify the type of metaphysics these principles presuppose, and he examines the extent to which this use of metaphysics can be justified and sustained in the current philosophical and political context.

The final two contributions examine even more applied issues in Kant's political philosophy with a view to illuminating the nature of Kant's practical philosophy more generally. According to Sharon Anderson-Gold, a Kantian framework for the rightfulness of national law requires a cosmopolitan framework of rights. Her contribution therefore explores the fundamental role played by a universal and unconditional set of rules in the grounding of more contingent and constructed legal frameworks, like that specific to a nation. Of course, the assumption here is not simply that such a universal and unconditional set of rules, which would constitute a cosmopolitan framework of rights, can be taken for granted and directly applied whenever it seems to be denied by national laws.

Oliver Eberl's contribution focuses precisely on this issue and on the currently dominant interpretations of Kant's response. He shows that these interpretations make a case for a right to regime change in rogue states by assuming the existence of a rightful order of international relations which is threatened by such states. In fact, Eberl argues, Kant only allows for a right to regime change as a preventive, collective self-defence measure under conditions of a state of nature. This right is a provisional one, part of a decentralized system of collective security similar to that stipulated in the Charter of the United Nations. Hence, Kant cannot be regarded as justifying a unilaterally performed regime change in a rogue state with the argument that it would serve universal and unconditional interests.

4. Further questions

This overview of the next twelve chapters of this volume brings into relief the significance of four sets of issues which are relevant for the project of a Kantian, critical practical philosophy. The first set of issues concerns the very nature of transcendental idealism, a position with epistemological and (even if only negatively) metaphysical implications, which may be required for an appropriate account of justification in conditions of pluralism and diversity.

The second set of issues centres on the relationship between Kant's theoretical and practical philosophies and, more generally, between an account of what happens in the world and an account of what ought to happen. Although Kant asserts a certain priority of practical over theoretical reason, in fact the idea of a critical metaphysics is developed by Kant in his theoretical philosophy; indeed, its development in the practical domain sometimes gives the impression that what Kant is doing is merely drawing the implications for the practical domain of the theory already formulated in the theoretical domain.

The third set of issues concerns more specifically a critical practical philosophy, in particular those aspects which refer to the justification of moral and political unconditional standards. While there are important parallels to be drawn between a Kantian theoretical and a Kantian practical critical philosophy, unless a distinct character is presented for each of these an appropriate account of the justification of *practical* standards cannot be articulated.

Finally, once such an account is formulated or at least once an approach to the issue of practical justification is identified, the question is how this account of approach can be applied – not only for the actual identification of specific justified standards, but for the application of justified standards to concrete circumstances.

In the context of the arguments of this volume, these sets of issues suggest several specific questions and areas of inquiry. As we have seen, Westphal's claim that Kant adopts a constructivist method of justification which can be defended without appeal to transcendental idealism seems to conflict strongly with Pihlström's claim that ethics and political philosophy are strongly connected with transcendental idealism. Yet any such conflict will depend on how we understand transcendental idealism, and also on how the relationship between moral (ethical and political) philosophy on the one hand and constructivism on the other is drawn.[18]

Moreover, Westphal's view seems to be in tension with Bernstein's claim that Rawlsian constructivism need not reject metaphysics altogether and may even rely on certain metaphysical aspects. This again raises questions about the nature of transcendental idealism and its relationship to metaphysics; but it also raises questions about what exactly we should take 'metaphysics' to refer to and mean. Furthermore, a distinction seems useful here between Kant's view of justification in moral philosophy and the constructivist account of justification.

An examination of the relationship between Kant's theoretical and practical philosophies therefore seems useful not only in order to determine the extent to which transcendental idealism, so important for Kant's theoretical philosophy, is to be found also in his practical philosophy, but also to determine the extent to which Kant's moral theory is in fact ultimately constructivist. As we have seen, the papers by Thorpe, Patrone and Ypi establish links between Kant's theoretical and practical philosophies with regard to the ideas of reason. Deligiorgi draws parallels more generally between sense experience and moral experience, and explores the role of moral 'experience' in the application of justified moral principles.

Such investigations of the links between the theoretical and practical domain suggest issues for research, issues which might, for instance, focus on the extent to which important elements of theoretical philosophy have a similarly important role in practical philosophy and vice versa. Examples here would concern the constitutive function of certain elements of mind (or reason, in the general sense), the condition of universality and universalizability, the normative force of theoretical and practical claims, the very status of the elements of the a priori structure of mind or of the self as the transcendental condition of these elements. In short, the general question which can be explored further in this respect refers to the aspects of Kant's theoretical philosophy which are relevant for his practical (moral and political) philosophy.

Another important question, which can be associated with the third set of issues mentioned above, refers to the specifically practical character of Kant's practical philosophy and to an appropriate account of practical justification. The papers by Baiasu, Garrath Williams and Howard Williams place themselves more directly in the practical domain and try to offer answers to aspects of this general question. To be sure, in this way, these papers will also point to significant differences between Kant's theoretical and practical philosophies, but they go beyond this point and try to present accounts respectively of practical justification, normativity and apriority. These connect with the previous two sets of issues mentioned above, but they represent a series of distinct questions focused more precisely on the nature of Kant's practical philosophy. One important question would be whether, apart from the standard of truthfulness discussed in Baiasu's text, there are other standards which function as a priori structures of practical reason and are constitutive of practical judgement.

A further topic is suggested by Garrath Williams's study of authorship and responsibility, which is a rich source of questions and issues for further exploration, including the nature of 'the intelligible' and the prospects for Kantian constructivism. Furthermore, the question of synthetic a priori practical propositions raised by Howard Williams in relation to very concrete political issues, such as property, the state or war, can be pursued further along two directions of inquiry. Thus, one may explore other similar concrete issues, or one may investigate more deeply the nature of the practical synthetic a priori.

Finally, the question of the application of Kant's practical philosophy to specific political issues such as those explored by Anderson-Gold and Eberl in their contributions to this volume suggests, first of all, further research into the very idea of application and the extent to which it is even appropriate to talk in this way in the context of Kant's critical philosophy. Moreover, here, issues of 'application' are interrelated with questions concerning judgement, and a discussion of this aspect of Kant's practical philosophy in connection with his third *Critique* would be another fruitful topic for the project of a critical practical philosophy. One can, of course, also fruitfully explore other specific political issues discussed by Kant and then draw the implications for current circumstances and situations.

5. Critical practical philosophy: a project

This chapter has introduced the idea of a critical practical philosophy, which would be able to offer an appropriate account of justification of unconditional ethical and political standards in conditions of pluralism and diversity, but without the strong metaphysical commitments of moral realism.[19] The idea of such a critical practical philosophy is the main result of the attempt in this volume to approach the question of metaphysics and politics in Kant in a way which would be relevant for various urgent issues we are facing today.

We began this chapter with an overview of some aspects of the history of metaphysics and its relationship to the issue of ethical and political justification. The main aim there was to illuminate the motivations behind the reluctant attitude seen in the way current moral philosophers relate to metaphysics. While metaphysics has sometimes been associated with theology and with a dogmatic argumentative style, we have seen that this association was brought into question very early on and was systematically undermined by Kant and post-Kantians.

In the second section, we have seen that this dominant attitude of reluctance towards metaphysics makes it difficult for moral philosophers to offer an appropriate account of ethical and political justification in the current context of pluralism and diversity. In fact, it turns out that an indiscriminate rejection of metaphysics is as detrimental as an indiscriminate acceptance.

To be sure, a reluctant attitude towards metaphysics may still be motivated by its traditional identification with theology. This attitude is, of course, compatible with the current revival of some traditional forms of metaphysics, which is usually associated with a commitment to knowledge through sciences or even to scientism. In general, as Kant says in the epigraph to this chapter, additional reasons for such a reluctant attitude can be found in our constant tendency to overstep the limits of our epistemic capacities and to make speculative claims, claims which, as such, cannot be justified. This applies equally well to a metaphysics related to theology or scientism.

However, the implication is a critical attitude towards metaphysics, not one of complete rejection. Hence, the project of a critical practical philosophy is that of an account of ethical and political justification and normativity which proceeds precisely from the attempt to identify the limits of our epistemic practical capacities, and thus to draw a line between what can be known and justified about morality – as well as what can be known or justified morally – and what cannot. Hence, this will also be a line dividing what is morally permissible from what is morally impermissible.

We regard this project as distinctive in the current philosophical landscape. So another potentially fruitful area for research would centre on the relationships between this project and other similar contemporary projects, such as discourse ethics, constructivism, contractarianism or pragmatist moral and political philosophy. It may not be immediately clear to what extent this project does anything more than develop an account of justification and normativity already present in Kant. However, our aim is not to formulate, come what may, a *new* project; we are rather interested in an account which is able to tackle some important ethical and political issues that confront us today. Whether this project turns out to be more or less Kantian is a secondary issue. What is clear so far is that Kant's texts offer an important source of inspiration for the project and an important starting point for the formulation and development of those elements that Kant was not able to discuss. We share his view that metaphysics – as a study 'after physics' which is not reducible to empirical claims and conceptual analysis – has a limited yet significant role to play in moral and political philosophy. This limited role has an objectivating function that offers us knowledge of some of the basic preconditions for effective social and political action.[20]

Notes

1 John Warrington, 'Editor's Introduction', in Aristotle, *Metaphysics*, ed. and trans. J. Warringon (London: Dent, 1961), viii.

2 Aristotle, *Metaphysics*, p. 154.

3 See, for instance, the Kantian interpretation of Aristotle's method in epistemology in Martha Nussbaum, *The Fragility of Goodness: Luck and Ethics in Greek Tragedy and Philosophy*, rev. edn (Cambridge: Cambridge University Press, 2001), pp. 240–63.

4 For instance, in Christian Wolff, *Vernünfftige Gedancken von Gott, der Welt und der Seele des Menschen, auch allen Dingen überhaupt* (*Deutsche Metaphysik*), ed. C. Corr, in *Gesammelte Werke*, ed. J. École, H. W. Arndt, C. Corr, J. E. Hoffmann and M. Thomann, vol. 2. (Hildesheim: Georg Olms, 1965).

5 See Etienne Gilson, *Being and Some Philosophers*, second edn (Toronto: Pontifical Institute of Mediaeval Studies, 1952).

6 Of course, Kant's practical philosophy is quite distinct from Wolff's universal practical philosophy, as Kant himself points out (*GMS* 4: 390–1).

7 E. J. Lowe, *The Possibility of Metaphysics: Substance, Identity and Time* (Oxford: Clarendon Press, 1998); David Lewis, *Papers in Metaphysics and Epistemology* (Cambridge: Cambridge University Press, 2001); Michael Loux, *Metaphysics: a Contemporary Introduction*, rev. edn (London and New York: Routledge, 2002); David Armstrong, *Truth and Truthmakers* (Cambridge: Cambridge University Press, 2004).

8 From a Kantian perspective, this view is a form of transcendental realism, a view that Kant systematically challenges in his critical works.

9 A contemporary Kantian might even echo William James's pragmatism, arguing that in *every* genuinely metaphysical dispute, some practical issue is, however remotely, involved: see James, *Pragmatism: a New Name for Some Old Ways of Thinking*, ed. F. H. Burkhardt, F. Bowers and I. K. Skrupskelis (Cambridge, MA: Harvard University Press, 1975), chs 2–3. In some situations of metaphysical reflection, the ethical aspects are, of course, less relevant than in others. For example, it is easier to make the case for the ethical value-ladenness of the metaphysics of personhood (e.g. personal identity) than of the issue of universals vs. tropes. Piecemeal analysis and careful attention to specific issues in relation to such controversies is needed. The main point here is that we may not be able categorically to disconnect metaphysical disputes from ethical considerations.

10 Hilary Putnam, *The Collapse of the Fact/Value Dichotomy and Other Essays* (Cambridge MA: Harvard University Press, 2002); *Ethics without Ontology* (Cambridge, MA: Harvard University Press, 2004).

11 Of course, here we refer to formal logic and to contradictions of the type A and non-A. For Kantians claim that morally impermissible principles and actions are contradictory in some sense,and some even claim in a 'logical' sense. Yet, most often, this does not mean a contradiction in formal logic. See, for instance, the distinction between logical, practical and teleological contradictions in Christine Korsgaard, 'Kant's Formula of the Universal Law', in *Creating the Kingdom of Ends* (Cambridge: Cambridge University Press, 1996). See also the recent discussion of universalizability in Kant and of the various types of contradiction used in the literature in Mark Timmons, 'The categorical imperative and universalizability', in C. Horn and D. Schoenecker (eds), *Kant's* Groundwork of the Metaphysics of Morals: *New Interpretations* (Berlin: De Gruyter, 2006).

12 The assumption here is that providing a justification for rules is a possible and worthwhile enterprise. This may, however, be contested. From the perspective of Richard Rorty's 'ethnocentrism', for instance, justification assumes at least one starting point on which parties in dispute should agree on, and one rule that they should accept and on the basis of which implications can then be formulated. Yet on Rorty's account, there is no such starting point and no such rule. Even the principle of non-contradiction is regarded as culturally specific and in principle revisable. Hence, on this account, the task is to persuade others of the practical value of such a rule and of the acceptability of such a starting point, rather than to try to justify them: see Rorty, *Philosophy and Social Hope* (London: Penguin, 1999); *Philosophy as Cultural Politics* (Cambridge: Cambridge University Press, 2007). On the meta-philosophical and epistemological underpinnings of Rorty's position, see for instance James Tartaglia, *Rorty and the Mirror of Nature* (London: Routledge, 2007). Two things are worth mentioning here. First, Rorty's account does not presuppose that any means by which others can be persuaded are to be used; so he wants to maintain a distinction between violent force and persuasion, but he does not think that this can be achieved by reference to some idea of rational justification. Secondly, however, it is unclear whether his account is able to offer such a distinction between persuasion and violent force.

13 The exception here seems to be the situation where a person disagrees with a certain rule and agrees after the rule is clarified. But, in fact, this is not at all an exception. The reason why the rule is now accepted is that the agent realizes that it is the same as a rule she already considered as right. The process of clarification does not add anything to the rule; it only helps the agent understand it.

14 On this, see the discussion in Section 4 below, as well as n. 14.

15 Moral realism is understood here by analogy with contemporary metaphysical realism, as discussed in Section 2 above. Moral realism would thus imply a metaphysical claim concerning the existence, independently from the mind, of some moral standards. Moreover, it would imply an epistemological claim concerning the possibility for us of discovering or acquiring knowledge of these standards as they are independently from us. There are, however, versions of moral realism which put emphasis on the epistemological, rather than the metaphysical, claim. It remains an open question whether they are appropriately considered as versions of moral realism, rather than of, say, moral cognitivism. The general question of what moral realism refers to also remains open. We would also like to point out that our intention here is not to deny the persuasiveness of an interpretation of Kant as a moral realist. Our claim is only that such an interpretation would deprive Kant's theory of most of what makes it philosophically interesting and challenging.

16 The papers in the next twelve chapters were invited for a Section on 'Political and Metaphysics in Kant', organized as part of the 2007 European Consortium for Political Research General Conference, which took place in Pisa in September. Howard Williams and Sorin Baiasu organized the Section.

17 For some texts dealing more directly with this issue, see John Rawls, 'Justice as fairness: political not metaphysical', *Philosophy and Public Affairs*, 14/3 (1985), 223–51; Jean Hampton, 'Should political philosophy be done without metaphysics?', *Ethics*, 99/4 (1989), 791–814; Katrin Flikschuh, *Kant and Modern Political Philosophy* (Cambridge: Cambridge University Press, 2000). See also Sorin Baiasu, 'Kantian metaphysics and the normative force of practical principles', *Journal of International Political Theory*, 3/1 (2007), 37–56.

18 Sami Pihlström, for instance, defends a pragmatic form of transcendental idealism in *Pragmatist Metaphysics: an Essay on the Ethical Grounds of Ontology* (London: Continuum, 2009). More generally, 'transcendental idealism' can be understood in various ways. Kant first formulated his critical philosophy and the theory of transcendental idealism in the context of what he called 'theoretical philosophy', more exactly in the *Critique of Pure Reason*. Recent commentators have attempted to clarify the relationship between Kant's theoretical philosophy and transcendental idealism, and perhaps the most influential interpretive lines to date are the works of Graham Bird, *Kant's Theory of Knowledge: an Outline of One Central Argument in the* Critique of Pure Reason (London: Routledge and Kegan Paul, 1962); and Henry Allison, *Kant's Transcendental Idealism: an Interpretation and Defence* (New Haven, CT: Yale University Press, 1983). But see

also Robert Pippin, *Kant's Theory of Form: an Essay on the* Critique of Pure Reason (New Haven, CT: Yale University Press, 1982); Paul Guyer, *Kant and the Claims of Knowledge* (Cambridge: Cambridge University Press, 1987); and Richard Aquila, *Representational Mind: a Study of Kant's Theory of Knowledge* (Bloomington: Indiana University Press, 1983). In spite of important differences, both Bird and Allison emphasise the relationship between Kant's theoretical philosophy and transcendental idealism, and both regard transcendental idealism as a non-dogmatic, legitimate form of philosophizing. Both agree that, with regard to the much-debated topic of the reality of things in themselves, all we can say epistemologically is that we cannot know them. Yet whereas Allison thinks the only conclusions which transcendental idealism can legitimately offer on this are epistemological – conclusions which, moreover, have only a negative character – Graham Bird seems to accept that transcendental idealism also affords us ontological considerations; these, to be sure, make no specific epistemological claims beyond the negative ones already mentioned, but they nevertheless tell us something about the world's reality structure. For other ways of distinguishing between transcendental idealisms, see Mark Sacks, *Objectivity and Insight* (Oxford: Oxford University Press, 2000). See also Adrian Moore's discussion of this issue in 'Transcendental constraints, transcendental features and transcendental idealism' (paper presented to the Mark Sacks Memorial Conference, 2009).

19 See, however, n. 11 above, where the possibility of metaphysically weaker forms of moral realism is introduced.

20 Stephen Engstrom seems to back up this line of argument in his recent *The Form of Practical Knowledge: a Study of the Categorical Imperative* (Cambridge, MA: Harvard University Press, 2009), vii–xv.

References

Allison, H., *Kant's Transcendental Idealism: an Interpretation and Defence* (New Haven, CT: Yale University Press, 1983).

Aquila, R., *Representational Mind: a Study of Kant's Theory of Knowledge* (Bloomington: Indiana University Press, 1983).

Aristotle, *Metaphysics*, ed. and trans. J. Warrington (London: Dent, 1961).

Armstrong, D., *Truth and Truthmakers* (Cambridge: Cambridge University Press, 2004).

Baiasu, S., 'Kantian metaphysics and the normative force of practical principles', *Journal of International Political Theory*, 3/1 (2007), 37–56.

Bird, G., *Kant's Theory of Knowledge: an Outline of One Central Argument in the* Critique of Pure Reason (London: Routledge and Kegan Paul, 1962).

Engstrom, S., *The Form of Practical Knowledge: a Study of the Categorical Imperative* (Cambridge, MA: Harvard University Press, 2009).

Flikschuh, K., *Kant and Modern Political Philosophy* (Cambridge: Cambridge University Press, 2000).

Gilson, E., *Being and Some Philosophers*, second edn (Toronto: Pontifical Institute of Mediaeval Studies, 1952).

Guyer, P., *Kant and the Claims of Knowledge* (Cambridge: Cambridge University Press, 1987).

Hampton, J., 'Should political philosophy be done without metaphysics?', *Ethics*, 99/4 (1989), 791–814.

James, W., *Pragmatism: a New Name for Some Old Ways of Thinking*, ed. F. H. Burkhardt, F. Bowers and I. K. Skrupskelis (Cambridge, MA: Harvard University Press, 1975).

Kant, I., *Critique of Pure Reason*, trans. W. S. Pluhar (Indianapolis: Hackett, 1996).

——, 'Groundwork of the Metaphysics of Morals', in *Practical Philosophy*, ed. and trans. M. J. Gregor (Cambridge: Cambridge University Press, 1996).

——, *Critique of Practical Reason*, trans. W. S. Pluhar (Indianapolis: Hackett, 2002).

Korsgaard, C., 'Kant's formula of the Universal Law', in *Creating the Kingdom of Ends* (Cambridge: Cambridge University Press, 1996).

Lewis, D., *Papers in Metaphysics and Epistemology* (Cambridge: Cambridge University Press, 2001).

Loux, M., *Metaphysics: a Contemporary Introduction*, rev. edn (London and New York: Routledge, 2002).

Lowe, E. J., *The Possibility of Metaphysics: Substance, Identity and Time* (Oxford: Clarendon Press, 1998).

Moore, A. W., 'Transcendental constraints, transcendental features and transcendental idealism' (paper presented to the Mark Sacks Memorial Conference, 2009).

Nussbaum, M., *The Fragility of Goodness: Luck and Ethics in Greek Tragedy and Philosophy*, rev. edn (Cambridge: Cambridge University Press: 2001).

Pihlström, S., *Pragmatist Metaphysics: an Essay on the Ethical Grounds of Ontology* (London: Continuum, 2009).

Pippin, R., *Kant's Theory of Form: an Essay on the* Critique of Pure Reason (New Haven, CT: Yale University Press, 1982).

Putnam, H., *The Collapse of the Fact/Value Dichotomy and Other Essays* (Cambridge, MA: Harvard University Press, 2002).

——, *Ethics without Ontology*, (Cambridge, MA: Harvard University Press, 2004).
Rawls, J., 'Justice as fairness: political not metaphysical', *Philosophy and Public Affairs*, 14/3 (1985), 223–51.
Rorty, R., *Philosophy and Social Hope* (London: Penguin, 1999).
——, *Philosophy as Cultural Politics* (Cambridge: Cambridge University Press, 2007).
Sacks, M., *Objectivity and Insight* (Oxford: Oxford University Press, 2000).
Tartaglia, J., *Rorty and the Mirror of Nature* (London: Routledge, 2007).
Timmons, M., 'The categorical imperative and universalizability', in C. Horn and D. Schoenecker (eds), *Kant's* Groundwork of the Metaphysics of Morals: *New Interpretations* (Berlin: De Gruyter, 2006).
Warrington, J., 'Editor's Introduction', in Aristotle, *Metaphysics*.
Wolff, C., *Vernünfftige Gedancken von Gott, der Welt und der Seele des Menschen, auch allen Dingen überhaupt* (*Deutsche Metaphysik*), ed. C. Corr, in *Gesammelte Werke*, ed. J. École, H. W. Arndt, C. Corr, J. E. Hoffmann and M. Thomann, vol. 2. (Hildesheim: Georg Olms, 1965).

2 • Kant's Moral Constructivism and Rational Justification

Kenneth R. Westphal

1. Introduction

Inevitably, my paper is a fragment of a much larger project; here I can only sketch briefly the context within which I hope to highlight a very important feature of Kant's constructivist method for identifying and justifying basic norms: uniquely, it resolves the Pyrrhonian Dilemma of the Criterion.

2. The Dilemma of the Criterion

Pyrrhonian Scepticism and the Dilemma of the Criterion have haunted philosophy, implicitly or explicitly, from Pyrrho to the present day. The modern natural law tradition within which Kant worked was no exception. Although Grotius is among the few who explicitly cite Sextus' Dilemma of the Criterion, the twin problems of enabling and regulating international commerce – especially by sea – by regulating international relations, and of achieving and maintaining peace after the Thirty Years War, demonstrated that such problems could no longer be solved by appeal to particular sectarian faiths. This presented the Dilemma of the Criterion *in concreto*, even to thinkers who preferred to neglect Sextus' writings. The Dilemma of the Criterion is this:

> [I]n order to decide the dispute which has arisen about the criterion [of truth], we must possess an accepted criterion by which we shall be able to judge the dispute; and in order to possess an accepted criterion, the dispute about the criterion must first be decided. And when the argument thus reduces itself to a form of circular reasoning the discovery of the criterion becomes impracticable, since we do not allow [those

> who make knowledge claims] to adopt a criterion by assumption, while if they offer to judge the criterion by a criterion we force them to a regress *ad infinitum*. And furthermore, since demonstration requires a demonstrated criterion, while the criterion requires an approved demonstration, they are forced into circular reasoning.[1]

The Dilemma of the Criterion is a serious problem for any theory or method of rational justification, yet in practical philosophy the only normative justification we can have is by reasoning. This Dilemma cannot be solved (in non-formal domains) by foundationalist or coherentist theories of justification, nor by 'reflective equilibrium'.[2] Other methods or bases of normative justification – such as an authority, a founding text, a tradition, intuitionism in its various forms, the feelings of pleasure and displeasure or other such inclinations – are equally subject to the Dilemma of the Criterion. Contractarian forms of justification falter (*inter alia*) because they too easily allow contractors to neglect or deny their responsibilities – their *duties* – by refusing to recognize or (hence) to negotiate about them, or by insisting on negotiating non-negotiable issues. Contractarianism can neither avoid nor resolve dogmatism.[3]

3. Kant's constructivism

The key point of Kant's constructivist theory of justification is to show that sufficient justifying grounds for a wrong act *cannot* be provided to all concerned (that is, affected) parties. Conversely, sufficient justifying grounds for omitting positive moral obligations cannot be provided to all concerned parties. In contrast, legitimate principles are ones for which sufficient justifying reasons *can* be given to all concerned parties. Instead of consent, Kant's theory of normative justification relies on *possible* consistency of human maxims or forms of outer action. Kant's basic criterion of right action, along with its various instances, is neither indicative nor hypothetical; it is *modal*. The modality of Kant's basic criterion is nicely formulated by O'Neill: 'When we think that others *cannot* adopt, *a fortiori cannot* consent to, some principle we cannot offer them reasons for doing so.'[4]

'Adopt' here means to be able to follow consistently the very same principle in thought or action on the same occasion as one proposes to act on that maxim. This is an issue of capacity and ability, not a psychological claim about what someone can or cannot bring him- or herself to believe or to do. Hence the possibility of adopting a principle differs fundamentally from 'accepting' one, in the common philosophical senses of 'believe', 'endorse' or 'agree to', which are central to contractarian and contractualist analyses. The key thought O'Neill identifies here is the central point of Kant's universalization tests. Kant's tests rule out any maxim that cannot possibly be adopted by others on the same occasion on which one proposes to act on that maxim. It focuses on whether others can adopt our very maxim, not whether they might adopt the same kind of maxim. Numerical (rather than generic) identity of the shared maxim is central to Kant's tests: he says expressly that it is *your own* maxim that is to be universalized.[5] What we can or cannot adopt as a maxim is constrained by the form of behaviour or its guiding principle (maxim), by basic facts about our finite form of rational agency and by basic features of our worldly context of action. This latter information is brought into Kant's universalization tests by using the Principle of Hypothetical Imperatives, namely, 'Who wills the end, wills also (necessarily, if he accords with reason) the sole means which are in his power' (*GMS* 4: 417).[6]

Though minimal, Kant's tests directly rule out maxims of coercion, deception, fraud and exploitation. In principle, such maxims *preclude* offering to relevant others – most obviously to victims – reasons sufficient to justify following those maxims (or the courses of action they guide) in thought or action.[7] This is signalled by the lack of the very possibility of consent, which serves as a criterion of illegitimacy. Consent itself, whether implicit, explicit or hypothetical, plays no role in Kant's tests, nor in his justification of either the basis or the results of his tests. Kant's tests use the possibility of consent to signal the crucial justificatory possibility of providing sufficient justifying reasons to all concerned parties. Obviating the very possibility of consent on anyone's part obviates the very possibility of offering sufficient justifying reasons to all concerned parties. Because for any maxim (or any course of action) to pass his univerzalisation tests requires that sufficient justifying reasons for that maxim or action *can* be given to *all* concerned parties for acting on that maxim on that very occasion, Kant's constructivism embodies at its core equal respect for all persons as free rational agents, that is, as agents who can determine what to think or to do by rationally assessing the merits of the case.[8] Ruling out maxims which fail to pass this universalization test establishes the minimum necessary conditions for resolving the problems of conflict and social coordination that generated the central concern of modern natural law with establishing normative standards to govern public life, despite deep disagreements among various groups about the substance of a good or pious life.[9]

Kant's justificatory strategy is constructivist because it makes no appeal to any antecedent source or kind of normative authority. Thus Kant's constructivist justification of practical principles at its core embodies the autonomy of reason as being both a necessary and a sufficient basis for identifying, justifying and thereby genuinely establishing legitimate norms. This is a key dimension of the autonomy of rational judgement: Kant's justificatory strategy appeals only to a fundamental principle of rational justification as such, that justifying a principle, policy, belief, institution or action requires that its proponent be able to provide sufficient justifying reasons to all other concerned parties, such that these parties can consistently adopt or follow the very same proposal in thought or action. Therefore, Kant's constructivist justification of practical principles is fundamentally social and intersubjective, because it is addressed to *all* concerned parties.[10] Our behaviour, both verbal and physical, is not coordinated naturally, nor transcendentally, nor transcendently. Consequently, any stable social practices or constructions, whether communicative, intellectual, political or physical, can only be based on principles which all parties can consistently follow in thought and in action.

To identify and to justify such principles requires, Kant contends, that we follow these maxims: always to think actively, to think consistently, to think (so far as possible) without prejudice, and to think from the standpoint of *everyone* else (*KU* 5: 294; *AA* 8: 145). These maxims are not algorithms, nor are they specific methods, but they are *sine qua non* for rationally cogent and justifiable thought, judgement and action. As O'Neill points out, these maxims are equally ones of communication, required so that we can communicate with everyone and not just our own partisan camp.[11] Thus Kant's justificatory strategy is fundamentally social. The nerve of Kant's constructivist strategy is to show that the modal capacity to provide justifying reasons to all relevant others is a very stringent requirement. One great advantage of Kant's minimalist strategy of justification is that it avoids familiar problems regarding agreement or acceptance, whether implicit, explicit or hypothetical.[12]

On the basis of this modal principle, Kant develops a powerful kind of constructivism in normative theory, not in the sense popularized by Rawls[13] but in the sense explicated by O'Neill.[14] Kant's constructivism articulates the content of a natural law theory, though it moots the issues of ontology (moral realism) and motivation that confront natural law theories. It justifies the objectivity and legitimacy of practical, action-guiding principles without appeal to moral facts, whether natural or non-natural. Kant's constructivist principle addresses neither a particular society with its norms (communitarianism), nor an 'overlapping consensus' of a pluralistic society (Rawls), nor the multitude of voices aspiring to communicate in accord with the requirements of an 'ideal speech situation' (Habermas), nor a plurality of potential contractors (for example Gauthier or Scanlon). These latter considerations are important, but are secondary to the basic framework principles of justice identified and justified by Kant's constructivism, which articulates the most basic rational principle of human thought and action as such. The principles required for legitimate contract cannot themselves be established by contract because – as Hume already recognized – any such contract presupposes rather than defines or justifies those principles.[15] Conversely, requiring consent to establish basic norms too easily allows for negligence or back-sliding through refusal to consent, including refusal to acknowledge relevant considerations and obligations.[16] Kant's constructivism establishes key norms to which we are committed, whether we like it or not, by our rational requirements to act in justified ways on the one hand, and by the limits of our very finite form of human agency and our worldly context of action on the other.[17] According to Kant, there is no public use of reason without this constructivist principle, which uniquely avoids presupposing any authority, whether ideological, religious, socio-historical or personal.

Saying that Kant's constructivism does not appeal to moral facts may invite a misunderstanding. Unlike most contemporary 'constructivist' programmes, Kant's constructivism is not committed to generating or 'constructing' the entire moral domain by appeal solely to empirical facts and non-moral principles. Facts about human finitude, such as our liability to injury, coercion or deceit are empirical facts. They are partially constitutive of our finite form of rational agency. They are *morally relevant* facts because as agents there is so much we can, and either should or should not do, to produce, avoid, exploit, avert or minister to them. The point of departure of Kant's constructivism is not the alleged rights of others, but rather our own *obligations* towards others (and ourselves) given that each of us is a free, rational and finite agent. *Ab initio* this version of constructivism moves within the moral domain because it begins with the problem of social coordination (if not conflict) and because restricting ourselves to those principles for which we can provide all relevant parties with sufficient justifying reasons is as much a principle of morals as it is a principle of rational justification *per se*. It is a (broadly) moral principle because it requires us to act only on those principles that can be rationally justified, and because it requires us to respect ourselves and all other persons as rational agents, as agents who can understand, develop, assess and act on rationally justified principles because we recognize and understand their justificatory grounds.[18]

4. Rational judgement, autonomy and spontaneity

The self-conscious 'I think' that matters most to philosophy is the 'I judge' that is central to rational thought and action in any of its forms. Only a strong sense of 'I judge' that involves critical assessment makes possible thought and reasoning, as contrasted with mere vocables, rhetoric, propaganda or rote following of protocols. Conversely, anyone who can or does engage in genuine inquiry and debate instantiates (more or less adequately) this strong sense of the term. Kant's investigation aimed to uncover the transcendental conditions that make self-conscious experience humanly possible.[19] My focus here is primarily on the kind of self-conscious judgement required to understand, to appreciate and to *assess* the point of any substantial piece of justificatory reasoning.

To judge rationally is not merely to decide. To judge rationally is to make whatever judgement is best warranted in view of all available relevant considerations, including evidence, counter-evidence, relevant principles of inference; relevant (as opposed to irrelevant or less relevant) analogies with other examples, cases or domains;

as well as alternative accounts or assessments of the issue, whether historical, contemporaneous or heretofore unconsidered cogent alternatives. To judge rationally is to assume responsibility for the warrant or justificatory status of one's conclusions. To assume responsibility for making judgements and for making any and every particular judgement is to exercise autonomy. The autonomy of rational judgement consists in regulating one's own thinking, deliberation, assessment, judgement and conduct in view of the various factors (including those just mentioned) that bear on the identification and justification of the correct, or at least the best justified conclusion about the matter at hand. This kind of 'self-regulation' of one's own thinking is literally a form of 'auto-nomy', of self-guided, self-motivated, voluntary and self-assessing use of rules, principles, laws and evidence, where the relevant 'laws' are the principles and guidelines of cogent justificatory reasoning by use of which one regulates one's own thinking. Thus one basic sense in which judgement is autonomous is that one forms one's own judgement, rather than merely adopting anyone else's judgement, advice or recommendation (much less command).

A second significant sense in which rational judgement is autonomous is that it is guided by the normative considerations of appropriate assessment, and use, of both evidence and principles of reasoning. If judgement as a physiological or psychological process is in some way causal, it nevertheless counts as *judgement* only in so far as it responds to such normative considerations, rather than merely to its causal antecedents as such. Judgement is a response to, not merely an effect of, its proper evidentiary and inferential antecedents. If justificatory processes turn out to be causal, they are justificatory not because they are causal, but because they satisfy sufficient normative constraints – defining or at least including *proper* functioning, *proper* inference and *proper* assessment – to provide *inter alia* rational justification. Because of this, Kant held that reason, rational judgement (a pleonasm), is spontaneous.[20] This point merits closer consideration.

Only rational spontaneity enables us to appeal to principles of inference and to make rational judgements, both of which are normative because each rational subject considers for him- or herself whether available procedures, evidence and principles of inference warrant a judgement or conclusion. In the theoretical domain of knowledge, *having* adequate evidence, proof or (in sum) justification requires *taking* that evidence, proof or justification to be adequate; in the practical domain of deliberation and action, *having* adequate grounds for action requires *taking* those grounds to be adequate. We *act* only insofar as we take ourselves to have reasons, even in cases of acting on desires, where we must (*ex hypothesi*) take those desires – by judging them to be so – as appropriate and adequate grounds for action. Otherwise we abdicate rational considerations and absent ourselves from what Sellars calls 'the space of reasons', and merely behave.[21] In that case, to borrow McDowell's terms,[22] we provide ourselves only with excuses and exculpations, but not reasons or justifications, for acting or believing as we do.[23] Kant's conception of rational spontaneity opposes empiricist accounts of beliefs and desires as merely causal products of environmental stimuli, and it opposes empiricist accounts of action according to which we act on whatever desires are (literally) 'strongest'. We think and act rationally only in so far as we judge the merits of whatever case is before us. This is the third aspect of the rational autonomy of judgement.[24]

5. Reason, justification and history

Rational judgement is fallible because it involves one's own 'perspectival' assessment, as it were, of the relevant evidence and principles, and the interrelations between these. Due to our fallibility and limited knowledge, both factual and inferential, any particular judgement anyone makes is justified only to the extent that one does one's utmost to exercise informed judgement on that occasion, *and* to the extent that one's judgement survives critical scrutiny by all concerned parties (including oneself). In this important regard, because we are finite, fallible reasoners and cognizers, the justification and the justificatory status of our conclusions is a social phenomenon. Because informed judgement is socially based, so is rational justification.[25] We are each responsible for the critical assessment of our own and of others' rational judgements. Genuine and fully rational judgement requires constructive mutual critical assessment of each and everyone's judgement. This is the point of Kant's four maxims of judgement cited previously.

Because constructivist rational justification is fallibilist, it dispenses with the illicit tendency to unilateral judgement embedded in foundationalist models of justification. The 'one size fits all' notion of universalization for which the Enlightenment has so often been criticized is simply foreign to Kant's views. Kant's constructivist, fallibilist social theory of rational justification is inherently a pragmatic and historical theory of rational justification because the justification it provides is fallible, because it is based on the present state of knowledge, because it is inherently provisional and because the list of relevant alternative accounts of any issue and the relevant considerations bearing on it increase historically. Thus rational justification is also fundamentally historical; only thereby, indeed, can it resolve the Dilemma of the Criterion because fallibilism provides a cogent, rigorous alternative to the foundationalist regress of justifying reasons.

The Dilemma of the Criterion puts paid to the sceptical regress inherent in foundationalist models of justification and to the circularity involved in standard coherence theories. Critical self-assessment and mutual criticism can be constructive by enabling us to assess, to revise or to replace any particular claim within any line of justificatory reasoning, as well as any link among such claims. For this reason, rational judgement is not trapped in vicious circularity, *pace* the Dilemma of the Criterion. Roderick Chisholm erred profoundly when he contended that there are only three possible solutions to the Dilemma of the Criterion, none of them satisfactory because each commits a *petitio principii*.[26] According to Chisholm, one can start with universal principles, or instead with particular claims; or one can sceptically deny that one could start legitimately with either universal or particular claims. Chisholm neglected the very possibility of constructive self- and mutual criticism of the kind enabled by Kant's account of the autonomy of reason and the autonomy of rational judgement. Kant's account of these forms of autonomy (summarized above) involves and justifies a pragmatic, social and historical account of rational justification in which even our presumed 'first principles' are subject to ongoing assessment as they are used again and again in new situations. Yet Kant's account of rational justification maintains strict objectivity about the identification and justification of our principles and particular claims, because on Kant's account their justification must be addressed to all concerned (that is, all affected) parties. This is central to respecting all persons as ends in themselves, that is as rational agents who can and ought to judge what is right for themselves. And when individuals unfortunately fail so to do, this too can only be identified and established by careful critical scrutiny of our own and of their reasonings. The alleged Dilemma of the Criterion is defeated by pragmatic fallibilism of precisely the kind that Kant was the first to identify and develop.[27]

Notes

1 Sextus Empiricus, *Outlines of Pyrrhonism*, ed. and trans. R. G. Bury (Cambridge, MA: Harvard University Press, 1934), II.4 §20; cp. I.14 §§116–17.

2 The so-called method of 'reflective equilibrium' suggested by Nelson Goodman, *Fact, Fiction, and Forecast* (Indianapolis: Bobbs-Merrill, 1965), p. 64), and popularized by Rawls, *A Theory of Justice* (Cambridge, MA: Harvard University Press, 1971) fares no better, because it does little or nothing to guide different philosophers to the same equilibrium between principles and intuitions, even if they share substantially the same sets of each. Goodman's formulation expressly concerns what we *do*, namely, that we trim data to fit our theories, and trim our theories to fit data. Nothing in his observations shows that we ought to do this, nor how we ought best to do it. Thus his remarks neither provide nor suggest a justificatory method. Furthermore, intuitions are not sufficiently well-ordered to ground stable equilibria – see Martin Perlmutter, 'Moral intuitions and philosophical method', in K. R. Westphal (ed.), *Pragmatism, Reason and Norms* (New York: Fordham University Press, 1998) – and there are deeply and apparently irreconcilable 'intuitions' (if that is indeed what they are) among (schools of) philosophers. Thus reflective equilibrium as such can scarcely avoid (sub-)cultural or historicist relativism; indeed, it may instead be a source – if not a instance – of it. 'Reflective Equilibrium' simply is not a method; it may be the best we can initially strive for in highly problematic domains, but even in such domains our goals must include devising genuine methods for the domain in question.

3 I discuss this issue in Westphal, 'Urteilskraft, gegenseitige Anerkennung und rationale Rechtfertigung', in H.-D. Klein (ed.), *Ethik als prima philosophia?* (Würzburg: Königshausen und Neumann, 2011), 171–93.

4 Onora O'Neill, 'Kant and the social contract tradition', in F. Duchesneau, G. Lafrance and C. Piché (eds), *Kant actuel: Hommage à Pierre Laberge* (Montréal: Bellarmin, 2000), p. 200; cp. Westphal, 'Do Kant's principles justify property or usufruct?', *Jahrbuch für Recht und Ethik/Annual Review of Law and Ethics*, 5 (1997), 141–94 (see especially sections 4 and 5).

5 Recall Kant's statements from the *Groundwork* of the Formula of Universal Law: 'Act only in accordance with that maxim through which you can at the same time will that it become a universal law' (*GMS* 4: 221), the formula of a Law of Nature: 'Act as if the maxim of your action were to become by your will a *universal law of nature*' (*GMS* 4: 421), the formula of Autonomy: '... act only so that the will can regard itself at the same time as giving universal law through its maxim' (*GMS* 4: 434), the Humanity Imperative (*GMS* 4: 429; the imperative is quoted below, n. 12) and the formula of the Realm of Ends: '... every rational being must act as if he were by his maxims at all times a lawgiving member of the universal kingdom of ends. The formal principle of these maxims is, act as if your maxims were to serve at the same time as a universal law (for all rational beings)' (*GMS* 4: 438). All translations above are from Kant, *Practical Philosophy*, trans. M. J. Gregor (Cambridge: Cambridge University Press, 1996). Each of these statements of the principle of Kant's test indicates that it is one's own maxim, not one's generic kind of maxim, that is to be universalized. Moreover, the requirement that one's maxim be universalized entails that others shall act on it on the very occasion on which you do (or propose to). Kant's test does not suffer from the common objection found in maxims that are 'tailored' to pass his univerzalisation tests, because through clever use of logically universal quantifiers they pertain de facto only to one person. There is much to criticize in such alleged counter-examples. The most basic Kantian rejoinder is that tailoring maxims in this way simply fails to engage in the kind of universalization that Kant's tests require. Hence tailored maxims fail as counter-examples, because they do not generate examples of Kant's univerzalisation tests to begin with. In effect, this is the point of insisting that Kant's test works on 'generic maxims' in Barbara Herman, *The Practice of Moral Judgment* (Cambridge, MA: Harvard University Press, 1993), chs 6–7. Likewise, it is no obstacle to Kant's tests that I might act on a maxim of exploiting you now, and you might act on that maxim with regard to me at another time. Patently this is not the kind of universalization required by Kant's tests. (It should not be necessary to remark on this point, but too often Kant's tests are seriously misunderstood.)

6 Translation from Kant, *Groundwork of the Metaphysics of Morals*, trans. H. J. Paton (New York: Harper and Row, 1964). For a detailed example of how Kant's procedure works, see Westphal, 'A Kantian Justification of Possession', in M. Timmons (ed.), *Kant's Metaphysics of Morals: Interpretive Essays* (New York: Oxford University Press, 2002), pp. 89–109.

7 O'Neill, *Constructions of Reason: Explorations of Kant's Practical Philosophy* (Cambridge: Cambridge University Press, 1989), pp. 81–125.

8 The modal formulation of Kant's tests, their focus on the very possibility of consent and my stress on maximizing the autonomy of one's own rational, justificatory judgement raises two subsidiary issues I mention here in order to set them aside. One concerns our frequent use of expert opinion (e.g. that of medical doctors, accountants or lawyers) precisely because they, unlike we their clients, are experts in the areas in which we seek advice. In such cases, there are very important issues about how we can best distinguish genuine from lesser or merely presumed experts, to which the present analysis of rational justification by rational judgement directly pertains. The other concern is whether in some cases it may be justifiable to submit to certain forms of coercion or deception. The most obvious examples of such cases are medical: how and under what circumstances might it be justifiable to remain ignorant of one's own diagnosed, fatal disease? Or likewise, for seriously obese patients to have their jaws wired together in order not to eat for a planned period of time? (There have been such cases in the USA.) Such cases also involve crucial issues about how such patients can most justifiedly select the expert treatment they require or at least receive. Issues about patient autonomy in medicine are intricate and important, though I do not believe they raise genuine objections to the present analysis. For discussion of patient autonomy and related matters, see Neil C. Manson and Onora O'Neill, *Rethinking Informed Consent in Bioethics* (Cambridge: Cambridge University Press, 2007). I thank Rüdiger Bittner for raising this point with me.

9 Jerome B. Schneewind, *The Invention of Autonomy* (New York: Cambridge University Press, 1998).

10 The key question about Kant's constructivist strategy is thus not whether it is individualist or collectivist, but rather what kind of collectivism or intersubjectivity is built into Kant's universalism. Kant distinguished 'disjunctive' (i.e. distributive) and 'collective' forms of universality (cp. *AA* 23: 322–3). Presently, I believe that Kant's constructivism involves distributive, not collective, forms of universality.

11 O'Neill, *Constructions of Reason*, pp. 24–7, 42–8.

12 This paragraph summarizes some thoughts from O'Neill, 'Kant and the social contract'; cp. *Towards Justice and Virtue: a Constructive Account of Practical Reasoning* (Cambridge: Cambridge University Press, 1996); 'Constructivism in Rawls and Kant', in S. Freeman (ed.), *The Cambridge Companion to Rawls* (Cambridge: Cambridge University Press, 2003); 'Autonomy, plurality and public reason', in N. Brender and L. Krasnoff (eds), *New Essays in the History of Autonomy* (Cambridge: Cambridge University Press, 2004); 'Self-legislation, autonomy and the form of law', in H. Nagl-Docekal and R. Langthaler (eds), *Recht, Geschichte, Religion: Die Bedeutung Kants für die*

Gegenwart, Sonderband der *Deutschen Zeitschrift für Philosophie* (Berlin: Akademie Verlag, 2004); cp. Westphal, 'Do Kant's principles justify property or usufruct?', sections 4, 5. The term 'rational justification' is in these contexts a pleonasm. In moral philosophy, 'externalist' accounts of justification are out of place. Aside from simple perceptual knowledge, providing justifying reasons is the sole mode of justification in matters moral, for reason-giving is the only form of justification that can avoid dogmatism, question-begging, infinite regress or the Dilemma of the Criterion. Appeals to other alleged sources of normativity (a founding figure, text or tradition) cannot avoid these problems. Whether or how rational justification can avoid these sceptical problems has not often been considered with sufficient care by philosophers. Kant's constructivist procedure does raise issues – to be sure, absolutely general ones – about how to distinguish cases in which sufficient justifying reasons can be and have been addressed to all relevant parties, even though some of these parties may refuse to accept these reasons, whether due to inability, incomprehension or bias. This important issue is addressed by Hegel's phenomenological method; see Westphal, *Hegel's Epistemological Realism*, Philosophical Studies Series, 43 (Dordrecht: Kluwer, 1989), pp. 126–8, although these brief remarks are rooted in the entire analysis. Hegel's analysis shows that Kant's constructivist procedure does not relapse into a consent theory.

13 Rawls, *A Theory of Justice*.

14 O'Neill, *Constructions of Reason*; *Towards Justice and Virtue*; 'Kant and social contract'; 'Instituting principles: between duty and action', in M. Timmons (ed.), *Kant's Metaphysics of Morals: Interpretive Essays* (New York: Oxford University Press, 2002); 'Autonomy, plurality and public reason'; 'Self-legislation, autonomy and the form of law'.

15 David Hume, *A Treatise of Human Nature*, ed. D. F. Norton and M. J. Norton (Oxford: Oxford University Press, 2000 [1740]), pp. 331–2.

16 Regarding some key shortcomings in consent theories, see O'Neill, 'Kant and the social contract', 185–91; Westphal, 'Constructivism, contractarianism and basic obligations: Kant and Gauthier', in J.-C. Merle (ed.), *Reading Kant's Doctrine of Right* (Cardiff: University of Wales Press, forthcoming).

17 Westphal, 'L'ispirazione tragica della dialettica fenomenologica di Hegel', trans. C. Ferrini, in L. M. Napolitano Valditara (ed.), *Antichi e nuovi dialoghi di sapienti e di eroi. Etica, linguaggio e dialettica fra tragedia greca e filosofia* (Trieste: Edizioni Università di Trieste, 2002), pp. 151–77.

18 Kant formulates 'respect' primarily as respect for the moral law (*GMS* 4: 400, 401n., 403, 424, 426, 436, 440, *KpV* 5: 73, 74–6, 78–86, 128,

132, 151, 157). Respect for the moral law is constituted by recognizing the Categorical Imperative as the fundamental moral principle and following what the Categorical Imperative requires *because* it is the fundamental principle of morals. Kant's Categorical Imperative is the fundamental principle of morals because it provides the fundamental criterial procedure for distinguishing between legitimate and illegitimate types of action by distinguishing among prohibited, permissible and obligatory types of action. To use Kant's Categorical Imperative and to follow its dictates thus requires using the constructivist method explicated here for identifying and justifying legitimate maxims. Kant is emphatic that only in so far as we use the Categorical Imperative and follow its dictates can and do we treat each and every person as an end in him- or herself, and not merely as a means. Doing this requires that we think and act only on the basis of justifiable, and indeed rationally justified, principles. A necessary and sufficient criterion of rationally justifiable or justified principles is that only for such principles can we offer all concerned parties sufficient justifying reasons to think or act as we do or propose to do. Kant also speaks of respect for persons, not just for the moral law; this is central to his formulation of the Humanity Imperative: 'So act in that you use humanity, whether in your own person or in the person of any other, always at the same time as an end, never merely as a means' (*GMS* 4: 429). Hence in Kant's view it is proper to speak of respect for persons, although he is very clear that human beings merit respect as persons only due to their 'personality' (*KpV* 5: 87), which is their capacity to perform their duties by using and following the dictates of the Categorical Imperative: 'All respect for a person is actually only respect for the [moral] law (of moral integrity etc.), of which the person provides us the example' (*GMS* 4: 401 n.; cp. 428, 435, 436, 439, 440; *KpV* 5: 87, 93). Kant's Categorical Imperative is a principle of reason. To use the Categorical Imperative requires that we each exercise our own capacity for rational judgement. For reasons developed herein, exercising our capacity for rational judgment requires constructive self-criticism and mutual critical assessment (§§6–9).

19 Westphal, *Kant's Transcendental Proof of Realism* (Cambridge: Cambridge University Press, 2004).

20 Allison, 'We can act only under the Idea of Freedom', *Proceedings and Addresses of the American Philosophical Association*, 71/2 (1997), 39–50.

21 Wilfrid Sellars, *Science, Perception and Reality* (London: Routledge and Kegan Paul, 1963), p. 169.

22 John McDowell, *Mind and World* (Cambridge, MA: Harvard University Press, 1994).

23 Note that I do not say that taking evidence to be adequate suffices for that evidence to be adequate! Some epistemologists bridle at the notion that having adequate evidence or grounds for belief requires taking that evidence or those grounds to be adequate. Yet there are many examples of people having memories or perceptions that in fact bear evidentially on a certain belief they hold, though they fail to recognise this evidential relation and so fail to base their belief on that evidence. Basing (or, *mutatis mutandis*, rejecting) beliefs on evidence requires taking that evidence to be both relevant and adequate.

24 Kant's 'Incorporation Thesis' – see Allison, *Kant's Theory of Freedom* (Cambridge: Cambridge University Press, 1990), pp. 5–6, 39–40 – that no inclination is a motive unless and until it is incorporated into an agent's maxim by being judged to be at least permissible (*RGV* 6: 24), is thus an instance of the more general principle (and third aspect) of autonomous judgement identified here. Empiricists continue to rely on a belief-desire model of action which stems directly from Hobbes, apparently without realizing that it is a relic of the seventeenth century. This simple model may suffice for various branches of economic or sociological theory, but theirs is not the task of providing an adequate account of the reasoning, deliberation and action by any specific agent. That we behave in ways which, when aggregated across groups, can be modelled on the basis of this simple belief-desire model does not prove that the belief-desire model is either correct or adequate as an account of individual human agency, quite aside from considerations of the extent to which heavily commercialized modern societies tend to train individuals to behave as if the belief-desire model applies to us. Behaving in such ways is great for sales, though hardly sufficient for a full human life. That Rawls (see *A Theory of Justice*) elected to argue on the basis of an essentially economic, belief-desire model of human agency was a strategic concession to empiricists who were sceptical about the principles of justice Rawls advocated. He sought to derive his conclusions from their premises. This is not to endorse those premises, which of course no Kantian would do. The belief-desire model provides no basis for understanding cognitive justification. To be consistent, its advocates would undermine their own claims to justification of their favoured model of human behaviour. This argument is similar to Kant's point in the *Groundwork* (*GMS* 4: 446–9) that we can only act if we presume ourselves to be free from causal determination, because only then can we make rational judgements. Yet the present argument is stronger: if psychological determinism were true, we could not know it, because we could not have rational grounds of proof for psychological determinism. (By 'psychological determinism' I mean that every mental event is strictly and causally determined to

occur when and as it does by distinct causal factors of whatever kind. The view I advocate grants that our psychology can be and surely is causally conditioned, though these causal conditions do not suffice for psychological determinism.) The belief-desire model of action forms one pillar of causal accounts of the mind and human behaviour. The use of causal locutions to describe mental processes is unsurprising, but causal theorists of the mind disregard the important question raised by Kant, that of whether we are entitled to a constitutive construal of our causal locutions in connection with mental phenomena. Kant argued cogently that we are not, because we are only able to make legitimate causal judgements about *spatio*-temporal objects and events (Westphal, *Kant's Transcendental Proof*, §§8, 9, 36, 61, 62). A second key point of Kant's argument is that the regulative principle of natural science, always to seek causal explanations of phenomena, does not itself justify a causal description of a phenomenon. A causal description of a phenomenon is only justified by a genuine causal explanation of it. Only an empirically justified causal explanation of a phenomenon can justify a constitutive interpretation of the causal locutions it uses to describe and explain the phenomenon in question. Even after a truly marvellous 'decade (or two) of the brain' in neurophysiology, it will take many more such decades even to begin to develop plausible causal explanations of mental contents, thoughts, beliefs, desires, reasonings or decisions. Contemporary causal theories of mind are running on unredeemed and, for the foreseeable future, unredeemable promissory notes. For an illuminating attempt to unravel many current confusions about 'naturalism' in these connections, see Joseph Rouse, *How Scientific Practices Matter* (Chicago: University of Chicago Press, 2002).

25 'Judgement' has largely fallen by the wayside in analytic epistemology, except for an innocuous sense of identifying common sense objects in one's environs. Kant insisted that rules require judgement for their application (*KrV* A132–4/B171–3). In effect, Wittgenstein's scepticism about rule-following makes the same point, that principles are not algorithms, and indeed that their use requires social training and context: see Ike von Savigny, 'Self-conscious individual versus social self: the rationale of Wittgenstein's discussion of rule following', *Philosophy and Phenomenological Research*, 51/1 (1991), 67–84; Frederick L. Will, *Pragmatism and Realism*, ed. Westphal (Lanham: Rowman and Littlefield, 1997), chs 7–9). Further support for the social basis of constructive self-criticism are discussed in Westphal, 'L'ispirazione tragica'; *Hegel's Epistemology: a Philosophical Introduction to the Phenomenology of Spirit* (Cambridge, MA: Hackett), esp. §§20, 24, 28, 35; 'Urteilskraft'. Related issues are discussed in Catherine Z. Elgin, *Considered Judgment* (Princeton, NJ: Princeton University

Press, 1999); Leslie P. Thiele, *The Heart of Judgment* (Cambridge: Cambridge University Press, 2006).

26 Roderick Chisholm, *The Foundations of Knowing* (Minneapolis: University of Minnesota Press, 1982), 65–7, 75.

27 I further develop the analysis begun here in Westphal, 'Urteilskraft'. I wish to thank the conference organizers for their kind invitation, which allowed me to crystallize thoughts, and also the philosophers in Bielefeld, Hannover and in Dortmund, especially Rüdiger Bittner, Martin Carrier, Michael Wolff, Paul Hoyningen-Huene and Brigitte Falkenberg for constructive discussion of the work in progress from which this paper draws. My research was generously supported by a fellowship from the Alexander von Humboldt Foundation, to whom I express my gratitude.

References

Allison, H., 'We can act only under the Idea of Freedom', *Proceedings and Addresses of the American Philosophical Association*, 71/2 (1997), 39–50.

——, *Kant's Theory of Freedom* (Cambridge: Cambridge University Press, 1990).

Chisholm, R., *The Foundations of Knowing* (Minneapolis: University of Minnesota Press, 1982).

Elgin, C. Z., *Considered Judgment* (Princeton, NJ: Princeton University Press, 1999).

Goodman, N., *Fact, Fiction, and Forecast* (Indianapolis: Bobbs-Merrill, 1965).

Herman, B., *The Practice of Moral Judgment* (Cambridge, MA: Harvard University Press, 1993),

Hume, D., *A Treatise of Human Nature*, ed. D. F. Norton and M. J. Norton (Oxford: Oxford University Press, 2000 [1740]).

Kant, I., *Groundwork of the Metaphysics of Morals*, trans. H. J. Paton (New York: Harper and Row, 1964).

——, *Practical Philosophy*, trans. M. J. Gregor (Cambridge: Cambridge University Press, 1996).

Manson, N. C. and O'Neill, O., *Rethinking Informed Consent in Bioethics* (Cambridge: Cambridge University Press, 2007).

McDowell, J., *Mind and World* (Cambridge, MA: Harvard University Press, 1994).

O'Neill, O., *Constructions of Reason: Explorations of Kant's Practical Philosophy* (Cambridge: Cambridge University Press, 1989).

——, *Towards Justice and Virtue: a Constructive Account of Practical Reasoning* (Cambridge: Cambridge University Press, 1996).

——, 'Kant and the social contract tradition', in F. Duchesneau, G. Lafrance and C. Piché (eds), *Kant actuel: Hommage à Pierre Laberge* (Montréal: Bellarmin, 2000).

——, 'Instituting principles: between duty and action', in M. Timmons (ed.), *Kant's Metaphysics of Morals: Interpretive Essays* (New York: Oxford University Press, 2002).

——, 'Constructivism in Rawls and Kant', in S. Freeman (ed.), *The Cambridge Companion to Rawls* (Cambridge: Cambridge University Press, 2003).

——, 'Autonomy, Plurality and Public Reason', in N. Brender and L. Krasnoff (eds), *New Essays in the History of Autonomy* (Cambridge: Cambridge University Press, 2004).

——, 'Self-legislation, autonomy and the form of law', in H. Nagl-Docekal and R. Langthaler (eds), *Recht, Geschichte, Religion: Die Bedeutung Kants für die Gegenwart*, Sonderband der *Deutschen Zeitschrift für Philosophie* (Berlin: Akademie Verlag, 2004).

Perlmutter, M., 'Moral intuitions and philosophical method', in K. R. Westphal (ed.), *Pragmatism, Reason and Norms* (New York: Fordham University Press, 1998).

Rawls, J., *A Theory of Justice* (Cambridge, MA: Harvard University Press, 1971).

Rouse, J., *How Scientific Practices Matter* (Chicago: University of Chicago Press, 2002).

Savigny, Ike von, 'Self-conscious individual versus social self: the rationale of Wittgenstein's discussion of rule following', *Philosophy and Phenomenological Research*, 51/1 (1991), 67–84.

Schneewind, J., *The Invention of Autonomy: a History of Modern Moral Philosophy* (Cambridge: Cambridge University Press, 1998).

Sellars, W., *Science, Perception and Reality* (London: Routledge and Kegan Paul, 1963).

Sextus Empiricus, *Outlines of Pyrrhonism*, ed. and trans. R. G. Bury (Cambridge, MA: Harvard University Press, 1934).

Thiele, L. P., *The Heart of Judgment* (Cambridge: Cambridge University Press, 2006).

Westphal, K. R., *Hegel's Epistemological Realism*, Philosophical Studies Series, 43 (Dordrecht: Kluwer, 1989).

——, 'Do Kant's principles justify property or usufruct?', *Jahrbuch für Recht und Ethik/Annual Review of Law and Ethics*, 5 (1997), 141–94.

——, 'L'ispirazione tragica della dialettica fenomenologica di Hegel', trans. C. Ferrini, in L. M. Napolitano Valditara (ed.), *Antichi e nuovi dialoghi di sapienti e di eroi: etica, linguaggio e dialettica fra tragedia greca e filosofia* (Trieste: Edizioni Università di Trieste, 2002).

——, 'A Kantian Justification of Possession', in M. Timmons (ed.) *Kant's Metaphysics of Ethics: Interpretive Essays* (New York: Oxford University Press, 2002).

——, *Hegel's Epistemology: A Philosophical Introduction to the Phenomenology of Spirit* (Cambridge, MA: Hackett, 2003).

——, *Kant's Transcendental Proof of Realism* (Cambridge: Cambridge University Press, 2004).

——, 'Urteilskraft, gegenseitige Anerkennung und rationale Rechtfertigung', in H.-D. Klein (ed.), *Ethik als prima philosophia?* (Würzburg: Königshausen und Neumann, 2011), 171–93.

——, 'Constructivism, contractarianism and basic obligations: Kant and Gauthier', in J.-C. Merle (ed.), *Reading Kant's Doctrine of Right* (Cardiff: University of Wales Press, forthcoming).

Will, F. L., *Pragmatism and Realism*, ed. Westphal (Lanham: Rowman and Littlefield, 1997).

3 • Political, not Metaphysical, yet Kantian? A Defence of Rawls

Alyssa R. Bernstein

Katrin Flikschuh asserts in her recent book, *Kant and Modern Political Philosophy* [KMPP] (2000),[1] that the assimilation of Kant into mainstream Anglo-American liberalism 'is due almost entirely' to John Rawls's book, *A Theory of Justice* [TJ] (1999);[2] but while giving Rawls credit for this, she also holds him to blame for the 'rejection of metaphysics' by contemporary liberal political philosophers, which has impaired their theorizing, she contends, by making it not only un-Kantian but also incoherent (KMPP: 2–6, 13). Flikschuh attributes to Rawls the position that metaphysics 'can be relegated to the domain of persons' private beliefs' and that 'metaphysics in political thinking' is 'permissible, if at all, only in the private sphere, never in the public sphere' (KMPP: 20–1). Against this position she argues that 'metaphysical thinking cannot be reduced to the level of merely private reflection' and that it has an 'indispensable and positive role . . . in political thinking,' as demonstrated by Kant's political philosophy (KMPP: 6).

I argue here that Flikschuh's criticisms of Rawls's political liberalism fail because she misinterprets it.[3] She presents little description or analysis of it, as she admits, justifying this omission by saying that she intends merely to consider Rawls's view on the role of metaphysics in political thinking (KMPP: 12). However, she fails to carry out this intention because she does not carefully examine how Rawls uses the term 'metaphysics,' nor why he takes the position he does on the relation between metaphysics and political philosophy; nor what he means by 'public reason,' nor what role this latter idea plays in his political liberalism. As a consequence, she argues against views Rawls does not hold, and in favour of views he does not oppose.

Flikschuh is surely right that 'much liberal theorising about social and distributive justice today might be less Kantian than it takes itself to be'; however, I believe that Rawls's political liberalism is more Kantian than Flikschuh and others take it to be (KMPP: 4).[4] Elsewhere I have undertaken to support this view with regard to Rawls's conception of the moral basis of a just system of international law, which he calls the law of peoples (Bernstein, 'Kant, Rawls, and Cosmopolitanism', 2009); thus I have rebutted the criticisms of it that Flikschuh makes in her book.[5] In the present article I undertake to rebut the rest of the criticisms of Rawls's political liberalism that Flikschuh makes in the same book.[6] Oddly, she does not dispute, discuss or mention what Rawls regards as the main Kantian features of his conception of justice; I discuss them below. I do not here argue against her interpretation of Kant, which constitutes most of her book.

I begin by presenting Flikschuh's characterization of Rawls's conception of metaphysics, after which I examine what Rawls says about metaphysics and Kantian constructivism. Then I present the first part of my defence of Rawls. Next I summarize certain aspects of Rawls's political philosophy, focusing on his idea of public reason. Then I present the second part of my defence of Rawls.

1. Flikschuh on metaphysics and Rawls

Flikschuh uses Stephan Körner's notion of a categorial framework to articulate and defend her own conception of metaphysics as 'a discipline of philosophical reflection about the world of public experience' (KMPP: 32). So understood, 'metaphysical thinking . . . constitutes a person's reflective reconstruction of their cognitive experience of the publicly accessible world, the intersubjectively valid structure of which the categorial framework aims to identify and to elucidate for the purpose of guiding thought and action' (KMPP: 35). Flikschuh discusses Körner's 'more general, though recognizably Kantian' conception of metaphysics, instead of Kant's own, because she wants to 'avoid both the complexities of transcendental idealism as well as its contested status', and she thinks that 'adopting' Körner's conception enables her 'to emphasise those aspects of Kant's metaphysics that are central to his political philosophy without committing [her] to an unqualified endorsement of transcendental idealism' (KMPP: 5).

Flikschuh claims that Rawls characterizes metaphysics as the expression of an individual's private beliefs about the world, and she describes the development of Rawls's views as 'the privatisation of Kantian metaphysical thinking' (KMPP: 12, 20). I disagree, both with her claim and with her (very brief) description of the development of Rawls's views. I explain why in the next two sections, first examining what Rawls says about metaphysics and Kantian constructivism in 'The Independence of Moral Theory' [IMT] and 'Kantian Constructivism in Moral Theory' [KCMT].[7]

2. Rawls on metaphysics: IMT and KCMT

In IMT, Rawls expands upon some remarks made in TJ about moral justification and objectivity.[8] He argues that 'much of moral theory,' which he distinguishes from moral philosophy as one of the latter's main parts, 'is, in important respects, independent from certain philosophical subjects sometimes regarded as methodologically prior to it', such as metaphysics, the philosophy of mind, epistemology, and the theory of meaning (IMT: 286, 302).

> Moral theory is the study of substantive moral conceptions, that is, the study of how the basic notions of the right, the good, and moral worth may be arranged to form different moral structures. Moral theory tries to identify the chief similarities and differences between these structures and to characterize the way in which they are related to our moral sensibilities and natural attitudes, and to determine the conditions they must satisfy if they are to play their expected role in human life. (IMT: 286)

Although 'no part of philosophy is isolated from the rest', moral theory 'has its own distinctive problems and subject matter' (IMT: 287). Moral theory is related to moral philosophy as logic and the foundations of mathematics are related to the philosophy of mathematics and the theory of meaning, or even as theoretical physics is related to the philosophy of physics, Rawls argues (ibid.). The theory of meaning is not methodologically prior to the rest of philosophy, though many have believed it to be so due to Frege, and epistemology is not methodologically prior to the rest of philosophy, though many previously believed it so due to Descartes.

Therefore it is not necessary first to resolve the problems of the theory of meaning, epistemology, metaphysics and the philosophy of mind before investigating and resolving the problems of moral theory. Moreover, the questions of moral philosophy that connect with metaphysics and the philosophy of mind, epistemology and the theory of meaning 'must call upon moral theory': we need to understand substantive moral conceptions in order to answer questions about the nature of persons and personal identity, freedom of the will, the existence of objective moral truths, and the analysis of moral concepts (ibid.). 'The present situation in moral philosophy calls for a . . . strengthening of our grasp of the structure of moral conceptions, and in many respects, this inquiry, like the development of logic and the foundations of mathematics, can proceed independently' (ibid.).

After defending his project of developing a particular substantive moral conception (justice as fairness), by arguing in IMT against those who think it necessary first to address metaphysical and meta-ethical questions, Rawls further develops this moral conception in KCMT. Here, summarizing the main points of the first two of KCMT's three parts, Rawls says that he has

> sketched the main idea of Kantian constructivism, which is to establish a connection between the first principles of justice and the conception of moral persons as free and equal. These first principles are used to settle the appropriate understanding of freedom and equality for a modern democratic society. The requisite connection is provided by a procedure of construction in which rationally autonomous agents subject to reasonable conditions agree to principles of justice. (KCMT: 340)

In the third part of KCMT Rawls considers 'how a Kantian doctrine interprets the notion of objectivity' (ibid.).

One of Rawls's main purposes in KCMT is to explain, as distinct from defend, his own variant of Kantian constructivism, since 'the Kantian form of constructivism is much less well understood than other familiar traditional moral conceptions, such as utilitarianism, perfectionism, and intuitionism', and 'this situation impedes the advance of moral theory' (KCMT: 303). In an effort 'to deepen our understanding of Kantian constructivism', Rawls contrasts it with the doctrine he calls 'rational intuitionism'.[9]

> For our purposes here, rational intuitionism may be summed up by two theses: first, the basic moral concepts of the right and the good, and the moral worth of persons, are not analyzable in terms of nonmoral concepts (although possibly analyzable in terms of one another); and, second, first principles of morals (whether one or many), when correctly stated, are self-evident propositions about what kinds of considerations are good grounds for applying one of the three basic moral concepts, that is, for asserting that something is (intrinsically) good, or that a certain action is the right thing to do, or that a certain trait of character has moral worth. These two theses imply that the agreement in judgment which is so essential for an effective public conception of justice is founded on the recognition of self-evident truths about good reasons. And what these reasons are is fixed by a moral order that is prior to and independent of our conception of the person and the social role of morality. This order is given by the nature of things and is known, not by sense, but by rational intuition. (KCMT: 343–4)

So understood, 'rational intuitionism is compatible with a variety of contents for the first principles of a moral conception', including utilitarian contents (KCMT: 344).

Kantian constructivism, like rational intuitionism, combines a conception of moral objectivity with a set of first principles; however, their conceptions of the person differ. Rational intuitionism requires only 'a sparse notion of the person, founded on the self as knower': since the content of the first principles is already fixed, 'the only requirements on the self are to be able to know what these principles are and to be moved by this knowledge' (KCMT: 346). By contrast, a Kantian view requires 'a more complex conception of the person, of a kind adequate to determine the content of [first] principles, together with a suitable moral psychology' (ibid.).

> [The procedures by which first principles are selected] must be suitably founded on practical reason, or, more exactly, on notions which characterize persons as reasonable and rational and which are incorporated into the way in which, as such persons, they represent to themselves their free and equal moral personality. Put another way, first principles of justice must issue from a conception of the person through a suitable representation of that conception . . .' (ibid.)

Such a representation is illustrated, Rawls says, by the procedure of construction in his own variant of a Kantian conception, justice as fairness (ibid.).

A Kantian constructivist view determines certain principles as 'most reasonable for those who conceive of their person as it is represented in the procedure of construction' (KCMT: 355).[10] In the case of Rawls's variant of Kantian constructivism, the principles of justice 'are the principles most reasonable for us, given our conception of persons as free and equal, and full cooperating members of a democratic society' (KCMT: 340).

> [The first principles of justice as fairness] single out what facts citizens in a well-ordered society are to count as reasons of justice. Apart from the procedure of constructing these principles, there are no reasons of justice. Put in another way, whether certain facts are to count as reasons of justice and what their relative force is to be can be ascertained only on the basis of the principles that result from the construction. (KCMT: 351)

Rawls describes these principles as 'reasonable' instead of 'true', he explains, 'not because of some alternative theory of truth, but simply in order to keep to terms that indicate the constructivist standpoint as opposed to rational intuitionism' (KCMT: 355). A constructivist view does not require any particular account of truth, for instance, idealist or verificationist as opposed to realist (KCMT: 351).

> Whatever the nature of truth in the case of general beliefs about human nature and how society works, a constructivist moral doctrine requires a distinct procedure of construction to identify the first principles of justice. To the extent that Kant's moral doctrine depends upon what to some may appear to be a constructivist account of truth in the *First Critique* (I don't mean to imply that such an interpretation is correct), justice as fairness departs from that aspect of Kant's view and seeks to preserve the overall structure of his moral conception apart from that background. (KCMT: 351–352)

The main idea of Kantian constructivism, Rawls emphasizes, is to establish a connection between the first principles of justice and a conception of moral persons as free and equal (KCMT: 340). In

TJ, Rawls said that according to Kant, 'a person is acting autonomously when the principles of his action are chosen by him as the most adequate possible expression of his nature as a free and equal rational being'; these principles are to be thought of as legislation for a kingdom of ends or an ethical commonwealth; and 'this moral legislation is to be agreed to under conditions that characterize men as free and equal rational beings' (TJ: 221–6). However, Kant did not adequately specify a particular set of principles of justice, so 'we need an argument showing which principles, if any, free and equal rational persons would choose and these principles must be applicable in practice' (TJ: 224). Rawls contends that his own conception of justice, justice as fairness, provides such an argument.

In developing justice as fairness, Rawls uses three model-conceptions (a moral person, a well-ordered society, the original position) in order to 'fix ideas', that is, to limit vagueness, ambiguity, and indeterminacy, and to establish a 'framework' within which to reason (KCMT: 307, 357). The general purpose of the model-conceptions of a moral person and a well-ordered society is 'to single out the essential aspects of our conception of ourselves as moral persons and of our relation to society as free and equal citizens' (KCMT: 308). The role of the original position is

> to establish the connection between the model-conception of a moral person and the principles of justice that characterize the relations of citizens in the model-conception of a well-ordered society. It serves this role by modeling the way in which the citizens in a well-ordered society, viewed as moral persons, would ideally select first principles of justice for their society. The constraints imposed on the parties in the original position, and the manner in which the parties are described, are to represent the freedom and equality of moral persons as understood in such a society. If certain principles of justice would indeed be agreed to (or if they would belong to a certain restricted family of principles), then the aim of Kantian constructivism to connect definite principles with a particular conception of the person is achieved. (ibid.)

If we start with the concept of a person as 'the basic unit of agency and responsibility in social life', and define a person as 'a human being capable of taking full part in social cooperation, honoring its ties and relationships over a complete life', we will specify this capacity differently depending on how we understand social cooperation or a complete life; 'and each such specification yields another conception of the person falling under the concept' (KCMT: 357). Given that Rawls is 'addressing the public culture of a democratic society,' and given his conception of the task of justifying a conception of justice, he aims to use 'a conception of the person implicitly affirmed in that culture, or else one that would prove acceptable to citizens once it was properly presented and explained' (KCMT: 306).

In a Kantian constructivist conception, Rawls argues, objectivity is compatible with autonomy (whether as Kant construes autonomy or as Rawls himself construes it in the terms of justice as fairness), but rational intuitionism is heteronomous.

> [I]t suffices for heteronomy that [first] principles obtain in virtue of relations among objects the nature of which is not affected or determined by the conception of the person. Kant's idea of autonomy requires that there exist no such order of given objects determining the first principles of right and justice among free and equal moral persons. Heteronomy obtains not only when first principles are fixed by the special psychological constitution of human nature, as in Hume, but also when they are fixed by an order of universals or concepts grasped by rational intuition, as in Plato's realm of forms or in Leibniz's hierarchy of perfections. (KCMT: 345)

Kant would have rejected rational intuitionism, Rawls contends,[11] because its notion of objectivity is not compatible with autonomy (ibid.;TJ: 221–6).

The original position, 'by setting up a definite framework within which a binding agreement on principles must be made', presents a specific problem that forces us 'to describe the parties and their mutual relations in the process of construction so that appropriate principles of justice result' (KCMT: 357). Since 'it seems quite likely that there are only a few viable conceptions of the person both sufficiently general to be part of a moral doctrine and congruent with the ways in which people are to regard themselves in a democratic society', and since it is possible that only one of these conceptions has 'a representation in a procedure of construction that issues in acceptable and workable principles, given the relevant general beliefs', there may be a single most reasonable conception of justice for a democratic society (KCMT: 355). Justice as fairness does not 'exclude the possibility of there being a fact of the matter about this'; it is 'compatible with objectivism in this sense' (KCMT: 355–6).

However, it does not presuppose that there is a single most reasonable conception, nor that there is more than one. It is open to the possibility that 'for us, there exists no reasonable and workable conception of justice at all', and that therefore 'the practical task of political philosophy is doomed to failure' (KCMT: 356). Below, I discuss Rawls's understanding of the practical task of political philosophy, after offering the first part of my reply to Flikschuh.

3. Reply to Flikschuh (I)

According to Flikschuh, what is '[m]ost striking about the development of Rawls's views on metaphysics in political thinking is the contrast between a relatively fixed, general conception of metaphysics and rather more shifting interpretations of Kant's moral theory in relation to that general conception' (KMPP: 21–2). She takes Rawls's conception of metaphysics to be 'a type of transcendent rationalism' (KMPP: 22).

> Rawls's understanding of the rational intuitionisms of Henry Sidgwick, G. E. Moore, and W. D. Ross shapes his own formulation of that view. He tends to generalise from his account of the British intuitionists to the metaphysical systems of Plato, Aristotle, Spinoza, and Leibniz. Hence it is fair to say that rational intuitionism constitutes Rawls's paradigm conception of metaphysics ... Since he views metaphysics by the lights of rational intuitionism, he must repudiate those aspects of Kant's moral theory that imply metaphysical commitments interpreted as a form of rational intuitionism. (ibid.)

Flikschuh does not specify which 'aspects of Kant's moral theory' Rawls 'must repudiate', nor does she provide much argumentative or textual support for her claim about how Rawls 'views metaphysics'. In fact, Rawls nowhere says that rational intuitionism is his 'paradigm conception of metaphysics', nor, I contend, is this implied by what he does say. Rawls uses the term 'metaphysics' in IMT, but there he merely argues that 'much of moral theory', which he distinguishes from moral philosophy as one of the latter's main parts, 'is, in important respects, independent from certain philosophical subjects sometimes regarded as methodologically prior to it', including metaphysics (IMT: 286, 302). Rawls hardly uses the term 'metaphysics' at all in KCMT, where he contrasts rational intuitionism with Kantian constructivism for the reasons I have explained above. Flikschuh does not examine Rawls's usage of the term 'metaphysics,' nor does she engage the arguments he makes in IMT and KCMT.

According to Flikschuh, 'Rawls's interpretation of Kant' can be divided into 'three broad phases', the first of which is his 'assimilation of Kant's metaphysics under rational intuitionism' in TJ (KMPP: 22). In fact, however, in TJ Rawls does not discuss Kant in relation to rational intuitionism, nor does he say much about Kant's metaphysics. Rawls does discuss 'intuitionism': he discusses the distinctive features of intuitionist views and argues that the only way to refute intuitionism is to present 'the sort of constructive criteria that are said not to exist' (TJ: 35). In the section of TJ entitled 'The Kantian Interpretation of Justice as Fairness',[12] Rawls discusses neither intuitionism nor rational intuitionism. Nowhere in TJ does he assimilate Kant's metaphysics under any form of intuitionism.

The second broad phase of 'Rawls's interpretation of Kant', according to Flikschuh, is his 'juxtaposition of rational intuitionism with Kantian constructivism' in KCMT (KMPP: 22). Specifying 'juxtaposition', Flikschuh claims that the two theses to which, as Rawls claims in this essay, rational intuitionists are committed[13] 'express a summary conception of metaphysics as the hypostatisation of an order of rationally intuited true ideas' (KMPP: 24). However, even if rational intuitionists are committed to such a conception of metaphysics, Rawls himself need not be, and I find little evidence that he attributes 'remnants of a rationalist metaphysics to Kant's ethics', contrary to Flikschuh's unsupported claim that he does so in KCMT (KMPP: 25). Moreover, although rational intuitionism proposes answers to questions that belong to metaphysics, and can properly be called a 'metaphysical doctrine', rational intuitionism cannot properly be called *a conception of metaphysics* as Rawls uses the term 'metaphysics', since he uses it to refer to a subfield in the academic discipline of philosophy.

The third broad phase of 'Rawls's interpretation of Kant', according to Flikschuh, is his 'juxtaposition of rational intuitionism and Kantian constructivism with political constructivism in *Political Liberalism*' (KMPP: 23). She says that Rawls's 'third and most recent position is of principal interest to [her] contention that he privatises metaphysics' (KMPP: 25). In *Political Liberalism* [PL],[14] Flikschuh contends, Rawls characterizes both rational intuitionism and Kantian constructivism as

> metaphysical doctrines representing two divergent possible comprehensive conceptions of the good. Neither is inadmissible so long as they do not enter the realm of public debate. Both must remain confined to a person's private view of the world. (KMPP: 26)

At this point it becomes necessary to explain Rawls's idea of public reason, for Flikschuh here misinterprets it. In order to explain it I must put it in the context of Rawls's political philosophy.

4. Rawls on the practical task of political philosophy

According to Rawls, the task of political philosophy in its 'practical role,' which arises from 'divisive political conflict and the need to settle the problem of order', is 'to focus on deeply disputed questions and to see whether, despite appearances, some underlying bases of philosophical and moral agreement can be uncovered'.[15] While the 'dominant tradition' has viewed political philosophy 'as part of moral philosophy, together with theology and metaphysics', Rawls's political philosophy has a different aim, in view of the fact that 'the normal result of the exercise of human reason within the framework of the free institutions of a constitutional democratic regime' is a plurality of reasonable yet incompatible comprehensive doctrines (PL: xvii–xix). Believing that it is impossible to maintain a shared adherence to one comprehensive doctrine except 'by the oppressive use of state power with all its official crimes and the inevitable brutality and cruelties, followed by the corruption of religion, philosophy, and science', Rawls develops a conception of political justice that takes reasonable pluralism to be a permanent condition of a democratic political culture.[16]

4.1. Reasonable pluralism, legitimate law, public reason

As Rawls explains in the two introductions in the paperback editions of PL, he began to modify the view he had presented in TJ (in

1971) because he came to see that the account of the stability of a well-ordered society offered in Part III of that book is not consistent with the rest of the view. According to that account of stability, in a well-ordered democratic society all or nearly all citizens endorse justice as fairness on the basis of a Kantian comprehensive philosophical doctrine, that is, a moral doctrine not limited to the domain of the political but general in scope. Only after publishing TJ did Rawls clearly draw the distinction between comprehensive doctrines and strictly political conceptions,[17] having realized that it is unrealistic to expect that all or nearly all citizens will ever endorse justice as fairness on the basis of the same comprehensive doctrine, even under the best of foreseeable conditions. This realization led Rawls to confront the following question: 'How is it possible that there may exist over time a stable and just society of free and equal citizens profoundly divided by reasonable though incompatible religious, philosophical, and moral doctrines?' (PL: xx, xxxvii). More sharply put, this question asks how it is possible 'for those affirming a religious doctrine that is based on religious authority, for example, the Church or the Bible, also to hold a reasonable political conception that supports a just democratic regime' (PL: xxxvii, xxxix). Rawls addresses this question in PL, construing it as a question about 'the essential conditions of a viable and just society' (ibid.).

Since citizens in a constitutional democracy exercise ultimate political power as a collective body, the fact of reasonable pluralism raises the question of what kinds of reasons citizens in a well-ordered democratic society may reasonably give one another when fundamental political questions are at stake: by what ideals and principles are citizens to exercise their power so that each can reasonably justify his or her political decisions to the other citizens?[18] Rawls answers this question by specifying 'the basic moral and political values that are to determine a constitutional democratic government's relation to its citizens and their relation to one another' (IPRR: 132). The nature of the political relation in a well-ordered democratic society is, according to Rawls, one of 'civic friendship', which is realized when citizens fulfil their duty of civility (IPRR: 135). This duty requires citizens to apply the criterion of reciprocity and employ public reason when deliberating about questions of constitutional essentials and matters of basic justice. 'The idea of political legitimacy based on the criterion of reciprocity says: Our exercise of political power is proper only when we sincerely believe that the reasons we would offer for our political actions – were we to state them as government officials – are sufficient, and we also reasonably think that other citizens might also reasonably accept those reasons' (IPRR: 137).

In PL Rawls discusses, 'from the point of view of the political', the main moral and philosophical ideas of a constitutional democratic regime, including: a free and equal citizen, legitimate exercise of political power, stability for the right reasons, a reasonable overlapping consensus, and public reason with its duty of civility (PL: xli). In so doing, he modifies some of the ideas used in TJ and introduces some new ideas. Among the modified ideas is that of the person: 'the idea of the person as having moral personality with the full capacity of moral agency is transformed into that of the citizen' (PL: xliii).

Although Rawls's conception of a just democratic society, justice as fairness, regards the citizen as a moral agent, it discusses only the political rights and duties of citizenship and their associated values: it considers the citizen as 'the political person of a modern democracy with the political rights and duties of citizenship, and standing in a political relation with other citizens' (PL: xlv). Citizens are free in virtue of their having the two moral powers and the associated powers of reason, and equal in virtue of having all of these powers 'to the requisite minimum degree to be fully cooperating members of society' (PL: 19). Further, citizens are free also in the following three senses: they conceive themselves and each other (1) as having not only the capacity for a conception of the good but also the right to view their persons as independent from and not identified with any particular scheme of final ends, so that 'their public or legal identity as free persons is not affected by changes over time in their determinate conception of the good'; (2) as 'self-authenticating sources of valid claims'; and (3) as 'capable of taking responsibility for their ends' (PL: 30, 32–3; JF: 21).

If citizens who endorse different comprehensive doctrines can appreciate what a political conception of democratic justice achieves, acquire an allegiance to it, and affirm its principles of justice as expressing political values that – under the reasonably favourable conditions that make democracy possible – are normally overriding, then the political conception of justice can be the focus of an 'overlapping consensus' of reasonable comprehensive doctrines.[19] When such an overlapping consensus exists, the political conception of justice is justifiable either in terms of any of these doctrines, or independently of all of them and simply in terms of the political ideas constituting the conception of justice. When this is the case, the members of the society can use what Rawls calls 'public reason' when offering justifications to one another for 'laws and policies that invoke the coercive powers of government concerning fundamental political questions' and for the basic structure of their shared social and political world. Justifications in terms of public reason can be offered to and freely accepted by all members of the society (IPRR: 165–6).

Rawls proposes that when questions of fundamental political justice are discussed in the public political forum, the idea of the politically reasonable should replace the idea of the whole truth (understood as including reasons drawn from a particular comprehensive doctrine).

> Since the idea of public reason specifies at the deepest level the basic political values and specifies how the political relation is to be understood, those who believe that fundamental political questions should be decided by what they regard as the best reasons according to their own idea of the whole truth – including their religious or secular comprehensive doctrine – and not by reasons that might be shared by all citizens as free and equal, will of course reject the idea of public reason. Political liberalism views this insistence on the whole truth in politics as incompatible with democratic citizenship and the idea of legitimate law. (IPRR: 138)

4.2. The public political forum, nonpublic political culture, and background culture

Whenever a question of fundamental political justice is at issue in a democracy, a citizen is to 'deliberate within a framework of what he or she sincerely regards as the most reasonable political conception of justice, a conception that expresses political values that others, as free and equal citizens[,] might also be expected reasonably to endorse' (IPRR: 140). In a representative government, citizens vote for representatives and not for particular laws, except when voting on referendum questions, which are rarely matters of basic justice. Ideally, 'judges, legislators, chief executives, and other government officials, as well as candidates for public office, act from and follow the idea of public reason and explain to other citizens their reasons for supporting fundamental political positions in terms of the political conception of justice they regard as the most reasonable' (IPRR: 135). Citizens who are not government officials ideally 'think of themselves *as if* they were legislators and ask themselves what statutes, supported by what reasons satisfying the criterion of reciprocity, they would think it most reasonable to enact'.[20] Ideally, all citizens and all government officials act from and follow public reason, so understood; when they do,

> the legal enactment expressing the opinion of the majority is legitimate law. It may not be thought the most reasonable, or the most appropriate, by each, but it is to be accepted as such. Each thinks that all have spoken and voted at least reasonably, and therefore all have followed public reason and honored their duty of civility. (IPRR: 137)

The idea of public reason applies to the public political forum, which Rawls divides into three parts:

> the discourse of judges in their decisions, and especially of the judges of a supreme court; the discourse of government officials, especially chief executives and legislators; and finally, the discourse of candidates for public office and their campaign managers, especially in their public oratory, party platforms, and political statements. (IPRR: 133–4)

The idea of public reason *does not apply* to the background culture, that is, the culture of civil society, which includes 'the culture of churches and associations of all kinds, and institutions of learning at all levels, especially universities and professional schools, scientific and other societies' (IPRR: 134 n. 13).[21] Nor does the idea of public reason apply to the media, for instance 'newspapers, reviews and magazines, television and radio and much else', which constitute 'the nonpublic political culture' (IPRR: 134 n. 13).[22] Thus the idea of public reason does not apply to what Jürgen Habermas and Seyla Benhabib call *the public sphere*, which is what political liberalism calls *the background culture* of civil society (IPRR: 142 n. 28).[23]

The public political culture of a democracy, as Rawls understands it, includes forms of discussion and expression that go beyond political deliberation, decision-making, and public justification. By contrast with the background culture, however, the public political culture involves an injunction to present public political reasons (IPRR: 152). This injunction, which Rawls calls 'the proviso', applies when reasons deriving from comprehensive doctrines are expressed in public political discussion: 'reasonable comprehensive doctrines, religious and nonreligious, may be introduced in public political discussion at any time, provided that in due course proper political reasons – and not reasons given solely by comprehensive doctrines – are presented that are sufficient to support whatever the comprehensive doctrines introduced are said to support' (IPRR: 152). Public reasoning, as distinct from witnessing, conjecture, and declaration, aims for public justification; it is argument that 'proceeds correctly from premises we accept and think others could reasonably accept to conclusions we think they could also reasonably accept' (IPRR: 155–6). On condition that the proviso is in due course appropriately satisfied in good faith, the introduction into public political discussion of religious and secular doctrines does not change the aim of public reasoning (IPRR: 153).[24]

According to Rawls, in a constitutional democracy 'the public conception of justice should be, so far as possible, independent of controversial philosophical and religious doctrines', and so 'to formulate such a conception we apply the principle of toleration to philosophy itself: the public conception of justice is to be political, not metaphysical' (JF:PM: 388). What Rawls means by 'the public conception of justice' is a conception of justice that serves as a democratic society's public standard of justification for all fundamental questions about the justice of the society's basic institutions. For the reasons explained above, no conception of justice that depends on a particular comprehensive doctrine can play this role.

It is important to note that accepting the principle of toleration following the European Wars of Religion in the sixteenth and seventeenth centuries did not involve ceasing to affirm the truth of one's own religion, but only declining to impose it forcibly, for the sake of peaceful coexistence, among other reasons. Similarly, accepting the principle of toleration as applying to political philosophy (to the extent that a public conception of justice for a democratic society must avoid asserting or presupposing the truth of any particular comprehensive doctrine) does not involve ceasing to affirm the truth of one's own comprehensive doctrine. 'Properly understood, . . . a political conception of justice need be no more indifferent . . . to truth in morals than the principle of toleration, suitably understood, need be indifferent to truth in religion' (IOP: 435). Rawls refrains from asserting that justice as fairness is true, or even that it would be true if an overlapping consensus on it were to develop; however, citizens may regard it as true in so far as it accords with their own general and comprehensive views.

Rawls's political conception of justice

> extends the movement of thought that began three centuries ago with the gradual acceptance of the principle of toleration and led to the non-confessional state and equal liberty of conscience. This extension is required for an agreement on a political conception of justice given the historical and social circumstances of a democratic society. . . . In applying the principle of toleration to philosophy itself it is left to citizens individually to resolve for themselves the questions of religion, philosophy, and morals in accordance with the views they freely affirm. (IOP: 437)

5. Reply to Flikschuh (II)

Flikschuh attributes to Rawls the view that we should 'set aside contentious philosophical differences when deliberating about principles of justice for a just social order' (KMPP: 20, 29–30). Here Flikschuh apparently overlooks the distinctions among Rawls's three methods of justification: using the original position to justify principles, seeking reflective equilibrium, and using public reason.[25] The requirements of public reason cannot be specified until the principles of justice have been determined, for which purpose Rawls uses the original position and reflective equilibrium.

Flikschuh also attributes to Rawls the views that 'metaphysics in political thinking' is 'permissible, if at all, only in the private sphere, never in the public sphere', and that '[p]ublicly voicing one's opposition to political constructivism on the grounds that it does not accord with one's religious and metaphysical beliefs cannot be tolerated'. She criticizes Rawls's position as making it difficult or impossible for professional metaphysicians to practice their vocation in Rawls's constitutional democracy.

> One would expect them to discuss, defend, and promulgate their conflicting metaphysical systems within the limits of the law, exercising toleration of each other's views as a matter of good liberal practice. But could one expect them to remain silent, or merely privately troubled, when it comes to questions of political justification and legitimation? (KMPP: 30)[26]

However, in fact Rawls does not hold that metaphysics is to be done only in private and never in any public settings (for example, in universities, in public lecture halls, in the pages of published books and journals), and does not argue that religious or metaphysical beliefs must not be expressed in public. The well-ordered society of justice as fairness is a liberal-democratic society with a constitutional regime that secures the full range of liberal rights and liberties, including freedoms of speech, press, assembly, thought, conscience and religion. The requirements of public reason apply to the public political forum but not to the background culture, which includes newspapers, reviews and magazines, television and radio, and so on. Rawls does not argue that criticism of political constructivism should be suppressed. What he opposes is oppressive, illegitimate use of political power.

Flikschuh attributes to Rawls the view that 'a person's religious and metaphysical beliefs are legitimate so long as they support political constructivism', that is, Rawls's political liberalism. But Rawls nowhere assesses religious or metaphysical beliefs as (il)legitimate; *a fortiori* he does not argue that a criterion of their legitimacy is whether they support political constructivism. What he does assess as (il)legitimate is the use of political power. Flikschuh does not examine his views on this topic, nor does she say much in her book about any of her own views on this topic.

6. Conclusion

Flikschuh's claim that 'political thought' or 'political justification' requires metaphysics is ambiguous: while it is surely true on some interpretation (for instance, at least one important question of political philosophy cannot be answered without determining the truth of at least one metaphysical proposition), and may well be true on another (for example, doing political philosophy well requires understanding Kant's moral and political philosophy, which requires at least some understanding of Kant's metaphysics), it is not true on all interpretations, including one that takes it as a claim about public reason and public justification as Rawls understands these ideas.

Rawls's political liberalism (which includes both justice as fairness and the law of peoples) specifies a particular interpretation of respect for persons and recognition of their inherent worth and dignity.[27] Rawls developed Kant's philosophy further, and went beyond it, in order to address issues Kant had not addressed.[28] Thus Rawls's political philosophy resulted from his doing metaphysics in a certain sense, namely, thinking through the relations among the metaphysical, ethical, and political questions addressed in the works of the philosophers he studied, including Kant. However, Rawls's published work does not include much in the way of proposed and defended answers to metaphysical questions. It addresses certain questions that are political and not metaphysical in the following three related yet distinct senses: (1) these political questions would remain unanswered even after the most relevant metaphysical questions (for instance, about the nature of the self and the nature of human freedom) were answered, and answering these metaphysical questions may require first developing moral theory further (i.e. metaphysics is not sufficient); (2) these political questions can be answered adequately for practical purposes without first settling the enduring controversies about those metaphysical questions (i.e. metaphysics is not necessary); (3) these political questions can be encountered and addressed by adherents of diverse comprehensive doctrines, religious or secular, whose lines of philosophical reasoning about metaphysical and ethical questions lead them all to endorse (a) a conception of citizens as free and equal persons and (b) a conception of society as a fair system of social cooperation; therefore a conception of justice appropriate to serve as a public standard of justification for a democratic society is one that is developed on the basis of these conceptions of person and of society, and does not presuppose the truth or falsity of any particular one of these comprehensive doctrines, thus does not preclude them from being part of an overlapping consensus on the political conception of justice.

Flikschuh claims that a political philosopher must work within a framework of principles, both theoretical and practical, which are systematically interrelated (KMPP: 33–5); however, Rawls nowhere denies this. Indeed, what he says in IMT about the relations between moral theory and the rest of philosophy, and in his later works about the relations between his political constructivism and comprehensive philosophical doctrines, is consistent with that claim. Flikschuh claims that Rawls rejects Kant's transcendental idealism; however, Rawls nowhere rejects it as false, although political liberalism avoids presupposing the truth of any particular comprehensive doctrine, including Kant's, for the reasons explained above. Flikschuh claims that Rawls uses the term 'metaphysics' to refer to rational intuitionism, and rejects metaphysics; however, Rawls does not use the term 'metaphysics' in that way, and when discussing rational intuitionism he does not claim that it is false, although he does argue that it is incompatible with autonomy (both as Kant construes autonomy and as Rawls himself construes autonomy in the terms of justice as fairness) and that Kantian constructivism offers a conception of objectivity better suited to the practical role of political philosophy as part of a democratic society's public political culture.

Rawls's main concern is not to develop a conception of justice that Kant scholars would all describe as Kantian, but instead to determine a satisfactory answer to what Rawls regards as the fundamental question of political philosophy for a modern constitutional democracy: the question of 'what principles of justice are most appropriate to specify the fair terms of cooperation when society is viewed as a system of cooperation between citizens regarded as free and equal persons, and as normal and fully cooperating members of society over a complete life' (JF: 176 n. 59). In order to develop a satisfactory answer, Rawls draws upon the works of Kant and Rousseau, among others, and he acknowledges the sources of the ideas he uses. Since the structure of Rawls's conception of justice differs so markedly from the structures of non-Kantian conceptions, and since his conception shares so many important features with Kant's moral and political philosophy, it makes sense for Rawls to describe his view as Kantian despite its divergences from Kant's own philosophy, which Rawls himself points out (PL: 99–101, 222 n. 9). It is interesting and worthwhile to consider precisely in what respects Rawls's conception of justice is (not) Kantian. In doing so, fans of Kant should be sure not to overlook the possibility that some differences from, or developments of, Kant's expressed views may indeed be justifiable, and may even be properly termed Kantian.[29]

Notes

1 Katrin Flikschuh, *Kant and Modern Political Philosophy* (Cambridge: Cambridge University Press, 2000). Henceforth cited in text as 'KMPP'.

2 John Rawls, *A Theory of Justice*, rev. edn (Cambridge, MA: Harvard University Press, 1999); first published in 1971. Henceforth cited in text as 'TJ'.

3 Since 1999, the year before Flikschuh's book was published, it has become much easier to obtain and study Rawls's writings and to avoid misunderstanding them, thanks to the publication of Rawls's *Collected Papers*, ed. S. Freeman (Cambridge, MA: Harvard University Press, 1999) as well as Samuel Freeman (ed.), *The Cambridge Companion to Rawls* (Cambridge: Cambridge University Press, 2003) and *Rawls* (New York: Routledge, 2007), to which I refer below.

4 Others who have made criticisms of political liberalism similar to some of Flikschuh's include Jean Hampton, Otfried Höffe, and Onora O'Neill. Within the limitations of the present short article I cannot fully address their criticisms. However, some of the arguments I direct to Flikschuh apply to one or more of these other critics as well. My discussion of public reason supplements the arguments made by Paul Weithman, 'Liberalism and the political character of political philosophy', in C. F. Delaney (ed.), *The Liberalism-Communitarianism Debate: Liberty and Community Values* (Maryland: Rowman and Littlefield, 1994), pp. 189–211, rebutting Jean Hampton, 'Should political philosophy be done without metaphysics?', *Ethics* 99/4 (1989), 791–814; Flikschuh cites Hampton but not Weithman.

5 'Rawls has shown a persistent lack of concern with Kant's political philosophy. This is so especially with regard to Kant's cosmopolitanism. In 'The Law of Peoples' – his only direct contribution to problems of international justice – Rawls explicitly distances his position from that of Kant, and opts for a qualified endorsement of existing international law instead' (Flikschuh, *Kant*, p. 183).

6 I do not address her criticism of Rawls's argument for the difference principle (as involving Hobbesian assumptions), since Paul Guyer convincingly rebuts similar criticisms in his essay 'Life, Liberty, and Property: Rawls and Kant', in D. Hüning (ed.), *Recht, Staat, und Völkerrecht bei Immanuel Kant* (Berlin: Duncker und Humblot, 1998). Flikschuh neither rebuts nor cites Guyer's essay.

7 Rawls, 'The independence of moral theory' (1975), henceforth cited in text as 'IMT'; 'Kantian constructivism in moral theory' (1980), cited as 'KCMT'; both reprinted in *Collected Papers*.

8 See Rawls, *A Theory of Justice*, pp. 15–19, 40–6, 452–5, 506–14.

9 '[I]n one form or another [this doctrine] dominated moral philosophy from Plato and Aristotle onward until it was challenged by Hobbes and Hume and, I believe, in a very different way by Kant. To simplify matters, I take rational intuitionism to be the view exemplified in the English tradition by Clarke and Price, Sidgwick and Moore, and formulated in its minimum essentials by W. D. Ross' (Rawls, 'Kantian constructivism', p. 343). Rawls adopts 'Ross's characterization of rational intuitionism, adjusted to allow for any number of first principles' (ibid., p. 343 n. 4).

10 How should people 'conceive of their person'? Rawls does not address this question in his political liberalism (which excludes the Kantian congruence argument of Part III of TJ), leaving it for others to address; on these topics, see Freeman, *Rawls*, chs 6–9, and Weithman, 'Liberalism'.

11 Recall that Rawls uses a modified version of Ross's characterization of rational intuitionism.

12 Flikschuh misquotes the title of this section as 'A Kantian Interpretation of the Original Position' (Flikschuh, *Kant*, p. 23).

13 Above, in section 2, these two theses are quoted from Rawls, 'Kantian constructivism', pp. 343–4.

14 Rawls, *Political Liberalism*, rev. edn (New York: Columbia University Press, 2005).

15 Rawls, *Justice as Fairness* (Cambridge, MA: Harvard University Press, 2001), pp. 1–2. Henceforth cited in text as 'JF'.

16 Ibid., p. 34.

17 See the discussion of this distinction in Freeman, *Rawls*, p. 332.

18 Rawls, 'The idea of public reason revisited' (1997), in *The Law of Peoples* (cited in text as 'IPRR'), p. 136.

19 See the discussion of the idea of a reasonable comprehensive doctrine in Freeman, *Rawls*, pp. 349–51.

20 'There is some resemblance between this criterion and Kant's principle of the original contract', as Rawls notes ('The idea of public reason revisited', p. 135 n. 16).

21 Regarding the background culture, see also *Political Liberalism*, p. 14.

22 Although this is a somewhat odd usage of 'nonpublic', it can be understood as referring to political discussions and debates that do not constitute political decision-making or the wielding of political power.

23 Here Rawls cites works by Habermas and Benhabib.

24 Moreover, Rawls here emphasizes, there is a positive ground for citizens' introducing their reasonable comprehensive doctrines into the public political culture.

25 See Thomas M. Scanlon, 'Rawls on justification', in S. Freeman (ed.), *The Cambridge Companion*.

26 In a footnote at this point in her text, Flikschuh cites Hampton, 'Should political philosophy be done without metaphysics?', as raising similar objections.

27 As Rawls says: 'without the principles of right and justice, the aims of benevolence and the requirements of respect are both undefined; they presuppose these principles already independently derived . . . Once the conception of justice is on hand, however, the ideas of respect and of human dignity can be given a more definite meaning. Among other things, respect for persons is shown by treating them in ways that they can see to be justified. But more than this, it is manifest in the content of the principles to which we appeal' (*A Theory of Justice*, p. 513).

28 See Alyssa R. Bernstein, 'Kant, Rawls, and Cosmopolitanism: *Toward Perpetual Peace* and *The Law of Peoples*', *Jahrbuch für Recht und Ethik/Annual Review of Law and Ethics*.

29 This article has developed from a paper I presented in September 2007 for the ECPR Kantian Standing Group's Section, entitled 'Politics and Metaphysics in Kant', of the 4th European Consortium for Political Research conference (Pisa, Italy, September 2007). For financial assistance enabling me to attend the conference, I thank the Ohio University Philosophy Department's Spetnagel Travel Fund and Ohio University's Institute for Applied and Professional Ethics. A generous fellowship from DePauw University, the 2007–8 Nancy Schaenen Visiting Scholar position at the Janet Prindle Institute for Ethics, enabled me to draft this article. Colin Manning provided research assistance and transcription. For valuable written comments or discussion I thank Sorin Baiasu, Monica Mueller, Hugo Omar Seleme, and Lucas Thorpe.

References

Bernstein, A., 'Kant, Rawls, and Cosmopolitanism: *Toward Perpetual Peace* and *The Law of Peoples*', *Jahrbuch für Recht und Ethik/Annual Review of Law and Ethics*, 17 (2009), 3–52.

Flikschuh, K., *Kant and Modern Political Philosophy* (Cambridge: Cambridge University Press, 2000).

Freeman, S. (ed.), *The Cambridge Companion to Rawls* (Cambridge: Cambridge University Press, 2003).

——, *Rawls* (New York: Routledge, 2007).

Guyer, P., 'Life, Liberty, and Property: Rawls and Kant', in D. Hüning (ed.), *Recht, Staat, und Völkerrecht bei Immanuel Kant* (Berlin: Duncker und Humblot, 1998).

Hampton, J., 'Should political philosophy be done without metaphysics?', *Ethics* 99/4 (1989), 791–814.

Larmore, C., 'Public reason', in S. Freeman (ed.), *The Cambridge Companion to Rawls* (Cambridge: Cambridge University Press, 2003).

Rawls, J., 'The independence of moral theory', reprinted in *Collected Papers* [1975].

——, 'Kantian constructivism in moral theory', reprinted in *Collected Papers* [1980].

——, 'Justice as fairness: political not metaphysical' (cited in text as 'JF:PM'), reprinted in *Collected Papers* [1985].

——, 'The Idea of An Overlapping Consensus' (cited in text as 'IOC'), reprinted in *Collected Papers* [1987].

——, 'The idea of public reason revisited', reprinted in *The Law of Peoples* [1997].

——, *The Law of Peoples* (Cambridge, MA: Harvard University Press, 1999).

——, *A Theory of Justice*, rev. edn (Cambridge, MA: Harvard University Press, 1999).

——, *Collected Papers*, ed. S. Freeman (Cambridge, MA: Harvard University Press, 1999).

——, *Justice as Fairness* (Cambridge, MA: Harvard University Press, 2001).

——, *Political Liberalism*, rev. edn (New York: Columbia University Press, 2005).

Scanlon, T. M., 'Rawls on justification', in S. Freeman (ed.), *The Cambridge Companion to Rawls*.

Weithman, P., 'Liberalism and the political character of political philosophy', in C. F. Delaney (ed.), *The Liberalism-Communitarianism Debate: Liberty and Community Values* (Maryland: Rowman and Littlefield, 1994).

4 • On the Conditions of Discourse and Being: Kantian, Wittgensteinian and Levinasian Perspectives on the Relation between Metaphysics and Ethics

Sami Pihlström

1. Introduction: 'Aristotelian' and 'Kantian' metaphysics – and ethics

Metaphysics is usually regarded as the most general inquiry into the structures of reality, 'Being qua Being' – as a 'category theory' in a realist, Aristotelian spirit.[1] Traditionally, metaphysics and ethics have been seen as two distinct areas of philosophy, metaphysics being the primary one. What I propose here is a rethinking of the relation between metaphysics and ethics. More than anyone else, it was Kant who paved the way for the kind of rethinking I will sketch. From a Kantian perspective, metaphysics cannot be practised as an inquiry into the world *an sich*; yet there is room for a *critical* conception of metaphysics, reconceived as an examination of the basic features of a *humanly categorized reality*, of the practice-embedded conditions necessary for us to be able to experience an objective, structured world. It is (only) this 'human world' that we may hope to be able to investigate metaphysically.[2]

If we cannot expect metaphysics (or science) to offer us a view of the world as it is in itself, we must carefully consider how exactly we contribute to 'making' the world, to 'structuring' it into what it is for us. If we take seriously the Kantian claim that our very notion of reality is crucially, unavoidably, a function of human ways of constituting reality, and if we extend this view to cover historically transformable categories instead of fixed a priori structures of cognition, in particular to human *practices*[3] – as pragmatists since William James and John Dewey have suggested – then the question arises to what extent these world-constituting practices involve moral elements. The issue goes deeper than the uncontroversial idea that different metaphysical positions may have different ethical implications. My question is whether metaphysics, in the Kantian 'critical' sense, might be *grounded* in ethical considerations, based on ethical premises. A contemporary Kantian prepared to utilize, say, James's pragmatism, might argue that in *every* genuine metaphysical dispute some practical issue is, however remotely, involved.[4]

One of the aims of the contemporary Kantian-cum-pragmatist metaphysician might be – in my view ought to be – the construction of a comprehensive argument, in more or less explicitly ethical terms,[5] against 'metaphysical realism' (to use Putnam's expression – or against what Kant called 'transcendental realism'),[6] an assumption that leads many philosophical theories ethically astray. Metaphysical realism, in brief, ignores 'the human world', yet none of its recent critics has emphasized the ethical aspect of this neglect.[7] For the early pragmatists, especially James (in his 1907 *Pragmatism*), the paradigmatic form of ethically 'blind' metaphysics was absolute, monistic idealism, represented by Hegelians; in our own days, it is rather reductive materialism and scientism that have inherited this role. We should ask, however, whether any attempt to defend the ethics-metaphysics entanglement – or the related entanglement of values with facts – is committed to antirealism, or whether a (pragmatic) form of realism is acceptable within a broader 'idealist' (Kantian) framework. There are two basic research hypotheses that must be critically tested as the metaphysics-ethics entanglement receives further scrutiny, a modest one and a more ambitious one: (1) metaphysics and ethics are (deeply) entangled within a Kantian transcendental conception of metaphysics, especially in a pragmatist (Jamesian) rearticulation (the *modest* hypothesis); (2) *any* metaphysics presupposes ethics (the *ambitious* hypothesis). Only the first one can receive any sort of elaboration and legitimation here.

This paper will examine the metaphysics-ethics intertwinement in a Kantian and twentieth-century setting. First, I will briefly examine the metaphysical status of Kant's 'postulates of practical reason' (section 2). I will then connect the discussion with the legacies of two leading twentieth-century thinkers – Ludwig Wittgenstein and Emmanuel Levinas – controversially interpreting their projects and those of their followers, especially Rush Rhees's Wittgensteinian ideas, as quasi-Kantian attempts to establish transcendental preconditions (and limits) of meaningful discourse, and hence of any humanly possible reality or being-in-the-world (sections 3–4). Kant's own views will be revisited by way of conclusion (section 5).

2. Kant's postulates: metaphysical, ethical, or both?

A paradigmatic case of a metaphysics built on ethics can be found in Kant's doctrine of the postulates of practical reason: the freedom of the will, the existence of God, and the immortality of the soul. Although Kant did not claim this doctrine to presuppose his transcendental idealism, there is a sense in which it does presuppose something rather similar: the world is not absolutely independent of us but is (as James might put it) responsive to our ethical (and generally valuational) needs and interests, 'in the making' through such needs and interests. *We* structure reality in terms of what the moral law requires; there is no ontologically pre-structured world we could engage with.[8] But *is* our structuring really metaphysical, or should we confine ourselves to a purely ethical, pragmatic account of the postulates? For Kant, the postulates 'structure' our faith rather than the world, but for pragmatist neo-Kantians this contrast is elusive.

This is not the proper place to go into the details of Kant's criticism of transcendental theology in the Ideal of Pure Reason in the Dialectics of the first *Critique* (*KrV* A567/B595ff.). Nor can I closely examine Kant's 'moral argument' for the existence of God and the immortality of the soul in the Canon of Pure Reason (*KrV* A795/B823ff.) and the Dialectics of the second *Critique* (*KpV* 5: 122ff.). I will discuss only the *metaphysical status* of Kant's postulates.

As mere ideas of pure reason, the concepts of God and the soul lack 'objective reality'. At best, they can be used regulatively, not constitutively. This, however, is only the point of view of theoretical, speculative reason. From the perspective of practical reason – which, famously, is 'prior to' theoretical reason for Kant (*KpV* 5: 119ff.) – there is some kind of 'reality' corresponding to these concepts. Their epistemic status, when transformed into postulates of practical reason, differs from the status of the constitutive transcendental conditions of human experience, such as the categories and the forms of pure intuition, explored in the Transcendental

Analytic and the Transcendental Aesthetic. The latter concepts, according to Kant, structure the experienceable, knowable world. However, the postulates also structure – in an analogical, not identical manner – the human world as a world of ethical deliberation and action. This 'structuring' is not 'merely ethical' in the sense of being devoid of metaphysical concerns, but also metaphysical (in a 'critical' sense: see the discussion of the entanglement of the ethical and the metaphysical above).

As a reading of Kant, this is controversial. However, Frederick Beiser (2006) offers an insightful interpretation of Kant's 'moral faith' as a metaphysical perspective on the reality of God and the soul. He insists that Kant's notion of the highest good, *summum bonum* (*KrV* A810–11/B838–9), is explicitly derived from the Christian tradition, especially Augustine and the idea of a 'City of God' (Beiser 2006: 593–9). These notions refer to a situation in which there is a harmony between the duties set by the moral law and the happiness of moral agents acting on the basis of, or out of respect for (not merely in accordance with) this law. Beiser summarizes Kant's argumentation (*KpV* 5: 124–32) as follows:

1. We have a duty to promote the highest good (*summum bonum*).
2. We have to presuppose the conditions for the possibility of the highest good.
3. God is a condition for the possibility of the highest good.
4. Therefore, we have to presuppose the existence of God.[9]

This, on Beiser's reading, is an argument *absurdum practicum*, as distinct from an argument *absurdum logicum*. Unlike the latter, it does not purport to show that denying the conclusion yields a logical contradiction, but rather that denying the conclusion results in a breach of duty. According to Beiser, the moral law and the faith based on the concept of the highest good, though epistemically independent of each other (since one can and must be committed to moral duty independently of the highest good and theism), are nevertheless logically dependent: the possibility of acting on the basis of the moral law presupposes moral faith, because it is a condition set by the law itself. We can know, independently of religious standpoints, that the moral law binds us, but we cannot (claims Beiser) really act on the basis of that law unless we presuppose God's existence and the immortality of the soul.[10]

I find this argument essentially pragmatist; it resembles James's reflections on the will (or right) to believe and the pragmatic need to postulate a divine reality.[11] Beiser, however, also sharply differentiates Kant's views from James's, construing the latter as 'merely pragmatic' and immanent, not genuinely metaphysical. He fails to see that James too can be interpreted as a pragmatically theistic metaphysician.[12]

God's existence and immortality, as postulates, are auxiliary presuppositions needed for morality; without them the highest good, set as a duty to us by the moral law, could not be realized. For Kant, these presuppositions are both subjectively necessary interests and objective requirements of morality as it arises 'from within' reason. We can never know anything about God or the soul *qua Dinge an sich selbst*; we can only 'know' (or must postulate) them as objects required for the purposes of practical reason, purposes 'higher' than those of theoretical reason. I believe Beiser is correct in emphasizing that Kant's defence of the postulates is not merely pragmatic or 'immanent', detached from metaphysics and the Protestant Christian tradition Kant had inherited and to which he contributed. The moral world in which the highest good is realized is comparable to the metaphysically loaded notions of the City of God and *corpus mysticum*.[13] Kant is genuinely a theist, maintaining that the possibility of morality – of pursuing what the moral law requires – presupposes a commitment to the existence of God, though this commitment can only be made legitimately from the standpoint of practical reason.

Moreover, Kant's defence of the postulates and 'moral faith' is a *transcendental* justification of a kind of metaphysics, though not *transcendent* metaphysics postulating mysterious objects for theoretical reason.[14] Its transcendentality is found within our practices of moral deliberation under the guidance of the categorical imperative. If theistic metaphysics and immortality are understood as requiring justification from the standpoint of speculative, theoretical reason, all that results is paralogisms and the errors involved in the traditional proofs of God's existence, mercilessly criticized in the first *Critique*. Yet practical reason may legitimately widen the scope of the ideas left problematic by theoretical reason, rendering their objects real (*KpV* 5: 132–6); the concepts and objects postulated by practical reason may even be constitutive, instead of being merely regulative as the ideas of pure reason must remain in their only theoretically legitimate use (*KpV* 5: 135). Thus practical reason may turn reason's ideas from merely regulative to constitutive use, which does not, however, make them dogmatic principles to be avoided by critical metaphysicians.[15]

I would even suggest that the Kantian metaphysician argues transcendentally for the need to postulate transcendent objects or principles (such as God), although their transcendence can only be legitimately postulated 'from within' the practices of morality that transcendentally require them.[16] No illegitimate speculation about the metaphysics of pre-given, practice-independent dogmatic principles or entities (structured prior to our moral point of view) is needed or even possible. The notion of transcendence is here rethought from the perspective of the metaphysics-ethics entanglement.[17]

3. A Wittgensteinian perspective: Rhees's transcendental argument

Having introduced our issues through these Kantian preliminaries and having identified one interesting case of the entanglement of ethics and metaphysics in Kant's doctrine of the postulates of practical reason, I now turn to two influential (though sometimes sidelined) paradigms in contemporary philosophy, defined by Ludwig Wittgenstein and Emmanuel Levinas together with their followers. My question is whether some of their central ideas can be seen as 'Kantian' transcendental ones, and whether, in particular, some paradigmatically Wittgensteinian or Levinasian views could be said to combine metaphysics and ethics in something like the manner outlined above. Perhaps one might even interpret the Levinasian and Wittgensteinian reflections as Kantian transcendental arguments in a broad sense.[18]

The issue I will take up is the *possibility of discourse* and the related problem of the *possibility of (humanly experienceable) being or reality*, or the necessary (transcendental) preconditions for these possibilities. I will not dwell on the transcendental background of Levinas's thought in Husserl's phenomenology or the dispute over Wittgenstein's Kantianism;[19] instead, I will propose a transcendental analysis of Levinas's fundamental idea of otherness, the ethical primacy of the other. A comparison with the way in which speaking to, or with, another person is constitutive of language and meaning in Rush Rhees's Wittgenstein-inspired thought is interesting here.[20] Thus, I will not directly discuss Wittgenstein himself but a Wittgensteinian thinker, Rhees, who transcends Wittgenstein's own views in crucial respects.[21] Levinas's and Rhees's reflections on otherness – on our relation to the other as ineliminably built into our being in the world into our being able discursively to structure the world we are in – synthesize ethics and metaphysics as profoundly as the Kantian postulates do.

Let us start with Rhees. A pivotal point in his recently published posthumous work, edited by D. Z. Phillips (another neo-Wittgensteinian philosopher of religion and ethical thinker), is that we have to go 'beyond Wittgenstein's builders', beyond the kind of simple language games Wittgenstein introduces in the *Investigations* (1953), especially §2.[22] Language and meaning are possible only against the background of a much broader agreement on a form of life than the one assumed in the case of the 'builders'. A richer context is required for there to be any meaningful communication. In particular, it is impossible that there should be only one single conversation; if there is, or has been, one conversation, there must have been, or must be able to be, several. This argument can be reshaped as a transcendental one: it is a necessary condition for the possibility of language or meaning (in the form in which we recognize it from within our linguistic practices), that language use not be isolated or 'narrow' in the way imagined in the case of the builders.

Rhees differs from several leading Wittgenstein commentators in explicitly defending a reading of Wittgenstein as concerned with fundamental philosophical questions regarding the possibility of language and discourse.[23] There *must* be, or must have been, much more variety and generality in language use than the kind of variety imagined, say, in the language game of the builders for us to be able to use language, to recognize our and others' attitudes and utterances as meaningful. In particular, what is relevant here is the fundamental linguistic experience of speaking *to* another (and *with* another). This facing of otherness requires what Wittgenstein (*Investigations*: II, iv) calls an 'attitude towards a soul' – which again brings us to the union of ethics and metaphysics. The attitude towards a soul is *not* based on any prior metaphysical theory of souls; nor, on the other hand, is it a 'mere' attitude detached from what the world (of other human beings) is taken to be like.

I will provide some textual evidence for a transcendental account of Rhees's reading of Wittgenstein.[24] Rhees often says that it is a task of philosophy to be concerned with the intelligibility of language, the possibility of understanding or the possibility of discourse (12–13, 65, 182–3). *Pace* 'grammatical' (non-transcendental) interpreters such as Thomas Wallgren, a properly Wittgensteinian philosophy of language makes statements about what is necessary for us to be able to understand linguistic expressions (69). The necessary condition – redescribable as a transcendental condition – for understanding and intelligibility is something that Rhees labels the 'background':[25]

> Unless people had something like a common background, they could not discuss. It is not enough simply that they should be masters of the same vocabulary and the same syntax . . . It seems as though there must be some sort of community of ideas before you can even say that people differ or that they disagree . . . this sort of community of ideas sets the limits within which communication is possible . . . The conditions for the possibility of discourse. (71)

Transcendental-sounding modal expressions occur crucially in this and other Rheesian passages. For our expressions to be meaningful, they must be connected with 'other things that *might* be said' but may not actually be said (105). A kind of *modal realism* is required. But the relevant modalities – possibility and necessity – need not be interpreted as involving concretely existing possible worlds,[26] nor as reducible to recombinations of the elements of the actual world.[27] They can be understood along Kantian lines, transcendentally, as involving features of the humanly categorized world – features that carry irreducible ethical and even political implications.[28]

The 'generality' of language is decisive in Rhees's account. 'If you are able to speak, that has something to do with the whole way in which you live' (113, 135, 173ff.). Rhees immediately asks why this should be so: 'Why *must* there be that connexion with the way one lives as opposed to the particular techniques which one may or may not exercise?' (113) A short answer is that this 'must' emerges from a transcendental reflection on the way we live and use language, as a result analogous to the 'must' of the Kantian categories, to their being necessarily involved in humanly possible experience – or, perhaps, analogous to the 'necessity' of postulating God and immortality in order to account for the kind of life the moral law requires. We may construe Rhees's reasoning as an instance of transcendental argumentation. He writes as follows:

> The principal question has been regarding my reasons for saying that you could not have one conversation unless you had others. I have been wanting to suggest that this was a logical matter; a logical impossibility . . . If I give the example of the two women having a conversation over the fence about the illnesses of their relatives, I have been wanting to suggest not only that there must have been other conversations but that there must have been conversations of other sorts . . . [This is] necessary if they are to speak and understand the sort of things that are said in that conversation; it would be true that they would speak in other connexions in the lives that they were leading as well . . . I might even question whether you could talk about the topic of the conversation at all, if this were the only topic. (173, 175, 183)

Rhees, then, affirms that the intelligibility of language, the possibility of discourse, is based on our habits and practices. These are the necessary 'background' of humanly possible meaning. The modal claims involved integrate transcendental and (broadly) pragmatically naturalist considerations. The structure of Rhees's transcendental argument might be reconstructed as follows:

1. There are (particular) conversations. (Premise, obvious from everyday experience.)
2. Necessarily, if (1) is possible, then there is a 'background' of other conversations (about the same and other topics).
3. But (1) is possible because actual.
4. Therefore, there *is* a 'background' of other conversations: there is 'generality' in language that cannot be reduced to mere calculus-like rules but must be understood as being based on the generality of human life with other people and the capacities involved in such life.

Premises (1) and (3) hardly need defence. The crucial transcendental work, transcendental reflection,[29] required for the argument to be sound must defend premise (2). We may see Rhees's entire book, together with Wittgenstein's own investigations (for instance about the impossibility of a private language), as constituting an argument for premise (2). This premise needs substantial reflection and cannot be supported by an obvious deductive reasoning. The same applies to traditional Kantian premises, such as 'necessarily, if cognitive experience of objects and events is possible, then objects and events stand in causal relations to one another', or 'necessarily, if morality is possible, the moral agent must be able to seek to realize the highest good'.

A problem with Rhees's views, however, is his manner of speaking about 'logical' possibility and impossibility. We can hardly say that the relevant transcendental possibilities, impossibilities or necessities here are logical in the sense in which, say, the law of contradiction is logically necessary. We may need an extended, broad notion of logical necessity (and, analogously, possibility), resembling 'metaphysical possibility' or necessity.[30] But the metaphysical cousin of logical possibility or necessity is hardly self-explanatory. We might, with some hesitation, call Rhees's modalities 'transcendental', ignoring the question of what kind of modalities are involved in transcendental reflection. (Perhaps we need Kant's own account of modality as a group of categories, but this cannot be examined here.)

Language, for Rhees, is entangled with an ethical way of being alive, of being in the world with others. 'Language is something that can have a literature', not just something that has rules like chess (164). The difference between humans and animals in this regard is not a contingent, empirically describable difference that might be otherwise (149–50). It is, rather, a transcendental feature of our form(s) of life, seen and (incompletely) understood from within those forms of life themselves. If human language without morality is impossible, then so is a (fully) human world without morality (and, by extension, political relations).[31] Thus the dependence of facts on values,[32] and of metaphysics on ethics, is transcendental. No facts are *possible* without valuational perspectives transcendentally constituting them as facts of objective reality. Nor are facts possible in the absence of a normatively organized and reorganizing, hence always politically relevant, human practice. This is a (more or less pragmatist) generalization of the Kantian theses that empirical things and facts transcendentally depend on the forms of intuition and the concepts of understanding provided by 'us' (the transcendental subjects), and that 'religious facts' such as

God's existence are by analogy transcendentally dependent on the moral law.

4. A Levinasian perspective: language and otherness

Levinas's views on the moral subject's relation to the Other also invite a transcendental reconstrual, despite his strategy of 'going beyond' transcendental phenomenology and the transcendental subject.[33] In a Levinasian picture, speaking *to* another in a face-to-face encounter with her/him, structured as an attitude toward a soul, is a necessary condition for the possibility of discourse. There is no humanly possible linguistic meaning, or discourse of any kind, without the prior encounter with, a face-to-face relation to, the other. There can be no mere 'naming', no mere description, without calling upon the other or being called into responsibility by the other, one's potential listener.[34] It is a precondition for the possibility of any discourse that the words uttered be words speakable to someone or with someone – the other – just as we saw Rhees argue that one must be able to speak to and with others if one is to be able to mean anything by one's expressions. The Levinasian 'going beyond' the primacy of the (transcendental) ego is comparable to the Wittgensteinian 'going beyond' the idea of a private language and the further Rheesian 'going beyond' the idea, still (according to Rhees) present in Wittgenstein, that a limited, specific discourse could amount to an entire language. The key insight is the increasing generality in and through my acknowledgement of my responsibility to, and for, the other, both in language use and in my life generally.

Let us collect textual evidence from Levinas's writings, as we did in Rhees's case. To be concise, I will focus on a few selected pieces available in English.[35]

Levinas writes: 'Language is born in responsibility. One has to speak, to say *I*, to be in the first person, precisely to be me (*moi*). But, from that point, in affirming this *me* being, one has to respond to one's right to be'.[36] Language, then, not only presupposes the other – the potential communication partner – but sets oneself, one's own being, into question. Levinas goes beyond the Wittgensteinian-Rheesian paradigm in emphasizing this fragility, the *potential ethical unacceptability*, of the 'I'. The 'transcendence' involved in language, not unlike Rhees's 'generality', is, for Levinas, responsibility.[37]

The fundamental connection between language and responsibility is epitomized in Levinas's distinction between 'saying' and the 'said', paralleling Wittgenstein's distinction between 'showing' and 'saying'. Saying, for Levinas, is related to the 'excess' involved in my responsibility for the other: 'it is by saying that sincerity – exposedness without reserve – is first possible'.[38] 'Saying' is something that only 'shows itself', in Wittgenstein's early terms of the *Tractatus*,[39] or something that must be 'passed over into silence' as something ethically fundamental that must not be trivialized through normal linguistic discourse. This ethical saying is 'serious nonsense', just like the ethical discourse Wittgenstein saw as running up against the limits of language.[40] My relation to the other, according to Levinas, is not just a matter of my thinking that s/he is, but of my speaking to her/him – of the 'impossibility of approaching the other without speaking', comparable to the 'attitude towards a soul'.[41] It is, first and foremost, my responsibility for her/his mortality and my (ethical) impossibility of abandoning her/him to die alone.[42] The face of the other is 'the original locus of the meaningful'.[43] Here, Levinas's rejection of traditional ontology crystallizes: 'The relation to the other is therefore not ontology'.[44]

Language, for Levinas, 'in its expressive function, addresses and invokes the other'.[45] There can be no language without the other – a transcendental statement again, with an irreducibly modal status. Transcendental-sounding modalities are found throughout Levinas's discussion, which always turns back to the fundamental role of the other. Being 'face to face' with the other, 'I can no longer deny the other: it is only the noumenal glory of the other that makes the face to face situation possible', a situation which is 'an impossibility of denying, a negation of negation', concretely inscribing 'thou shalt not murder' on the face of the other.[46] One might, as in Rhees's case, wonder what kind of impossibility (logical, transcendental, metaphysical?) Levinas has in mind when speaking about, say, the 'impossibility to question' the 'supreme ethical principle' of being attentive to the suffering of others.[47] Perhaps we may again set this problem aside by admitting that his modal notions are peculiarly ethical, irreducible to any allegedly more fundamental necessities or (im)possibilities.[48]

Even so, Levinas distinguishes too sharply between ethics and metaphysics (ontology) when claiming that the former is inevitably lacking from the latter and that ethical responsibility must be 'otherwise' than being. On the contrary, the irreducibility and ubiquity of the ethical[49] is what makes ethics 'metaphysical'. Thus, the fundamental unity and entanglement of ethics with metaphysics might be emphasized in Levinasian terms. Simply by being, by 'being there' (anywhere), I am already involved in the questioning of the justification of being itself, my own being in particular: 'This is the question of the meaning of being: not the ontology of the understanding of that extraordinary verb, but the ethics of its justice. The question *par excellence* or the question of philosophy. Not "Why being rather than nothing?", but how being justifies itself.'[50] These questions can well be phrased as questions of (transcendentally reconceptualized) metaphysics, rather than going beyond metaphysics or ontology. When Levinas suggests that ethics is 'not a moment of being' but 'otherwise and better than being, the very possibility of the beyond',[51] he offers insightful, beautiful redescriptions of human beings' way(s) of being in the world, instead of leading us beyond being. His is, moreover, a transcendental redescription drawing attention to features of human life that cannot be eliminated in so far as we are able to understand our lives in their present meaning.

Here it is especially interesting to note the parallels between Levinas's ethics of otherness – his views on ethics as the first philosophy – and Rhees's Wittgensteinian account of the conditions of discourse in the communicative encounter with the other. In the Wittgensteinian framework too, there is always a prior transcendental commitment to the possibility of a listener – the other to whom, with whom, one may speak.[52] Both Levinasian and Wittgensteinian insights into our need to assume a relation to otherness prior to epistemic relations – a fundamentally ethical, yet also metaphysical, relation at the root of our being – are reinterpretable as (re)descriptions of a transcendental necessity rendering language, meaning or discourse possible 'from within' a form of life (practice) already structured through continuous engagement in meaningful discourse. This is also a transcendental necessity rendering possible the very being of human beings and of the world they are (able to be) in. There is no humanity – or even world – apart from this relation to otherness. Hence the Wittgensteinian-Levinasian thematization of otherness is an inquiry into the conditions necessary for the possibility of a human world, going to the heart of 'critical' (Kantian) metaphysics of the humanly, especially ethically, categorized reality whose basic tasks and hypotheses were sketched above.

5. Back to Kant: concluding reflections

How do these reflections compare with Kant's? I have interpreted some recent philosophical approaches as 'Kantian', or 'transcendental' in a broad sense. I now briefly return to the ways in which metaphysics and ethics (and politics) are related in Kant's own thought.

My move from issues in Levinas and Rhees back to Kant, especially his discourse on 'radical evil' in Book I of the *Religionsschrift* (*RGV* 6: 19–53), is motivated not only by the fact that Levinas claims to 'feel particularly close' to 'the practical philosophy of Kant'[53] but also by the following. Both Levinas and Rhees (and D. Z. Phillips) agree with Kant (*MpVT*) on the ethical need to oppose any traditional *theodicy*, theoretical approaches to the 'meaningfulness' of evil and suffering.[54] An ethically responsible discourse on evil – a truly ethical response to evil, especially evil and suffering inflicted upon another human being – is not theoretical in the theodicists' sense, but belongs to the realm of Levinasian 'saying' instead of the neutrality and the possibly resulting violence or injustice of the 'said'. When trying to speak about evil and suffering ethically, or when trying to base our metaphysics of evil upon a sound ethical basis, we must, again, speak *to* the other. Otherwise we risk committing ourselves to the evil we seek to understand. This is a metaphysico-ethical truth about a structural feature of our ways of being human. It is not an ahistorical, apodictically certain metaphysical truth, because it is (for Levinas) primarily the Holocaust – a concrete historical event in which real human beings were involved – that made theodicies impossible.[55] Nevertheless, after the Holocaust, we may understand that 'the justification of the neighbor's pain is certainly the source of all immorality' and that theodicies seeking such justifications are not just impossible but 'odious', contributing to the evil they attempt to justify or explain away.[56] Even transcendental insights into the human world may depend on historical contingencies, such as the Holocaust, which may reopen our eyes to acts humans are capable of, acts beyond reason and understanding.

Kant's theory of radical evil need not be understood as opposed to, say, Hannah Arendt's notion of the banality of evil.[57] Rather, our tendency to be involved in evil, banal or not – that is, to adopt freely maxims contrary to the moral law, or freely to choose our own happiness at the cost of moral virtue and thus deliberately subordinate morality to the interest of our own well-being – may be seen as 'radically' rooted in human nature. The group of problems invited by this position is, again, both metaphysical and ethical (and political). We cannot strictly separate the metaphysical and the ethical elements of Kant's theory of evil any more than we can separate the one from the other in our reflections above on the possibility of language as being dependent on our relations to others. Kant, Rhees and Levinas are trying to say things about what the (human) world is like, and how it ought to be transformed. The Kantian discourse on evil can be seen as a metaphysical theory of the (human) world as much as the postulates can. This is one more example of the entanglement thesis that we have seen both Levinas and Rhees (on a Kantian reinterpretation) maintain. The postulates of practical reason, or radical evil, are no more concepts or ideas moving us 'beyond ontology' in Kant than the relation to the other is such a move in Levinas, if my transcendental rearticulation of his position is taken seriously.

I have introduced a sufficient number of examples to consider once more the status – and the possible different versions – of my 'entanglement thesis'.[58] It might be asked, for instance, whether the ethics-metaphysics entanglement is itself *metaphysical* or merely *conceptual*, that is, whether it is based on an anti-metaphysically realist rejection of any robustly mind- or scheme-independent reality (connected with the further claim that our schemes of categorizing reality are value-laden), or whether it is only a thesis about the entanglement of factual and evaluative components in 'thick' ethical concepts and statements employing them. This dichotomy between the ontological order ('metaphysics') and the conceptual one is, however, itself problematic. For the kind of Kantian pragmatist I have imagined as a potential advocate of the fact-value and metaphysics-ethics entanglement(s), there is no principled distinction to be drawn between the merely conceptual and the robustly ontological versions of the entanglement thesis. After all, the thesis itself amounts to a rejection of the very idea of a reality whose ultimate metaphysical structure *could* be ethically neutral.[59]

Another question is whether metaphysical theses are epistemically grounded in or justified by ethical premises, or whether the 'grounding' of such theses is ethical in a stronger – metaphysical! – sense. In the latter case, metaphysical theses would be made true by the ethical consequences they have, rather than merely being rationally acceptable because of such consequences. Again, from the perspective of the entanglement thesis (in its relatively strong versions), this is a distinction without difference. In Kant, it may be uncontroversial that the grounding of metaphysics – theism and immortality – lies in ethics, in the sense that we are practically justified in maintaining the relevant theses which are originally reached in the realm of theoretical reason independently of ethics. In the other authors considered above, this is *not* clear. It may be misleading to regard the relevant metaphysical ideas as being available to us prior to the contribution of practical reason: we cannot just place originally ethically neutral ideas into an ethical perspective, examining whether we can ground them ethically. We cannot so much as arrive at them independently of ethical considerations. In particular, the Levinasian (or Rheesian) account of otherness is so thoroughly shot through with moral concern that it would be quite impossible to separate a thesis purely metaphysical in origin from its ethical legitimation process. If our views about other human beings and the need to be responsible towards them are 'made true' by anything, they are made true by our ethically shaped being in the world.

The kind of ethically structured conditions for the possibility of discourse we have perceived are not *just* conditions for the possibility of language, for the 'conceptual order' or for the acceptance of certain metaphysical beliefs, but also conditions of being itself – conditions for the possibility of any *human* being or reality we are capable of finding ourselves experiencing, surrounded by, or immersed in. At least, they are conditions for our being able to find ourselves so. The limits of *mere* ontology are reached; there is a need for an ethical intervention at the heart of the metaphysical quest. However, my basic point is that reaching the limits of mere ontology does not lead us beyond ontology – neither in Wittgensteinian nor Levinasian nor Kantian context.

The 'going beyond' ontology may thus be seen as an attempt to bring ethics back into the centre of metaphysics. This is what any Kantian worthy of the name ought to do, in so far as the human conditions for the possibility of cognizing and representing reality are thoroughly ethical. Thus, while the account I have given of the relation between metaphysics and ethics requires loosening and reinterpreting standard assumptions surrounding transcendental philosophy, my proposal should be seen as maintaining a basically Kantian approach. It is supposed to acknowledge the entanglement and interdependence of the two objects of wonder and unconditional respect that Kant famously invokes in the closing of the second *Critique* (*KpV* 5: 161–2): the starry heavens (metaphysics) and the moral law (ethics).[60]

Notes

1 For recent contributions, see for example E. J. Lowe, *The Possibility of Metaphysics: Substance, Identity and Time* (Oxford: Clarendon Press, 1998), ch. 1; David Lewis, *Papers in Metaphysics and Epistemology* (Cambridge: Cambridge University Press, 2001); Michael Loux, *Metaphysics: a Contemporary Introduction*, rev. edn (London and New York: Routledge, 2002), ch. 1; David Armstrong, *Truth and Truthmakers* (Cambridge: Cambridge University Press, 2004), chs 1–2.

2 I have developed this idea, connected with my pragmatist rearticulation of Kantian transcendental philosophy, in several earlier publications: see Pihlström, 'Methodology without metaphysics? A pragmatic critique', *Philosophy Today*, 48 (2004), 188–215; *Pragmatic Moral Realism: a Transcendental Defense* (Amsterdam and New York: Rodopi, 2005); 'Metaphysics with a human face: William James and the prospects of pragmatist metaphysics', *William James Studies*, 2, *http://williamjamesstudies.press.uiuc.edu/*; *Pragmatist Metaphysics: an Essay on the Ethical Grounds of Ontology* (London: Continuum, 2009).

3 Pihlström, *Naturalizing the Transcendental: a Pragmatic View* (Amherst, NY: Prometheus/Humanity Books, 2003), chs 1–2; 'Recent reinterpretations of the transcendental', *Inquiry*, 47 (2004), 287–314.

4 See William James, *Pragmatism: a New Name for Some Old Ways of Thinking*, ed. F. H. Burkhardt, F. Bowers and I. K. Skrupskelis (Cambridge, MA: Harvard University Press, 1907), especially chs 2–3; Pihlström, *Structuring the World: the Issue of Realism and the*

Nature of Ontological Problems in Classical and Contemporary Pragmatism, Acta Philosophica Fennica, 59 (Helsinki: The Philosophical Society of Finland, 1996), ch. 3; 'Metaphysics with a human face'; *'The Trail of the Human Serpent is over Everything': Jamesian Perspectives on Mind, World, and Religion* (Lanham, MD: University Press of America [Rowman and Littlefield Publishing Group], 2008). In some situations of metaphysical reflection, the ethical aspects are, of course, more remote than in others. For example, it is easier to make the case for the ethical value-ladenness of the metaphysics of personhood (e.g. personal identity) than of the issue of universals vs. tropes. Piecemeal analysis and careful attention to specific issues in relation to such controversies is needed. The main point here is that we cannot categorically disconnect metaphysical disputes from ethical considerations.

5 The notions 'ethical' and 'moral' are used broadly here, roughly equivalently with 'practical' (in a Kantian sense). At a meta-level, moreover, the superiority of the view acknowledging the entanglement of metaphysics and ethics may itself be ethically defended: there may be moral reasons, or morally better reasons, for maintaining that metaphysics needs ethical grounding than for maintaining the opposite. Here, I am crucially indebted to Kenneth Westphal's Kantian-cum-Hegelian reflections on fallibilist and anti-foundationalist justification of reason and its normative principles (reflexively by means of reason itself). Cp. Westphal's contribution to this volume, and see Pihlström, *Naturalizing the Transcendental*, ch. 5.

6 I am afraid that Westphal's realism 'sans phrase', though defended in a Kantian transcendental way, is eventually a form of metaphysical realism, though not transcendental realism in Kant's sense. This point cannot be argued here (but see Pihlström, *Naturalizing the Transcendental*).

7 See e.g. Hilary Putnam, *Realism with a Human Face*, ed. J. Conant (Cambridge, MA and London: Harvard University Press, 1990), ch. 1; Henry Allison, *Kant's Transcentental Idealism: an Interpretation and Defense*, rev. edn (New Haven, CT: Yale University Press, 2004), ch. 2.

8 I am to some extent relying on the Putnamian critique of the 'ready-made world' (Putnam, *Realism with a Human Face*; Pihlström, *Structuring the World*), but I do not assume Putnam's specific views ('internal realism' or its followers). Some of the metaphors I use have a Putnamian (or Jamesian) origin, though.

9 Frederick C. Beiser, 'Moral faith and the highest good', in P. Guyer (ed.), *The Cambridge Companion to Kant and Modern Philosophy* (Cambridge: Cambridge University Press, 2006), p. 604.

10 Ibid., pp. 606–7.

11 James, *The Will to Believe and Other Essays in Popular Philosophy*, ed. F. H. Burkhardt, F. Bowers and I. K. Skrupskelis (Cambridge, MA: Harvard University Press, 1897); *Pragmatism.*

12 Beiser, 'Moral faith', p. 610. This misconstrual may result from the fact that Beiser focuses only on 'The Will to Believe', ignoring James's discussions of our need for a moral order and the ethically 'energizing' function of theism (see the essays 'The Sentiment of Rationality' and 'The Moral Philosopher and the Moral Life', in ibid.; cp. *Pragmatism*, especially chs 3 and 8). James's argument for the practical requirement of theism is more empirical and psychological than Kant's a priori approach; yet a case for a pragmatic-transcendental reconstruction of Jamesian ideas can be made (Pihlström, *'The Trail of the Human Serpent'*).

13 Beiser, 'Moral faith', pp. 597, 618–19). Although this is no study on James, it might also be suggested that there are Kantian overtones in James's (*Pragmatism*, ch. 3) notion of an 'eternal moral order', which he sees as a deep human need. Cp. ibid., ch. 8 for a 'meliorist' view of the possible yet not inevitable 'salvation' of the world (see also Pihlström, 'Metaphysics with a human face'; *'The Trail of the Human Serpent'*).

14 Beiser, 'Moral faith', 589–90.

15 See Beiser, 'Moral faith', pp. 613, 620; in addition to Beiser's paper, see the recent discussions of the relevance of Kant's Christian and metaphysical ideas in Philip Rossi, 'Kant's philosophy of religion', in E. Zalta (ed.), *Stanford Encyclopedia of Philosophy* (2005), *http://plato.stanford.edu/entries.kant-religion/* (accessed April 2007); Byrne, *Kant on God* (Aldershot: Ashgate, 2007); Stephen Palmquist, *Kant's Critical Religion* (Aldershot: Ashgate, 2000; updated online version at *http://www.hkbu.edu.kk/~ppp/ksp2*).

16 Pihlström, 'Recent reinterpretations of the transcendental'; *'The Trail of the Human Serpent'.*

17 I have here provided only one example of the Kantian metaphysics-ethics(-politics) entanglement. See Lucas Thorpe's and Howard Williams's contributions to this volume for additional – and more fully developed – cases of such entanglement, especially in Kant's political philosophy.

18 See the papers on transcendental arguments in Robert Stern (ed.), *Transcendental Arguments: Problems and Prospects* (Oxford: Clarendon Press, 1999); see also Ralph C. S. Walker, 'Kant and transcendental arguments', in Guyer, *The Cambridge Companion to Kant*, pp. 238–68; Pihlström, *Naturalizing the Transcendental*, chs 2–3; 'Recent reinterpretations of the transcendental'.

19 See Pihlström, *Naturalizing the Transcendental*; 'Shared language, transcendental listeners, and the problem of limits', in Pihlström (ed.), *Wittgenstein and the Method of Philosophy*, Acta Philosophica Fennica, 80 (Helsinki: The Philosophical Society of Finland, 2006); Kenneth R. Westphal, 'Kant, Wittgenstein, and transcendental chaos', *Philosophical Investigations*, 28 (2005), 303–23; Thomas Wallgren, *Transformative Philosophy: Socrates, Wittgenstein, and the Democratic Spirit of Philosophy* (Lanham, MD: Lexington Books [Rowman and Littlefield Publishing Group], 2006).

20 Rush Rhees, *Wittgenstein and the Possibility of Discourse*, ed. D. Z. Phillips (Oxford: Blackwell, 2006).

21 Rhees was a leading figure in the 'Swansea school' of Wittgenstein interpretation; other prominent thinkers in this tradition (broadly understood) include, among others, Peter Winch, D. Z. Phillips, Raimond Gaita and Lars Hertzberg. I will not take any stand on the *interpretative* accuracy of these philosophers' (even Rhees's) understanding of Wittgenstein. I will focus on the systematic issues instead of historical interpretations.

22 Ludwig Wittgenstein, *Philosophical Investigations*, trans. G. E. M. Anscombe (Oxford: Blackwell, 1958).

23 D. Z. Phillips, 'Introduction', in Rhees, *Wittgenstein*, xxvii, xxxi–xxxii.

24 The page numbers given in brackets in the following section all refer to Rhees, *Wittgenstein*.

25 See also, for an analogous idea, Charles Taylor, *Philosophical Arguments* (Cambridge, MA and London: Harvard University Press, 1995); see also the discussion in Pihlström, 'Shared language'.

26 Lewis, *Papers in Metaphysics*.

27 Armstrong, *Truth and Truthmakers*.

28 Sometimes Rhees speaks with less confidence in, or less carefully with respect to, the modal status of his ideas: 'If you are speaking now, you will speak in other connexions' (*Wittgenstein*, p. 213). This factual, empirical-sounding, non-transcendental formulation is, however, an exception in his otherwise richly modal discussion.

29 On the importance of transcendental reflection on our (human) cognitive capacities and incapacities in Kant, see Westphal, *Kant's Transcendental Proof of Realism* (Cambridge: Cambridge University Press, 2004), especially ch. 1. I am disconnecting the notion of transcendental reflection from its immediate Kantian context.

30 Lowe, *The Possibility of Metaphysics*, ch. 1.

31 I am not claiming that politics is reducible to ethics. I am just suggesting that the language we use for categorizing the world we live in is ethically (and, generally, valuationally) structured, and that it would be difficult or impossible to sharply separate the political dimensions of that structuredness from its 'merely' ethical dimensions.

32 Putnam, *The Collapse of the Fact/Value Dichotomy and Other Essays* (Cambridge, MA and London: Harvard University Press, 2002); *Ethics without Ontology* (Cambridge, MA and London: Harvard University Press, 2004).

33 I say this with as much, or as little, confidence in transcendental interpretations of Levinas as in transcendental interpretations of Wittgenstein, understanding that it is extremely controversial whether Levinas can fruitfully be construed as a transcendental philosopher; see e.g. Bernasconi 2002: 234–5.

34 Lars Hertzberg, 'On the need for a listener and community standards', in L. Hertzberg and M. Gustafsson (eds), *The Practice of Language* (Dordrecht: Kluwer, 2001); Pihlström, 'Shared Language'.

35 Emmanuel Levinas, *The Levinas Reader*, ed. S. Hand (Cambridge, MA *and* Oxford: Blackwell, 1989); *Outside the Subject*, trans. M. B. Smith (London: The Athlone Press, 1993 [1987]); *Entre Nous: Thinking-of-the-Other*, trans. M. B. Smith and B. Harshav (London and New York: Continuum, 2006 [1991]). On *interpretative* issues regarding Levinas's major works, *Totality and Infinity* (1961) and *Otherwise than Being or Beyond Essence* (1974), see several essays in Simon Critchley and Robert Bernasconi (eds), *The Cambridge Companion to Levinas* (Cambridge: Cambridge University Press, 2002).

36 Levinas, *The Levinas Reader*, p. 82.

37 Ibid., p. 109.

38 Ibid., p. 183.

39 Wittgenstein, *Tractatus Logico-Philosophicus*, trans. D. F. Pears and B. F. McGuinness (London: Routledge and Kegan Paul, 1974 [1921]).

40 Critchley, 'Introduction', in Critchley and Bernasconi, *The Cambridge Companion*, p. 19.

41 Levinas, *Entre Nous*, p. 6;

42 Ibid., pp. 124–5, 160–1.

43 Ibid., p. 124.

44 Ibid., p. 7.

45 Ibid., p. 28.

46 Ibid., p. 30.

47 Ibid., p. 81.

48 Pihlström, *Pragmatic Moral Realism*.

49 Ibid.

50 Levinas, *The Levinas Reader*, p. 86.

51 Ibid., p. 179; *Entre Nous*, p. 174.

52 Hertzberg, 'On the need for a listener'.

53 *Entre Nous*, p. 9.

54 For Levinas's opposition to theodicy, see Levinas, *Entre Nous*, pp. 81ff.; Richard J. Bernstein, *Radical Evil: a Philosophical*

Interrogation (Cambridge: Polity Press, 2002); Paul Davies, 'Sincerity and the end of theodicy: three remarks on Levinas and Kant', in Critchley and Bernasconi, *The Cambridge Companion*, especially pp. 170–4; cp. also Pihlström, *'The Trail of the Human Serpent'*, ch. 4.

55 *Entre Nous*, pp. 84–5.

56 Ibid.

57 Hannah Arendt, *Eichmann in Jerusalem: a Report on the Banality of Evil*, reprinted in *The Portable Hannah Arendt* (New York: Vintage, 2004 [1963]). See Bernstein, *Radical Evil*, for an approach crucially informed by both Kant and Arendt; see also Susan Neiman, *Evil in Modern Thought: an Alternative History of Philosophy* (Princeton, NJ: Princeton University Press, 2002); Phillip Cole, *The Myth of Evil* (Edinburgh: Edinburgh University Press, 2006) for recent discussions of Kant's theory of radical evil.

58 These remarks have been inspired by Mark Timmons's comments on an earlier draft of my paper.

59 This is not to say that it would be uninteresting to consider weaker versions of the thesis, such as versions in which the dualism between the ontological 'order of being' and the (merely) conceptual order is preserved, but this paper has been mainly concerned with the entanglement idea in its full force, as developed through Kantian, pragmatist, Wittgensteinian and Levinasian insights.

60 This paper grows out of my research project, 'The Ethical Grounds of Metaphysics' (Academy of Finland, 2008–11). I am grateful to Heikki A. Kovalainen and Henrik Rydenfelt for insightful formulations of issues pursued within that project and thus for some of the ideas that have found their ways into this paper. I also thank Sorin Baiasu for inviting me to contribute to the Kant session of the 4th ECPR conference (Pisa, Italy, September 2007), as well as Hanne Appelqvist, Katerina Deligiorgi, Leila Haaparanta, Heikki Kannisto, Toni Kannisto, Olli Koistinen, Heikki J. Koskinen, Vesa Oittinen, Lucas Thorpe and Howard Williams for Kantian comments and conversations. I am particularly grateful to Sorin Baiasu, Mark Timmons and Ken Westphal for their engaging comments on earlier drafts.

References

Allison, H. E., *Kant's Transcentental Idealism: an Interpretation and Defense*, rev. edn (New Haven, CT: Yale University Press, 2004).

Ameriks, K., 'The critique of metaphysics: the structure and fate of Kant's dialectic', in Guyer, *The Cambridge Companion to Kant.*

Arendt, H., *Eichmann in Jerusalem: a Report on the Banality of Evil*, reprinted in *The Portable Hannah Arendt* (New York: Vintage, 2004 [1963]).

Armstrong, D. M., *Truth and Truthmakers* (Cambridge: Cambridge University Press, 2004.

Beiser, F. C., 'Moral faith and the highest good', in Guyer, *The Cambridge Companion to Kant.*

Bernasconi, R., 'What is the question to which "substitution" is the answer?', in Critchley and Bernasconi, *The Cambridge Companion to Levinas.*

Bernstein, R. J., *Radical Evil: a Philosophical Interrogation* (Cambridge: Polity Press, 2002).

Byrne, P., *Kant on God* (Aldershot: Ashgate, 2007).

Carr, D., *The Paradox of Subjectivity: the Self in the Transcendental Tradition* (Oxford: Oxford University Press, 1999).

Cole, P., *The Myth of Evil* (Edinburgh: Edinburgh University Press, 2006).

Critchley, S., 'Introduction', in Critchley and Bernasconi, *The Cambridge Companion to Levinas.*

Critchley, S. and Bernasconi, R. (eds), *The Cambridge Companion to Levinas* (Cambridge: Cambridge University Press, 2002).

Davies, P., 'Sincerity and the end of theodicy: three remarks on Levinas and Kant', in Critchley and Bernasconi, *The Cambridge Companion to Levinas.*

Grier, M., *Kant's Doctrine of Transcendental Illusion* (Cambridge: Cambridge University Press, 2001).

Guyer, P. (ed.), *The Cambridge Companion to Kant and Modern Philosophy* (Cambridge: Cambridge University Press, 2006).

Hertzberg, L., 'On the need for a listener and community standards', in L. Hertzberg and M. Gustafsson (eds), *The Practice of Language* (Dordrecht: Kluwer, 2001).

James, W., *The Will to Believe and Other Essays in Popular Philosophy*, ed. F. H. Burkhardt, F. Bowers and I. K. Skrupskelis (Cambridge, MA: Harvard University Press, 1897).

——, *Pragmatism: a New Name for Some Old Ways of Thinking*, ed. F. H. Burkhardt, F. Bowers and I. K. Skrupskelis (Cambridge, MA: Harvard University Press, 1907).

Kant, I., *Kritik der reinen Vernunft*, ed. R. Schmidt (Hamburg: Felix Meiner, 1990 [1781/1787]).

——, *Critique of Practical Reason*, in M. J. Gregor (ed.), *Practical Philosophy* (Cambridge: Cambridge University Press, 1996 [1788]).

——, 'Über das Misslingen aller philosophischen Versuche in der Theodizee'. In English: 'Concerning the possibility of a theodicy and the failure of all previous philosophical attempts in the field', in A. Wood and G. Di Giovanni (eds), *Religion and Rational Theology* (Cambridge, Cambridge University Press, 1996 [1791]).

——, *Die Religion innerhalb der Grenzen der blossen Vernunft*. In English: *Religion within the Boundaries of Mere Reason*, in A. Wood and G. Di Giovanni (eds), *Religion and Rational Theology* [1794].

Levinas, E., *The Levinas Reader*, ed. S. Hand (Cambridge, MA and Oxford: Blackwell, 1989).

——, *Outside the Subject*, trans. M. B. Smith (London: The Athlone Press, 1993 [1987]).

——, *Entre Nous: Thinking-of-the-Other*, trans. M. B. Smith and B. Harshav (London and New York: Continuum, 2006 [1991]).

Lewis, D., *Papers in Metaphysics and Epistemology* (Cambridge: Cambridge University Press, 2001).

Loux, M. J., *Metaphysics: a Contemporary Introduction*, rev. edn (London and New York: Routledge, 2002).

Lowe, E. J., *The Possibility of Metaphysics: Substance, Identity and Time* (Oxford: Clarendon Press, 1998).

Neiman, S., *Evil in Modern Thought: an Alternative History of Philosophy* (Princeton, NJ: Princeton University Press, 2002).

Palmquist, S., *Kant's Critical Religion* (Aldershot: Ashgate, 2000; updated online version [2007] at *http://www.hkbu.edu.kk/~ppp/ksp2*).

Phillips, D. Z., 'Introduction', in Rhees, *Wittgenstein*¸ pp. xxv-xliv.

Pihlström, S., *Structuring the World: the Issue of Realism and the Nature of Ontological Problems in Classical and Contemporary Pragmatism*, Acta Philosophica Fennica, 59 (Helsinki: The Philosophical Society of Finland, 1996).

——, *Naturalizing the Transcendental: A Pragmatic View* (Amherst, NY: Prometheus/Humanity Books, 2003).

——, 'On the Concept of Philosophical Anthropology', *Journal of Philosophical Research*, 28 (2003), 259–85.

——, 'Methodology without metaphysics? A pragmatic critique', *Philosophy Today*, 48 (2004), 188–215.

——, 'Recent reinterpretations of the transcendental', *Inquiry*, 47 (2004), 287–314.

——, *Pragmatic Moral Realism: a Transcendental Defense* (Amsterdam and New York: Rodopi, 2005).

——, 'Shared language, transcendental listeners, and the problem of limits', in Pihlström (ed.), *Wittgenstein and the Method of Philosophy*,

Acta Philosophica Fennica, 80 (Helsinki: The Philosophical Society of Finland, 2006).

——, 'Synthesizing Traditions: Rewriting the History of Pragmatism and Transcendental Philosophy', *History of Philosophy Quarterly*, 23 (2006), 375–90.

——, 'Metaphysics with a human face: William James and the prospects of pragmatist metaphysics', *William James Studies*, 2 (2007), *http://williamjamesstudies.press.uiuc.edu/*.

——, *'The Trail of the Human Serpent is over Everything': Jamesian Perspectives on Mind, World, and Religion* (Lanham, MD: University Press of America [Rowman and Littlefield Publishing Group], 2008).

——, *Pragmatist Metaphysics: an Essay on the Ethical Grounds of Ontology* (London: Continuum, 2009).

Putnam, H., *Realism with a Human Face*, ed. J. Conant (Cambridge, MA and London: Harvard University Press, 1990).

——, *The Collapse of the Fact/Value Dichotomy and Other Essays* (Cambridge, MA and London: Harvard University Press, 2002).

——, 'Levinas and Judaism', in Critchley and Bernasconi, *The Cambridge Companion to Levinas*, pp. 33–62.

——, *Ethics without Ontology* (Cambridge, MA and London: Harvard University Press, 2004).

Rhees, R., *Wittgenstein and the Possibility of Discourse*, ed. D. Z. Phillips (Oxford: Blackwell, 2006).

Rossi, P., 'Kant's philosophy of religion', in E. Zalta (ed.), *Stanford Encyclopedia of Philosophy* (2005), *http://plato.stanford.edu/entries.kant-religion/* (accessed April 2007).

Stern, R. (ed.), *Transcendental Arguments: Problems and Prospects* (Oxford: Clarendon Press, 1999).

Taylor, C., *Philosophical Arguments* (Cambridge, MA and London: Harvard University Press, 1995).

Walker, R. C. S., 'Kant and transcendental arguments', in Guyer (ed.), *The Cambridge Companion to Kant*, pp. 238–68.

Wallgren, T., *Transformative Philosophy: Socrates, Wittgenstein, and the Democratic Spirit of Philosophy* (Lanham, MD: Lexington Books [Rowman and Littlefield Publishing Group], 2006).

Westphal, K. R., *Kant's Transcendental Proof of Realism* (Cambridge: Cambridge University Press, 2004).

——, 'Kant, Wittgenstein, and transcendental chaos', *Philosophical Investigations*, 28 (2005), 303–23.

Wittgenstein, L., *Tractatus Logico-Philosophicus*, trans. D. F. Pears and B. F. McGuinness (London: Routledge and Kegan Paul, 1974 [1921]).

——, *Philosophical Investigations*, trans. G. E. M. Anscombe (Oxford: Blackwell, 1958 [1953]).

5 • One Community or Many? From Logic to Juridical Law via Metaphysics

Lucas Thorpe

There are, I believe, at least five 'core' notions of community in Kant's mature work that are all modelled on the category of community, introduced as the third category of relation in the first *Critique*. In the Third Analogy and the *Metaphysical Foundations of Natural Science*, Kant develops an account of physical interaction. In his pre-critical writings and the cosmology sections of his metaphysics lectures he provides an analysis of the metaphysical idea of a 'World' understood as a community of individuals in interaction. In his ethical works we find the ideal of a realm of ends understood to be an ideal moral community, and in his political writings the ideal of a political community governed by juridical laws. Finally, we find the theological ideal of a community of holy beings, which Kant sometimes calls 'the kingdom of heaven'. In addition we find a number of other senses of community whose relation to the category of community are less clear, for example the notion of ethical community presented in religion and the notion of a *sensus communis* in the *Critique of Judgement*. The five 'core' notions of community, then, are:

1. The *scientific* notion of interaction. This concept is introduced in the *Third Analogy* and developed in the *Metaphysical Foundations of Natural Science.*[1]
2. A *metaphysical* idea. The idea of a world of individuals (monads) in interaction. This idea was developed in Kant's pre-critical period and can be found in his metaphysics lectures.
3. A *moral* ideal. The idea of a realm of ends.
4. A *political* ideal. The idea of a juridical community (or community of communities) governed by juridical laws.
5. A *theological* ideal. What Kant calls 'the kingdom of heaven', and which can be thought of as a community of holy beings, or angels.

In this paper I will examine the relationship between the first, second and fourth of these notions. My argument is that Kant's notion of a juridical community governed by juridical laws is modelled on the metaphysical idea of the world. This metaphysical idea of a world is, in turn, modelled on the category of community introduced in the first *Critique* and developed in his logic lectures. As far as I am aware, Kant himself does not use the phrase 'juridical community'. The *Metaphysics of Morals* is divided into a Doctrine of Right and a Doctrine of Virtue. The Doctrine of Right is itself divided into sections on Private Right and Public Right. The main topic in the Private Right is Kant's account of the metaphysic of property and the nature of what I call juridical laws. Public Right on the other hand has to do with those laws that are necessary for bringing about a condition of Private Right, or what Kant sometimes calls 'the rightful condition'.[2] For human beings the existence of Public Right is a necessary condition for the possibility of Private Right, but it would seem that we could conceive of a community, say a community of angels, where there was Private Right but no need for Public Right. What I call a juridical community is the idea of a community governed by Private Right, abstracting from what is needed to bring such a community into existence. The notion of a juridical community as employed in this paper, then, is more abstract than the notion of a human political community that involves the idea of a state and laws governing the nature of the state and relations between states.

A central aspect of my interpretation has to do with explaining what Kant means by *juridical* laws. By juridical laws, I mean those laws that are part of what Kant calls private, as opposed to public, right.[3] Kant claims that juridical laws are necessarily coercive, and this is often taken to mean that such laws are essentially enforceable through the use of force – either actual force or the threat of force (punishment).[4] Although this is the standard reading of what Kant means by coercion, I believe such an account is clearly mistaken, since for Kant juridical laws are coercive in the sense that they necessitate or obligate. Thus in talking about 'powers of coercion' in his ethics lectures, Kant explains perfect obligation as 'an obligation where the agent can be necessitated to an act of duty by another's choice' (*V-Eth/Vigil* 27: 289). Such laws could even govern a community of angels. For example, if in an ideal community governed by juridical law one individual lends another individual a particular object and then asks for it back, the second individual is *necessitated*, or *coerced*, to return it. The threat of punishment is not needed for a law to be coercive in this sense. It is in this sense that (ideal) juridical laws are coercive. A similar criticism of the standard reading of 'coercion' in Kant has been offered by Arthur Ripstein, who points out that Kant's 'initial, and indeed, paradigmatic, example of coercion is the right of a creditor to demand payment from a debtor, a right to compel payment, not a right to punish nonpayment'.[5] My claim about the relationship between Kant's metaphysics and his politics is that it is the existence of laws that are coercive in this sense that allows for real metaphysical interaction in a juridical community: for interaction, understood metaphysically, requires that the agent be able to 'determin[e] the active power of the substance being acted upon' (V-MP/Mron 29: 823), and the existence of coercive juridical laws enables me to 'determine another's choice by my choice' (*MS* 6: 271).

Before presenting my argument in more detail, let me first say a few words about Kant's understanding of metaphysics. My claim is that Kant's idea of a political community is not essentially a practical idea but a theoretical one, namely the idea of a community of individuals in interaction, an idea that Kant refers to in his theoretical works as the idea of a world, or 'the intelligible world'. The development of this idea was originally part of Kant's monadology and meant to solve a theoretical problem that Leibniz had been unable to solve. Kant began his philosophical career as an unorthodox Leibnizian, and he spent much of the 1750s and 1760s trying to develop a monadology. Unlike Leibniz, Kant was committed to the position that monads can really interact, and he believed that any adequate monadology must be able to explain how a set of monads could constitute a 'world' in any meaningful sense. In particular, like many eighteenth-century German metaphysicians he believed that the idea of a world is the idea of a composite, and so that any adequate monadology must be able to explain the possibility of monadic composition, a possibility Leibniz had been unable to explain.

The problem of monadic composition, for both Leibniz and Kant, is to explain how a number of independent individuals can come together and form one thing. For both of them, this is a metaphysical problem. Ultimately, Leibniz was unable to explain adequately how a substantial composite was possible and bequeathed this problem to Kant. Kant's solution to Leibniz's problem of composition was inspired by Rousseau. A set of independent individuals can only form a true composite substance if each member of the composite is responsible for the laws that provide the composite with its unity. That is, in a composite substance, each member of the composite must be autonomous. Kant names our idea of such a composite substance an 'intelligible world' or a realm of ends (*Reich der Zwecke*).

Although in the 1750s and 1760s Kant, like Leibniz, believed that the purpose of metaphysical speculation was to provide us with a true account of the way the world actually is, over time his attitude to metaphysical speculation diverged from that of Leibniz. He came to see that such speculation cannot give us insight into the way things are; it cannot provide us with objective knowledge. For the critical Kant, metaphysical speculation involves an analysis of our ideas of pure reason and is not able (or intended) to provide us with knowledge of the putative objects of such ideas. However, although such metaphysical speculation cannot provide us with any knowledge of the way the world is, it can provide us with an 'image' of the way the world could and should be. The idea of a world of individuals in interaction (the idea of a community governed by juridical laws) is not a possible object of our faculty of intuition (and, as a result, is not a possible object of cognition); it *is*, however, a possible object of our faculty of desire, that is to say it is a possible object of choice, for we can choose to be a member of such a world. Indeed, Kant believes that it is simply a fact that this theoretical idea, the idea of being an autonomous member of a community, presents itself to our faculty of desire as something of immeasurable value.[6]

This paper has three main sections. In the first I examine the category of community as presented in the first *Critique*, and in the second the idea of a world discussed in his metaphysics lectures. In the final section I show how these logical and metaphysical conceptions of community play an important role in his conception of a juridical community.

1. The category of community in the *Critique of Pure Reason*

In the *Critique of Pure Reason*, Kant introduces the category of community as the third category of relation. The structure of the table of categories is derived from the table of judgements, and this table is divided into four classes, into judgements of quantity, of quality, of relation and of modality. The categories of the third class, then, are derived from the judgements of relation. According to Kant there are three types of relational judgement: categorical judgements (A is B), hypothetical judgements (if *p* then *q*) and disjunctive judgments (*p* or *q* or *r*). The categories of substance and accident are derived from the categorical form of judgement, the categories of cause and effect from the hypothetical form of judgement and the category of community, which either is or involves the idea of reciprocal influence, from the disjunctive form of judgement.[7]

Kant believes that the category of community (and as a result the notion of interaction) is to be sharply distinguished from that of cause and effect, for they are derived from different forms of judgement. We understand the importance of this claim by considering an alternative way of conceptualizing interaction. Defenders of such an alternative conception of interaction would argue that we can fully capture what is involved in interaction in the following terms: when two entities, say *x* and *y*, interact, *x* has a causal relation to *y* and *y* has a causal relation to *x*. Kant does not deny that this partially captures what is involved in the relation of interaction,[8] but he does not believe that it is the full story, for he believes that when a number of entities interact they (1) constitute a whole and (2) mutually exclude one another. These two factors are essential to the relation of interaction and cannot be captured by appealing to the ideas of ground and consequence or to the hypothetical form of judgement. Thus in his commentary to the table of categories in the *Critique of Pure Reason*, Kant compares the causal relation to the relation of interaction with community and points out that in the case of simple causation the relation is one of subordination, whereas in the case of interaction the relation is one of coordination (*KrV* B112). What he means by this is that in a causal relation the consequence is subordinated to the ground. For this reason the ground-consequence relation is the principle of the series, for the relation of ground and consequence can provide us with a well-ordered chain of causes and effects. The relation of community, on the other hand, cannot be understood in terms of the idea of subordination, for when a number of entities are members of a community they are not subordinated to one another but are coordinated with one another. The concept of coordination cannot be understood in terms of mutual subordination. When entities are coordinated with one another they are parts of a whole and mutually exclude one another. Thus Kant explains that the relation of community or interaction

> is an entirely different kind of connection from that which is to be found in the mere relation of cause to effect (of ground to consequence), in which the consequence does not reciprocally determine the ground and therefore does not constitute a whole with the latter (as the world-creator with the world). The understanding follows the same procedure when it represents the divided sphere of a concept as when it thinks of a thing as divisible, and just as in the first case the members of the division exclude each other and yet are connected in one sphere, so in the later case the parts are represented as ones to which existence (as substances) pertains to each exclusively of the others, and which are yet connected in one whole. (*KrV* B113)

In the first sentence of this passage Kant distinguishes the concept of causation from that of interaction, and focuses on the fact that in the case of interaction the entities in interaction 'constitute a whole'.[9] To understand the second sentence of this passage it is necessary to have a closer look at Kant's account of the disjunctive form of judgement. A disjunctive judgement has the form: '*x* is A or B or C'. Kant explains this form of judgement in the *Critique of Pure Reason* in the following terms: 'in all disjunctive judgments the sphere (the multitude of everything that is contained under it) is represented as a whole divided into parts (the subordinate concepts)' (*KrV* B112). He makes his point a little more clearly in his logic lectures. In his *Jäsche Logic*, for example, he explains that 'disjunctive judgments represent various judgments as in the community of a sphere and produce each judgment only through the restriction of the others in regard to the whole sphere' (LogJäsche 9: 107). A disjunctive judgement, then, is a judgement in which a number of judgements somehow restrict one another and fill up a (logical) sphere.

It is, then, from the disjunctive form of judgement that we get the concept of 'exclusion'. Kant makes this clear in his commentary to the table of categories. In this section he compares the disjunctive form of judgement with the hypothetical (if . . . then) form of judgement, and argues that

> in all disjunctive judgments the sphere (the multitude of everything that is contained under it) is represented as a whole divided into parts (the subordinate concepts), and since none of these can be contained under any other, they are thought of as coordinated with one another, not subordinated, so that they do not determine each other unilaterally, as in a series, but reciprocally, as in an aggregate (if one member of the division is posited, all the rest are excluded, and *vice versa*). (*KrV* B112)

Earlier in his commentary on the table of categories, Kant explains that the categories he has listed do not provide a complete list of the a priori concepts of the understanding, for there are also derivative concepts, which Kant calls 'predicables', that can be derived from the categories.[10] Under the category of community Kant lists two 'derivative concepts' or predicables: presence and resistance (*KrV* A82/B108). The reason why resistance is a predicable of the category of community is because our (pure, unschematized) concept of resistance is to be understood in terms of exclusion, and we understand the notion of exclusion a priori through our grasp of the disjunctive form of judgement. What we mean if we claim that one thing resists another is that if (or in so far as) the thing is posited all the rest are excluded. As we shall see, the fact that resistance is a predicable of the category of community has important implications for Kant's account of interaction, for he conceives of interaction in terms of the withdrawal of resistance, which given his analysis of community implies that only members of a community can interact.

The category of community, then, allows us to understand the notion of a number of impenetrable individuals (concepts) filling a conceptual space (another concept) and excluding other individuals (concepts) from their part of the conceptual space, without any appeal to the space of intuition. The fact that Kant believes the concept of resistance to be a predicable of the category of community will play an important role later in this paper, because Kant believes that the only way to conceive intelligibly of interaction is in terms of the withdrawal of resistance. And, as we shall see, this conception of interaction as the withdrawal of resistance is also to be found in his political writings, where Kant explains the possibility of the transfer of property in terms of the withdrawal of resistance.

It is also worth remembering that in the Third Analogy, Kant argues that the application of the category of community to experience is necessary for us to make judgements of simultaneity. He argues that 'things are simultaneous if in empirical intuition the perception of one can follow the perception of the other reciprocally' (*KrV* A211/B256–7). Indeed, the notion of simultaneity is so closely connected to the category of community that Kant changed the title of the Third Analogy from 'The Principle of Community' (*KrV* A211) in the first edition to 'The Principle of Simultaneity, According to the Law of Interaction, or Community' (*KrV* B256) in the second. The notion of simultaneity also plays an important role in Kant's account of the exchange of property in the Doctrine of Right in the *Metaphysics of Morals*. Here Kant explains that the exchange of property 'is possible only through a common will by means of which the object is always under control of one or the other' and he repeatedly stresses that this act of exchange must be simultaneous. Thus, for example, he argues that the acts of promise and acceptance 'cannot be represented as following one upon another . . . but as proceeding from a single common will (this is expressed by the word simultaneously) (*MS* 6: 273). The language here makes it clear that Kant is quite self-consciously conceiving of the exchange of property in terms of the category of community presented in the first *Critique*.

2. Community in Kant's metaphysics lectures

Let us now turn to Kant's discussion of community and interaction in his metaphysical writings. My main claim in this section is that the idea of a world of individuals in interaction (an intelligible world) can only be the idea of a community of autonomous individuals governed by laws that they have given themselves, that create resistance and that hence allow the agents to 'determine the active power' of patients. The reasons for this are that (1) a community of individuals can only really be unified if each individual member of the community is the source of the laws that provide the community with its unity (that is, each member must be autonomous) and (2) these laws must be laws that create resistance because, in Kant's view, the only way of conceiving of interaction is in terms of the withdrawal of resistance by the agent that allows a dead power in the patient to become a living power. In the following section we will see that juridical laws are laws that introduce precisely such resistance.

(1) I will begin by defending the claim that for Kant only autonomous individuals can truly interact and be real members of a world or community. For Kant our idea of a world is the idea of a substantial composite.[11] He makes his commitment to this clear in the cosmology sections of his metaphysics lectures. The first point he makes is that our idea of a world is the idea of a whole. Thus he argues that 'a multitude of substances without connection makes no world. One must thus not define world: the universe of substances, but rather the whole of them' (*V-MP/Dohna* 28: 657). However, he also argues that for substances to constitute a world they must form what he calls a *real* as opposed to an *ideal* whole. Kant believes that any composite must have both a form and matter, and hence there are two conditions that distinguish a real from an ideal whole, a material condition and a formal condition. (a) The material condition for existence of a real whole is that the parts of a real whole must be true individuals. This condition, which Kant sometimes posits in terms of the proposition that the world must be a substantial whole, implies – he believes – that spatial wholes, for example, are merely ideal wholes.[12] This material condition for real wholeness is a major motivation for Kant's claim that space is ideal. (b) The formal condition is that the unity of the whole must be 'real' rather than 'ideal', and the guarantee of the reality of the unity is the existence of 'real' connection(s).What is most significant here is Kant's account of this formal condition, for when we are thinking of a world of monads it is assumed that the material condition is met: the matter of the world is composed of the individuals that make up the world. In explaining this condition he writes that 'substances are the matter of the world, the formal aspect of the world consists in their connection (*nexu*) and indeed in a real connection (*nexu reali*). The world is thus a real whole (*totum reale*), not ideal' (*V-MP-L2/Pölitz* 28: 581). Our idea of a world is the idea of a *real* as opposed to an *ideal* whole in this sense.[13]

Elsewhere, Kant is a bit more explicit about this distinction. He argues that

> the connection (*nexus*) is ideal if I merely think the substances together, and real if the substances actually stand in interaction (*commercio*). // The form of the world is a real connection (*nexus realis*) because it is a real whole (*totum reale*) . . . Isolated substances, however, never

> constitute a whole (*totum*), then they must also be a real whole (*totum reale*). For were they ideal, then surely they could be represented in thought as a whole (*totum*), or the representations of them would constitute a whole (*totum*); but things in themselves would still not constitute a whole on this account. (V-MP/Mron 29: 851)

An ideal whole is a whole that can be 'represented in thought' as a whole. In such a whole the unity only exists in the mind of the observer. In a real whole, in contrast, the unity must be intrinsic to the whole. Although Kant himself does not explicitly make this claim, I suggest that what this means is that the individuals that constitute the whole must be responsible for the unity of the whole. Now, if we believe that laws are exactly the sort of thing that can supply unity to a group of individuals, then a real whole will be one in which the individuals that make up the whole are the source of the laws that provide the whole with its unity. That is, a real whole will be a realm of ends and the only way of being a member of such a whole is to be an autonomous being, that is, a being that is the giver or source of the laws that provide the whole with its unity.

(2) I will now defend the claim that Kant thought that interaction is only possible if there are laws that 'allow the agent to determine the active power of the patient'. This will be important for my discussion of Kant's account of juridical community as this is exactly what coercive juridical laws make possible, and in the following section I will show how this model lies behind his account of the transferral of property in his political writings.

The problem with conceptualizing interaction is fairly simple. Following Leibniz, Kant thinks that the idea of an individual (substance) is the idea of something essentially active. There is, however, a problem in explaining how two essentially active beings can act upon one another, for we must be able to give an account of how an essentially active substance can suffer or be passive. Kant himself addresses this problem in his metaphysics lectures, explaining that 'that substance suffers ([is] passive) whose accidents inhere through another power'. He then asks 'how is this passion possible, since it was said earlier that it [i.e. the passive/suffering substance] is active insofar as its accidents inhere'. (V-MP/Mron 29: 823)

The problem is not merely that Kant conceives of individual substances as essentially active, but that following Leibniz he is committed to the view that an accident (or more generally what Kant refers to as a 'determination') can only truly inhere in or belong to a substance if the substance is the active cause or ground of the accident. I name this doctrine the Principle of Active Inherence.[14] It is Leibniz's acceptance of this principle that lies behind his claim that monads are windowless and it also lies behind Kant's rejection of 'physical influence': the view, popular in the early eighteenth century, that action should be understood in terms of determinations flowing from the agent into the patient.[15] If we accept the Principle of Active Inherence, though, it is not clear how one individual can ever be the cause of any change in another individual. If a determination can only be a determination of individual *b* if *b* is the active ground or cause of the determination, how can another substance ever be the cause of a change in *b*? Leibniz's solution was to admit defeat and conclude that one substance cannot be the cause of a change in another.

Kant's solution to this problem would be to claim that we can understand the idea of an individual being acted upon without appealing to the untenable notion of accidents flowing from one individual into another, in terms of the agent 'determining the active power of the substance being acted upon' (V-MP/Mron 29: 823).[16] This account of action does not violate the Principle of Active Inherence, because the patient's determination inheres in the patient due to the patient's own power. This power, however, has been determined by the agent. And Kant explains the notion of one agent 'determining the power' of another in terms of the withdrawal of resistance.[17] On this model, one individual substance (the agent) is the 'cause' of a change in another individual substance (the patient) if the change in the patient is the result of the agent withdrawing its resistance. The patient remains, however, essentially active, for the determination is the result of its power.

3. Political/juridical community

I will now briefly outline Kant's account of Private Right in the *Metaphysics of Morals* and explain how his analysis of a community of property owners is modelled on the category of community and the account of interaction in his metaphysics lectures.[18]

Because we own things it seems natural to assume that ownership should be understood as a relationship between an individual and an object. For Kant, however, this is a fundamentally mistaken way of conceiving of property, for to *own* something is to have a (legitimate) right to it, and to have a legitimate right to something is not to be understood in terms of the relationship between an individual and a thing owned, but instead in terms of the owner's relation to other agents. To claim a right is to claim that others should recognize your possession and not interfere with your use of the object. It is to claim that others should not *resist* your use of an object, and Kant believes that such a claim can only be made against others who have commonly willed the same set of juridical laws. To have a property right ultimately involves an intelligible relationship,[19] and such intelligible rights are only possible in the civil condition. Such a condition, which for Kant is an ideal that can never be realized but only approached asymptotically, is only possible if the juridical laws are willed by all members of the community. Thus Kant explains that

> A unilateral will cannot serve as a coercive law for everyone with regard to possession that is external and therefore contingent, since that would infringe upon the freedom in accordance with universal laws. So it is only a will putting everyone under obligation, hence only a collective general (common) and powerful will, that can provide everyone this assurance. (*MS* 6: 256)

In an ideal juridical community each member consents to the laws of the community, and it is the existence of these laws that makes us all members of the same community; indeed, it is only the existence of such commonly willed laws that makes (fully legitimate) property rights possible.[20] The existence of juridical rights, then, presupposes the existence of juridical laws, and it is the existence of such laws that allows us to act upon one another in an intelligible juridical way. Thus, as the start of his discussion of Contract Right Kant explains that

> My possession of another's choice, in the sense of my capacity to determine it by my own choice to a certain deed in accordance with laws of freedom (what is externally mine or yours with respect to the causality of another), is a right (of which I can have several against the

> same person or against others); but there is only a single sum (system of laws), contract right, in accordance with which I can be in this sort of possession. (*MS* 6:271)

Here Kant defines a (contractual) right in terms of 'the possession of another's choice'. The language here is very similar to the language he uses to explain action in his metaphysics lectures. There, he argued that the agent must have a capacity to 'determin[e] the active power' of the patient. Here, he claims that to have a right is to possess 'a capacity to determine the choice of another'. And he argues that an individual can only possess such a capacity if there is a system of juridical laws and others (a) recognize and (b) affirm these laws. These laws are not physical laws but juridical laws, the existence of which depends upon them being freely taken up by each individual member of the community. Kant explains that 'my capacity to determine another's choice by my own choices' is called a right and that it is the existence of juridical laws that makes rights possible and, consequently, allows one individual to act upon ('determine the choice of') another. Laws that assign rights are called juridical (or coercive) laws. Such laws make interaction possible because they are the basis of resistance between individuals. Kant repeatedly stresses the relationship between juridical laws and the notion of resistance. For example, in his ethics lectures he argues that

> The universal law of reason can alone be the determining ground of action, but this is the law of universal freedom; everyone has the right to promote this, even though he effects it by *resisting* the opposing freedom of another, in such a way that he seeks to prevent an *obstruction*, and thus to further an intent . . . The other, however, *obstructs* the action by his freedom; the latter I can curtail and *offer resistance* to, insofar as this is in accordance with the laws of coercion; so *eo ipso* I must thereby *obstruct* universal freedom by the use of my own. From this it follows that . . . the right to coerce the other consists in *restricting* his use of freedom, insofar as it cannot co-exist with universal freedom according to universal law; and this is the right of coercion. . . // Since nobody can exercise a right to coerce, who has not obtained a right thereto from a higher ground, which consists, however, in one's own freedom and its congruence with the freedom of everyone according to universal law, it is clear that the right to coerce can only be derived from the idea of law itself. (*V-Eth/Vigil* 27: 523; my emphasis)

We should read such passages bearing in mind Kant's account of action in his metaphysical work, for he believes that all action should be understood in terms of the withdrawal of resistance. Here Kant argues that that the right to coerce 'consists in' (legitimately) resisting the freedom of others, and that such a right (that is, the possibility of resistance) can only be derived from the 'idea of law itself'. In other words, Kant is suggesting in this passage that it is juridical laws that make resistance, and hence interaction (understood in terms of the withdrawal of resistance), possible.

Only if such a community (or civil condition) exists can an individual really own property and 'transfer' her/his property to another. In so doing individuals are able to act upon one another through mutual consent. The activity of the agent (giver) is the withdrawal of an impediment, the activity of the patient (receiver) is an active uptake. In the transferral of property, then, a property right does not flow from the giver to the receiver. Rather, in the context of a commonly willed set of property laws, one party renounces a right while the other party simultaneously actively takes up the right. As previously noted, Kant's stress on simultaneity here should make it clear that he is modelling his account of the transferral of property on the category of community. Kant is very careful to make it clear that in the 'transferral' of property there has to be more than merely the 'abandoning' or 'renouncing' of a right by the giver. I suggest that Kant's reason for stressing this is his metaphysical commitment to the Principle of Active Inherence. For the receiver really to possess a right (s)he has to be the active ground of the right. Thus Kant explains that transferral of property 'is only possible through a common will by means of which the object is always under the control of one or the other, since as one gives up his share in the common undertaking [*Gemeinschaft*] the object becomes the other's through his acceptance of it (and so by a positive act of choice)' (*MS* 6: 271).

Just as, in general, a determination can only belong to a substance if the substance is the active ground of the determination, property can only belong to an individual if the individual is the active ground of the right. In an act of exchange, then, it is not as if the donor actively gives and the recipient passively receives. Instead, the receiver must be actively asserting a claim to an object and the donor merely withdrawing her/his (legitimate) claim to it, withdrawing resistance to the recipient's claim. This is why Kant stresses that the recipient must accept the property 'by a positive act of choice'. Acquiring a right to property is not something that can occur passively; instead, the recipient must actively assert a claim, even in the case of receiving a gift. Such considerations lie behind Kant's claim that in the legal sense, strictly speaking all commissive acts are really omissive. Thus he argues that

> all coercive or juridical laws are prohibitive, and rely on the principle of not withholding from the other what belongs to him (*neminem laede*). (For the fact that both commissive and omissive actions are equally necessary for the performance of actions in a physical sense, makes no difference, since all commissive actions are omissive, *in sensu juris*.) (*V-Eth/Vigil* 27: 512)

Thus although on the phenomenal level an act such as paying a debt may appear to be an action on the part of the debtor,[21] on the legal level all that is happening is that the debtor is allowing his creditor to use what is legally hers. In paying back the loan, the debtor has not really given his creditor anything. Kant believes that such an analysis can be applied to all property transactions and not merely to cases of repaying a debt. Thus he explains that 'I cannot give the other anything – he already has what belongs to him; . . . you are to leave the other his own, take nothing, abstain from all actions whereby you would detract from his rights' (*V-Eth/Vigil* 27: 512).

To conclude: I have argued that Kant's account of juridical community, the idea of a community of property owners, is modelled on the category of community introduced in the first *Critique* and his account of interaction found in his metaphysics lectures. At the very least, I hope I have shown that there are interesting parallels between Kant's political philosophy and his metaphysics of community and interaction, and that a study of Kant's logic and metaphysics can help us understand key aspects of his Doctrine of Right.

Notes

1 Examining the relation between the scientific account of interaction and Kant's account of a juridical community is beyond the scope of

this paper, although Kant himself notes their relationship in the *Metaphysics of Morals*, arguing that '[t]he law of a reciprocal coercion necessarily in accord with the freedom of everyone under the principle of universal freedom is, as it were, the *construction* of that concept, that is, the presentation of it in pure intuition a priori, by analogy with presenting the possibility of bodies moving freely under the law of the *equality of action and reaction*' (*MS* 6: 232).

2 Thus, in the first sentence of Public Right, Kant explains that 'the sum of all laws which need to be promulgated generally in order to bring about rightful conditions is *public right*' (*MS* 6: 311).

3 This usage of 'juridical' is not entirely consistent with Kant's usage of 'juridical' as he seems to use this term to apply to the whole of the Doctrine of Right, both Private Right and Public Right.

4 Thus, for example, Allen D. Rosen argues in *Kant's Theory of Justice* (Ithaca, NY: Cornell University Press, 1993), p. 83, that '[e]nforceability through coercion is therefore the essence of a juridical duty or law':.

5 Arthur Ripstein, 'Authority and coercion', *Philosophy and Public Affairs*, 32/1 (2004), 2–35. See also Ripstein, 'Kant's legal and political philosophy', in T. Hill (ed.), *A Companion to Kant's Ethics* (Oxford: Blackwell, forthcoming).

6 Thus, Kant explains that the civil condition 'is that condition which reason, *by a categorical imperative*, makes it obligatory to strive after' (*MS* 6: 318). For a fuller discussion of this see Thorpe, 'What's the point of studying ethics according to Kant?', *Journal of Value Inquiry*, 40 (2006), 461–74.

7 Kant's account of the disjunctive form of judgement has received rather a bad press in the contemporary literature. Thus Paul Guyer, for example, writes in *Kant and the Claims of Knowledge* (Cambridge: Cambridge University Press, 1987), p. 452, that '[a]s is often pointed out, Kant's connection of the real relation of reciprocal influence with the logical notion of exclusive disjunction is the most tenuous piece of his metaphysical deduction of the categories'. .

8 '[T]he third category always arises from the combination of the first two in its class' (*KrV* B110). In the case of the category of community, which is the third category of relation, the first and second categories are substance and causation. So community involves substances in causal relations, but cannot be reduced to the notion of mutual causation.

9 This is not the case in the ground-consequence relation. Kant appeals to the example of God, the 'world-creator'. God is the ground or cause of the world, but God and the world do not constitute a whole. If God were thought of as interacting with the world, however, God and the world would constitute a whole. Here I disagree with Schneewind, who

argues that Kant advocates the 'astonishing claim . . . that God and we share membership in a single moral community only if we all equally legislate the law we are to obey': Jerome B. Schneewind, *The Invention of Autonomy: a History of Modern Moral Philosophy* (Cambridge: Cambridge University Press, 1998), p. 513; see also p. 554.

10 Thus, Kant explains that 'the categories, as the true **ancestral concepts** of pure understanding, also have their equally pure **derivative concepts**' (*KrV* A81–2/B107)

11 Kant calls our idea of a world 'the intelligible world'. Kant makes this clear in the *Critique of Pure Reason* where he claims that 'the *mundus intelligibilis* is nothing but the concept of a world in general, abstracting from all conditions of intuiting it' (*KrV* A433/B461). He makes a similar point in his metaphysics lectures from the same period when he claims that 'a foreigner called it fantasy to speak of the intelligible world (*mundo intelligibili*). But this is just the opposite, for one understands by it not another world, but rather this world as I think of it through the understanding' (V-MP/Mron 29: 850).

12 'The world is thus a substantial whole (*totum substantiale*), hence not merely ideal. We can think of diverse ideal wholes (*tota idealia*), but they do not constitute a world, e.g., I can represent to myself a syllogistic whole (*totum syllogismorum*), an accidental whole (*totum accidentale*), or a whole in space, etc.; but these are mere ideal wholes (*tota idealia*), which consist of concepts. But the world is a real whole (*totum reale*), which consists of concepts' (V-MP/Mron 29: 851).

13 He frequently makes similar points. See, for example, *Metaphysik* L2 (*V-MP-L2/Pölitz* 28: 196) and *Metaphysik Dohna* (*V-MP/Dohna* 28: 657).

14 Thus Kant claims that '[w]e can never be merely passive, but rather every passion is at the same time action . . . Every substance is self-active, otherwise it could not be substance . . . The substance being acted upon (*substantia patiens*) is acting in itself (*eo ipso agens*), for the accident would not inhere if the substance had no power through which it inhered in it, hence it also acts' (V-MP/Mron 29: 823).

15 For a more detailed account of this, see Thorpe, 'Is Kant's realm of ends a *unum per se*? Aquinas, Suárez, Leibniz and Kant on composition', *The British Journal for the History of Philosophy* (forthcoming).

16 Here Kant writes: 'What then is genuine passivity? The acting substance (*substantia agens*) determines the power of the substance being acted upon (*substantiae patientis*) in order to produce this accident, therefore all passivity (*passio*) is nothing more than the determination of the power of the suffering substance by an outer power' (V-MP/Mron 29: 823).

17 Thus Kant explains that one individual 'determines the power' of another when it removes an impediment which allows what he calls a 'dead

power' to become a 'living power'. For example, in Metaphysics L2 he argues that 'with a faculty we imagine only the possibility of power. Between faculty and power lies the concept of endeavor (*conatus*; *Bestrebung*). When the determining ground for an effect is internally sufficient, then it is a dead power. But when it is internally and externally sufficient, then it is a living power. Power which is merely internally sufficient, without being able to produce the effect, is always opposed to an opposing power which hinders its effect, an impediment (*impedimentum*). Thus as soon as the impediment (*impedimentum*) is removed, the dead power becomes living. (*V-MP-L2/Pölitz* 28: 565).

18 See also Howard Williams's paper in this volume which supports my view that according to Kant property has a metaphysical character.

19 Thus Kant talks of 'intelligible possession (*possessio noumenon*)', and explains that property relations are 'purely intellectual' (*MS* 6: 273).

20 This idea of a juridical community is, of course, an ideal. In Kant's language, such a community is intelligible. The laws that actually exist have not actually been (and given their unjust nature, especially when regarded from a cosmopolitan perspective, could not be) commonly willed by the whole human race. This is why Kant believes that all property rights as they exist in the phenomenal world are provisional.

21 'In terms of physical forces [i.e. on the phenomenal level], the payment of a debt is nothing else but an action *commissiva*' (*V-Eth/Vigil* 27: 512).

References

Guyer, P., *Kant and the Claims of Knowledge* (Cambridge: Cambridge University Press, 1987).

Ripstein, A., 'Authority and coercion', *Philosophy and Public Affairs*, 32/1 (2004), 2–35.

——, 'Kant's legal and political philosophy', in T. Hill (ed.), *A Companion to Kant's Ethics* (Oxford: Blackwell, forthcoming).

Rosen, A. D., *Kant's Theory of Justice* (Ithaca, NY: Cornell University Press, 1993).

Schneewind, J. B., *The Invention of Autonomy: a History of Modern Moral Philosophy* (Cambridge: Cambridge University Press, 1998).

Thorpe, L., 'What's the point of studying ethics according to Kant?', *Journal of Value Inquiry*, 40 (2006), 461–74.

——, 'Is Kant's realm of ends a *unum per se*? Aquinas, Suárez, Leibniz and Kant on composition', *The British Journal for the History of Philosophy* (forthcoming).

6 • Kant's *Rechtslehre* and Ideas of Reason

Tatiana Patrone

1. Introduction

Since Kant is notoriously interested in bringing his philosophical system into an *architectonic* unity, the project of relating his political philosophy to his metaphysics promises to be rewarding. The Preface and the Introduction to *The Metaphysics of Morals* bridge Kant's political doctrine and the practical part of his corpus; throughout *Rechtslehre* we find numerous references to Kant's accounts of reason, freedom and morality; even where explicit references are missing, Kant's terminology and arguments bear resemblance to his critical works. Of the many respects in which Kant's philosophy of right can be related to his critical doctrine, I will discuss one. In what follows, I will focus on the relation between concepts of private right and concepts of public right, a relation which (as I will argue) closely resembles the relation between concepts of understanding and ideas of reason in the 'Transcendental Dialectic'.

What prompts this discussion is the fact that Kant generally calls concepts of public right *Ideen*, *Vernunftideen* and *Vernunftbegriffe*. In interpreting these notions as ideas of reason, Kant seems to emphasize that in transition from the 'state of nature' to the 'civil condition' *via* entering into the 'original contract', we are not dealing with historical events, but rather with philosophical idealizations. But since Kant develops a peculiar account of theoretical and practical reason, and since 'idea of reason' (in Kant) is a technical term, calling certain representations 'ideas of reason' comes with heavy baggage. After all, one third of the first *Critique* (the 'Transcendental Dialectic') is dedicated to reason's representations, and Kant devotes a full section of the 'Transcendental Dialectic' to paying tribute to Plato's notion of 'idea', the notion that captures the nature and the importance of reason's representations.

In this paper, I claim that the key concepts of public right are ideas of reason in Kant's technical sense. More specifically, I look into the parallel between Kant's account of ideas of reason in the first *Critique* and his account of concepts of private and public right in *Rechtslehre*. I claim that concepts of public right bring into a systematic unity concepts of private right, and thereby make possible the coherent application of concepts of private right to empirical objects, much as the transcendental ideas of reason bring into a systematic unity concepts of understanding, and thereby make possible their coherent application.

This introduction is followed by four sections. (2) I begin by discussing Kant's account of ideas of reason in the first *Critique*. Here, I focus on his claim that ideas are 'necessary' representations that serve to bring concepts of understanding into a systematic unity. (3) I then turn to Kant's *Rechtslehre* and, after a brief inventory of Kant's terms and arguments, I argue that there is an important difference between Kant's arguments for the 'objective validity' of concepts of private right and of concepts of public right. (4) Next, I go over the steps of one of the deductions in *Rechtslehre* – the deduction of 'intelligible possession' and (5) I discuss Kant's justification of two ideas of public right – 'civil union' and the 'will of all united'. What will emerge from this exegesis, I hope, is an account of the relation between concepts of private right and concepts of public right, an account that will look remarkably similar to Kant's arguments in the first *Critique*. Concepts of private right resemble concepts of understanding in that they are supported by *deductions* and in that they can be made applicable to the realm of experience coherently and correctly only with the help of *ideas of reason*. Concepts of public right, on the other hand, resemble the ideas of reason in that, first, they are justified by an appeal to the 'interests' of reason and, second, in that they serve the goal of bringing into a systematic unity concepts of understanding.

2. Ideas of reason and concepts of understanding

One of the key accounts in the first *Critique* concerns the interaction between our cognitive faculties. Following Kant, we can spell out this interaction by appealing, first, to the principles that govern the use of each faculty and, second, to the representations that correspond to these faculties. Each of our faculties, Kant claims, is responsible for certain kinds of representations. Roughly, to the faculty of sensibility correspond *intuitions*; to the faculty of understanding correspond *concepts*; and to the faculty of reason correspond *ideas*. At the beginning of the 'Transcendental Dialectic' Kant provides a 'progression of representations' which contains the record of all our 'cognitions':

> The genus is **representation** in general. Under it stands the representation with consciousness [*perceptio*]. A **perception** that refers to the subject as a modification of its state is a **sensation**; an objective perception is a **cognition**. The latter is either an **intuition** or a **concept**. The former is immediately related to the object and is singular; the latter is mediated, by means of a mark, which can be common to several things. A concept is either an **empirical** or a **pure concept**, and the pure concept, insofar as it has its origin solely in the understanding (not in a pure image of sensibility), is called *notio*. A concept made up of notions [*ein Begriff aus Notionen*], which goes beyond the possibility of experience, is an **idea** or a concept of reason. (*KrV* A320/B376–7)[1]

From this 'progression of representations' we see that ideas of reason are (1) 'concepts made up of notions' that (2) go 'beyond the possibility of experience'. Setting aside the genesis of ideas of reason (that is, 'concepts made up of notions'), let us look into the second feature that Kant highlights in this passage.

The full definition of the term 'idea of reason' that supplements Kant's 'progression of representations' is this: 'by an idea I mean a necessary concept of reason for which no congruent object can be given in the senses' (*KrV* A327/B383).[2] (Thus what Kant now includes in the definition of ideas is that they are *necessary* concepts of reason.) First and foremost, ideas of reason *transcend* the realm of experience and have 'no congruent objects' *in* experience. Kant's argument for this claim, briefly, amounts to the following: reason's main principle is 'to find the *unconditioned* for conditioned cognitions of the understanding, with which its unity will be completed' (*KrV* A307/B364; my emphasis). Since the 'unconditioned' cannot be given *in* the senses, this principle urges reason to go *beyond* the realm of the senses. And when reason *postulates* the unconditioned as a given it transgresses the boundaries of what can be known.

Although they are transcendent, ideas are *necessary* concepts of reason. The principle of reason to search for the unconditioned drives it to postulate the representations that correspond to the unconditioned, and it drives reason to do so *necessarily*. Indirect evidence of reason's predicament to search for answers that it cannot obtain in principle is provided by the history of metaphysics: the history of futile arguments concerning what we cannot know (God, for example). In A328/B384, Kant calls ideas of reason 'problems without solutions', and in Avii he says:

> [Human] reason has the peculiar fate in one species of cognitions [pertaining to its *ideas*] that it is burdened with questions which it cannot dismiss, since they are given to it as problems by the nature of reason itself, but which it also cannot answer, since they transcend every capacity of human reason.

The *persistence* of some metaphysical problems seems to show that reason is *necessarily* driven by its fruitless pursuit of the unconditioned.

However, the main argument for the 'necessity' of reason's ideas comes from a close look at the *principle* of reason. According to Kant, we can get an insight into reason's *modus operandi* from looking at what Kant calls the 'logical use of reason'. In A321/B378, Kant claims that 'we can expect that the *form of the syllogisms* will contain the *origin* of special concepts that we may call pure concepts of reason or transcendental ideas'. In fact, it is the form of the syllogisms that lets us uncover the very principle of reason, and the consistent application of this principle, according to Kant, ultimately leads reason to postulate the unconditioned as given and to assume (mistakenly) that its reference can be an object of knowledge.

In its negative task, the 'Transcendental Dialectic' exposes the flaws of the arguments based on reason's peculiar representations and the positive account of reason gives us the guidelines for the *proper* application of reason's ideas. Far from being willing to discard ideas, Kant argues that in spite of their transcendent nature they are indispensable for our cognition. Ideas of reason, he claims, ought to be used as *regulative principles* that bring concepts of understanding into a systematic unity. Thus, in the Appendix to the 'Transcendental Dialectic', Kant says that reason, while it 'does not create any concepts (of objects)' that can be applied in experience, does '*order* [these concepts] and gives them that unity which they can have in their greatest possible extension' (*KrV* A643/B672). Kant then adds that the 'law of reason to seek unity is necessary, since without it we would have no reason, and without that, no *coherent use of the understanding*, and, lacking that, no *sufficient mark of empirical truth*' (*KrV* A651/B679).

Let me emphasize again the aspect of Kant's account that interests us here. According to Kant, there is a demarcation between concepts of understanding and ideas of reason. Ideas are a priori representations of the 'unconditioned', and while they do not apply to empirical objects they are nonetheless necessarily generated through the application of reason's main principle to search for the unconditioned that corresponds to every given conditioned cognition. Furthermore, in spite of the fact that ideas cannot be applied to objects, they *can* (and *ought to*) be applied to concepts of understanding. Ideas function as regulative principles that bring concepts of understanding into a systematic unity, without which we would have no 'coherent use of the understanding' and no 'mark of empirical truth'.[3] In what follows, I will trace similar arguments in *Rechtslehre*. We will see that reason's ideas in the practical realm play essentially the same role of organizing concepts of private right into a coherent system.

3. Terms and arguments in *Rechtslehre*

The terminological distinction that will interest us here is the distinction between concepts of *private* right and concepts of *public* right. To the first set belong the three cornerstone concepts of Part I of *Rechtslehre* – the concepts of 'intelligible possession', of 'original acquisition' and of 'acquisition by contract'.[4] To the second set belongs a long list of concepts, for instance 'civil union', 'original contract' and the 'will of all united'. The first set of concepts, I will argue, functions in *Rechtslehre* in the same way that the pure concepts of understanding do in the first *Critique*: concepts of *private* right are the conditions *sine qua non* of our practical judgements. On the other hand, concepts of *public* right are akin to ideas of reason – they are the regulative principles that bring concepts of private right into a systematic unity.

Although Kant is not quite consistent in his terminology throughout *Rechtslehre*, he does consistently justify the application of concepts of private right quite differently from the application of the concepts of public right. To use Kant's jargon, the 'objective validity' of *all* and *only* concepts of private right is supported by *deductions*, while the application of concepts of public right is argued for on quite different, morally normative grounds. I will return to this issue shortly. For now, let me say that the difference in Kant's *arguments* supports a prima facie distinction between the status of concepts of private right and of public right: concepts of private right are akin to concepts of understanding, while concepts of public right resemble ideas of reason.

Here, then, is a brief catalogue of Kant's terms in *Rechtslehre*. As already mentioned, concepts of *Privatrecht* are 'intelligible possession' (to which Kant also refers as 'merely rightful possession', 'possessio noumenon', 'nonempirical possession' and 'non-physical possession'), 'original acquisition' and 'acquisition by contract'. Kant provides transcendental deductions for these concepts of private right in §6, §17 and §19 of *Rechtslehre* respectively.

On the other hand, we find that the term 'idea' (or one of its synonyms) is applied to the following concepts of *public* right: 'civil constitution', 'original contract', 'original community of land', 'right of nations', 'state', 'civil union', 'community of all nations', 'head of state' (and 'sovereign'), 'original possession in common', 'will of all united', 'peaceful community of all nations', 'punitive justice' and 'right'.[5] Aside from these, Kant also says that the command 'obey existing authority' is an idea of reason (*MS* 6: 319).

Let me now briefly outline firstly what is at stake in each of Kant's deductions, and secondly what his main strategy is in the normative arguments for the application of concepts of public right.

The main task of a Kantian deduction is to show that an a priori concept is applicable to empirical objects. In the first *Critique*, Kant says that a deduction is an 'explanation of the way in which concepts can relate to objects *a priori*' (*KrV* A85/B117); and in the second *Critique*, he explains that a deduction is 'the justification of [a concept's] objective and universal validity and the discernment of the possibility of the synthetic proposition [employing this concept] *a priori*' (*KpV* 5: 46). Furthermore, his understanding of the point of a deduction does not change in *Rechtslehre*. He writes:

'the *theory* that it is possible to abstract from [the empirical conditions] without giving up possession of the promise is itself the *deduction* of the concept of acquisition by contract' (*MS* 6: 273).[6] In a deduction, then, Kant's aim is to show that an a priori concept can be applied to empirical objects. Furthermore, Kant argues that in some sense these concepts *ought* to be applied to empirical objects. And so in *Rechtslehre*'s three deductions, Kant's task is the following: after discussing the *empirical factors* concerning possession, acquisition and contract-making, he shows how a priori propositions about them are possible. Specifically, Kant firstly goes over the spatio-temporal features (or 'limiting conditions') of possession, acquisition and contracts,[7] and secondly shows that these features fail to capture the essence of possession, acquisition and contract-making. Only an a priori account that *abstracts* from the spatio-temporal limitations of these concepts can explain the possibility of judgements concerning our rights of possession etc. Deductions of concepts such as 'intelligible possession', 'original acquisition' and 'acquisition by contract', then, involve arguments to the conclusion that it is *possible* to abstract from the spatio-temporal features of possession, acquisition and contract-making, and that it is possible to give an a priori account of these concepts.

We find no deductions of concepts of *public* right, on the other hand. In fact, Kant does not provide explicit arguments either for his claim that certain representations are *ideas of reason* or for his claim that they must be used as regulative principles. There is little doubt, however, that he regards concepts of public right as ideas and that he is convinced that we must use them as regulative principles. In 6: 315–16, for instance, Kant says that 'the original contract is [an] *idea* of [the act by which a people forms itself into a state]' and that 'in terms of [this idea] *alone* we can think of the legitimacy of a state'. And in 6: 371–2, he claims that a rightful constitution 'must be counted among *ideas*, to which no object given in experience can be adequate', and that 'the *idea* of a civil constitution, which is also an absolute command that practical reason, judging according to concepts of right, gives to every people, is *sacred* and *irresistible*'. We see in both passages that Kant holds ideas of reason to be essential for a political doctrine: it is 'in terms of the original contract *alone* that we can think of the legitimacy of the state', and the idea of the civil constitution is '*sacred*' and '*irresistible*' since it is an '*absolute* command' of practical reason.

I believe that the general strategy for justifying claims that concepts of public right – as *ideas of reason* – ought to be used in our political discourse can be discerned in the following passage. Here, Kant discusses another concept, the concept of a *state*, which also functions as a regulative principle. He writes:

> A state is a union of a multitude of human beings under the laws of right. Insofar as these are *a priori* necessary as laws, that is, insofar as they follow of themselves from concepts of external right as such, its form is the form of a state as such, that is, of *the state in idea, as it ought to be in accordance with pure principles of right*. This idea serves as a norm (*norma*) for every actual union into a commonwealth. (*MS* 6: 313; my emphasis)

In this passage, the connection is made between a concept as a regulative idea and the 'principles of right'; the normative status of this concept is based on its relation to *Rechtsprinzipien*, that is to say the principles of right (or, more precisely, the Universal Principle of Right) ultimately justify the claim that 'state' is an idea of reason and that it must be used as a *norma*. As we will see, Kant holds the Universal Principle of Right to be the following: 'an action is right if it can coexist with everyone's freedom in accordance with a universal law' (*MS* 6: 230). But before we turn to reason's political ideas and the arguments in support of their application, let us trace the steps of one of the deductions in *Rechtslehre*, the deduction of 'intelligible possession'.

4. Kant's *deduction* of 'intelligible possession'

As we saw, the task of a deduction is to show that an a priori concept is applicable to empirical objects. In *Rechtslehre*, at issue is the application to empirical objects of concepts of 'intelligible possession', 'original acquisition' and 'acquisition by contract'. The structure of the three deductions in §6, §17 and §19 respectively is essentially the same, and so I will now focus on the deduction of the first concept, the concept of 'intelligible possession'. In order to show that 'intelligible possession' can be applied to the spatio-temporal world, Kant first needs to show that 'intelligible possession' is indispensable for practical judgements of possession in general. The place to start, then, is to consider our mundane judgements of possession and to discern their underlying structure. Kant's aim here is to show that (perhaps contrary to appearances) our ordinary judgements of possession presuppose the a priori concept of possession. This would show, as I put it earlier, that the a priori concept of possession is a condition *sine qua non* of our practical judgements.

Above, I said that the concept of possession is the most important concept of private right. In fact, it is arguably the cornerstone of *Rechtslehre*. Let me explain. According to Kant, the general task of *Rechtslehre* is 'with mathematical exactitude' to determine 'what belongs to each' (*MS* 6: 233). This might seem to narrow the scope of Kant's doctrine: surely (we might argue) there are important rights that go beyond the concept of *possession*. But Kant understands the concept of possession rather widely. For him, claims of possession range from claims to 'corporeal things' to claims to 'others' *choices*', and to claims to 'others' *statuses* in relation to me' (*MS* 6: 247). Thus, claims of possession include all of the following propositions: (1) 'This copy of the *Groundwork* is mine' (a claim to the ownership of an *object*); (2) 'You ought to φ since you promised me you would' (a claim to the ownership of one's *choice*); and (3) 'This man is my husband' (a claim concerning one's *status* in relation to the agent). We can see, therefore, that when Kant says that possession is the central topic of *Rechtslehre*, he has in mind a fairly large set of claims concerning rightful relations among persons.What, then, can we say about the common structure of the claims of possession? According to Kant, it is plain that in making judgements of possession we are not making empirical claims. Consider, for instance, the judgement (1) 'This copy of the *Groundwork* is mine'. Claims such as (1) are not claims concerning which copy I happen to hold in my hands; rather, no matter which copy of the *Groundwork* I am physically holding, it is only *my* copy that is actually *mine*. The basis for the concept of possession, Kant concludes, is independent of the spatio-temporal relations between the agent and the physical object. Kant calls the empirical concept involved here 'holding', and he calls the a priori concept underlying the judgement of possession 'intelligible (or merely rightful) possession'. In so far as the concept of intelligible possession is *pure*, Kant believes, it requires a special kind of justification for its application to empirical objects, that is, a *deduction*.

The key to the possibility of applying an a priori concept to the spatio-temporal world, Kant argues, lies in the postulate of practical reason with regard to rights. In its positive formulation, the postulate says that 'it is possible for me to have any external object of my choice as mine' (*MS* 6: 246), and in its negative form, the postulate says that the *impossibility* of using external objects as mine or yours is 'contrary to right'. Giving up the concept of possession, Kant further argues, would result in no less than a 'contradiction of outer freedom with itself' since giving up the concept of possession would 'annihilate [objects of choice] in a practical respect' (*MS* 6: 246). Notice that the issue here does not concern giving up or retaining the empirical concept of *holding*. Instead, it concerns employing the concept of *possession* that has an 'intelligible' side. Kant's aim, therefore, is to show that our freedom would arrive at a 'contradiction with itself' were we to give up the possibility of making rightful claims to external objects etc.

Were we to give up our concept of possession, he believes, we would rob ourselves of the ability to use external objects as our own and to make claims upon other persons' choices or statuses. If all external objects were such that they could not be appropriated and used rightfully, our faculty of volition would be entirely vacuous: we would have the capacity to make choices but we would have no means to exercise this capacity rightfully. As agents living in the spatio-temporal world, we must be able to exercise our choices – we must be able to appropriate, to own and to use external objects; most importantly, we must be able to do this *rightfully*. This is what Kant means by saying that the *im*possibility of rightful claims of possession would 'annihilate [objects of choice] in a practical respect': the precepts of practical reason would become unintelligible were rightful relations among persons *im*possible. Kant concludes, therefore, that on pain of my 'outer freedom' contradicting itself, it must be 'possible for me to have [an] external object of my choice as mine'.

The deduction is complete with the justification of the postulate of practical reason with regard to rights. Kant explains:

> No one needs to be surprised that theoretical principles [such as this postulate of reason][8] about external objects that are mine or yours get lost in the intelligible and represent no extension of cognition, since no theoretical deduction can be given for the possibility of the concept of *freedom* on which they are based. It can only be inferred from the *practical law of reason* (the *categorical imperative*) as a *fact of reason*. (*MS* 6: 252; my emphasis)

In his justification of the postulate itself, therefore, Kant appeals to a host of concepts and arguments from his theoretical and practical philosophy. The postulate of reason, he says, is based (1) on the concept of *freedom*, which is inferred from (2) the *practical law of reason*, where 'practical law of reason' is (3) the *categorical imperative* and the concept of freedom can be 'inferred' from that practical law of reason as (4) a *fact of reason*. In short, Kant argues that the possibility of the use of the concept of possession can be based upon *an* ethical theory according to which it is possible to apply a priori concepts to the spatio-temporal world. That is, it can be based upon *his* ethical theory since his ethical theory *does* explain how a priori concepts ('intelligible possession' et al.) can be applied to the spatio-temporal objects. (It goes without saying that *The Metaphysics of Morals* is not the proper place to justify this ethical theory itself; the task of this justification is carried out mainly by the *Critique of Practical Reason* and by the *Groundwork*.)

5. 'Civil condition' and 'the will of all united'

Even if we know that concepts of private right are to be understood as a priori, we still need to know when they are applied correctly, that is, *rightfully*. This new leg of the argument begins with Kant's interpretation of the claim that possession, acquisition and contract-making can be thought of in abstraction from the spatio-temporal conditions. Roughly, Kant interprets all relations of possession as relations *among wills of persons* rather than as relations between persons and physical objects. That is, to say that I make a *rightful* claim of possession is to say that there is a relation in conformity with the right in which I stand to the wills of all other persons. And this relation amounts to the following: while I have a *right* to my copy of the *Groundwork*, everyone else has a *duty* not to interfere with my use of it. And so Kant says:

> Practical reason requires us to think of possession *apart from* possession of [an] object of my choice in appearance (holding it), to think of it not in terms of empirical concepts but of concepts of understanding, those that can contain *a priori* conditions of empirical concepts. Upon this is based the validity of such a concept of possession (*possessio*

> *noumenon*), as a *giving of law* that holds for everyone; for such lawgiving is involved in the expression 'this external object is *mine*', since by it an obligation is laid upon all others, which they would not otherwise have, to refrain from using the object. (*MS* 6: 253)

Any claim of possession, therefore, involves *universal legislation*. If correct, this claim establishes the *right* of the owner and the corresponding set of *duties* for others. What we now need are the necessary conditions for this universal legislation to be legitimate. This challenge brings us to Kant's account of concepts of public right, that serve as regulative principles of reason and guide us in the rightful application of concepts of private right.

Kant argues that provided that it is possible for us at all to have external objects as our own, the rest of the system of juridical rights 'can afterwards be adduced in an analytic way' (*MS* 6: 255). That is, once we establish the practical reality of concepts of private right, we can deduce analytically the conditions under which these concepts are rightfully applicable to experience. And since the three deductions in Part I of *Rechtslehre do* establish the practical reality of concepts of private right, nothing prevents us from deriving further claims concerning the *rightful* application of these concepts to empirical objects. Let us now look into two concepts of public right – 'civil union' and the 'will of all united' – that serve as necessary conditions for the rightful application of concepts of private right.

According to Kant, we have a duty to form a civil union. In particular, Kant holds, we have an unconditional duty to escape from the 'state of nature':

> It is true that the state of nature need not, just because it is natural, be a state of *injustice*. But it would still be a state *devoid of justice*, in which when rights are in dispute, there would be no judge competent to render a verdict having rightful force. (*MS* 6: 312)

Far from making an empirical argument to the conclusion that people's desires tend to come into conflict and that in the absence of a 'competent judge' violence will be the only way to resolve them, Kant makes a conceptual point concerning unilateral and omnilateral volition. No claim of possession, he believes, can be legitimate if it is based on a *unilateral* willing. The will that falls short of being *omnilateral* in principle cannot be a 'competent judge' in establishing whether a claim of possession is rightful or not. The 'competent judge' in any legislation, according to Kant, is the *will of all united*, and one of the necessary conditions for the existence of such a will is forming a *state*.[9]

The reason Kant considers a unilateral will to be incapable of universal legislation is that a unilateral will 'cannot serve as a coercive law for everyone with regard to possession since that would infringe upon freedom in accordance with universal laws' (*MS* 6: 256). Essentially, any unilateral volition amounts to imposing one's will on the wills of others, and such imposition necessarily 'infringes upon freedom' of others. In contrast to this, omnilateral volition proceeds from the *general* will, and this kind of volition is genuinely legislating. The point, of course, is that 'omnilateral' in Kant is synonymous with 'universal' and 'a priori.' Thus, Kant concludes that it is 'only a collective general will that can provide everyone the assurance' that no one's freedom is going to be violated (*MS* 6: 256).[10] We can see that crucial for the unity of the wills is the *principle* according to which this unity is brought about. Thus, by the 'will of all united' Kant understands the 'will of all united a priori', where the point of unity merely reflects the standpoint of reason in general.

Consequently, the duty to enter into a civil union follows from the claim that only in a civil condition do we have an omnilateral will that can make legitimate claims concerning possession, acquisition and contract-making. Once again, Kant's point concerns the relation between the 'civil union' and the 'will of all united': while in the state of nature volition is in principle *unilateral* (and thus not genuinely universally legislating), in the civil union we have the omnilateral will that can render legitimate claims of possession and so on.

Kant calls 'civil union', 'state' and 'the will of all united' *ideas of reason*, and we are now in a position to see clearly what justifies the application of this term. Recall that an idea of reason is a representation that corresponds to reason's universal principle to 'find the unconditioned for conditioned cognitions of the understanding' (*KrV* A307/B364). If we consider the concept of private right, 'intelligible possession' and the practical propositions in which it can be used (for instance, 'this copy of the *Groundwork* is mine'), we see that the concept, as well as the judgements in which it may be included, is a *conditioned*; that is, its rightful application depends on some further conditions (for example, it would depend on the way I *acquired* the book). And the *totality* of such conditions and thus the *unconditioned* is, for Kant, entering into a civil union. Nothing falling short of this condition can serve as the unconditioned for the claims of possession: to secure a claim of possession nothing but the general will would suffice, and a union of private wills into a general will is only possible in a civil condition.

Since Kant's term (the 'unconditioned') may suggest that *the* unconditioned must be only one, and that there cannot be a set of conditions each member of which is *an* unconditioned, we ought to ask whetherunconditionality implies uniqueness for Kant.[11] Once we find the unconditioned for 'conditioned' claims of possession (for example, the idea of a 'will of all united *a priori*'), the argument might go, it is unclear why we should need any *further* conditions (such as the idea of a civil union) to expand on the series of conditions for the rightful application of concepts of possession. After all, if the 'will united *a priori*' is an *unconditioned*, then it must be the case that it requires *no* further conditions. For Kant, however, to say that the 'will of all united *a priori*' is an unconditioned is not to say that the 'will of all united *a priori*' is subject to no further conditions *absolutely*, that is to say in every respect. Recall that ideas are representations that correspond to the principle of reason in accordance with which it strives for the unconditioned; such striving, however, can be applied to different *series* of conditions. (This explains, for instance, why Kant discerns *three* transcendental ideas of reason in the first *Critique*.) Therefore, ideas in *Rechtslehre* are unconditioned in *some* respects, but they allow (and in fact require) further conditions in other respects. Very briefly, the *absolute* totality of conditions for the rightful application of concepts of private right consists in what Kant calls 'perpetual peace', that is a condition in which states (each with its rightful, republican constitution) are united in a *congress*, and where a 'public right of nations [is] realized, one to be established for deciding their disputes in a civil way' (*MS* 6: 351). This idea of perpetual peace completes the series of conditions for the rightful application of concepts of private right *absolutely*, or in *every respect*. But unfortunately the exploration of this idea would take us far beyond the scope of this paper.

6. Conclusion

My aim was to develop a reading of Kant's *Rechtslehre* emphasizing that the key concepts of his political theory are *ideas of reason.* My main focus was on Kant's account of how concepts of private right are related to concepts of public right. This relation, I argued, resembles the relation between concepts of understanding and ideas of reason that Kant explores in the first *Critique.* We started out by looking into Kant's 'progression of representations' and his claim that ideas of reason correspond to what he calls the 'unconditioned'. In virtue of this fact, ideas of reason have no 'congruent objects' in the realm of experience. Nonetheless, while ideas cannot be directly applied to empirical objects, they do apply to concepts of understanding. While I did not go over the details of Kant's argument to this conclusion, I highlighted the claim that reason's ideas allow us to bring concepts of understanding into a systematic unity. The latter, according to Kant, is crucial, since this systematic unity provides us with a 'sufficient mark of empirical truth' (*KrV* A651/B679).

We saw that a similar account can be found in Kant's *Rechtslehre* with respect to concepts of private right and concepts of public right. Kant invites us to treat concepts of private right as a priori concepts. He claims that rather than focusing on the empirical conditions under which these concepts can be applied to empirical objects, we need to *abstract* from these conditions. Thus, the physical holding of an external object does not exhaust possession. Instead, Kant argues, the relation of possession is a relation among persons' wills rather than the relation between a person and an object. According to Kant, therefore, concepts of private right are not empirical but 'intelligible' (a priori). This means that in order to adjudicate the claims of possession we need to look beyond the spatio-temporal relation between a person and an object and to assess the rightfulness of the relation among persons' wills. With the claim that concepts of private right are a priori comes a special task of showing that it is both possible and necessary to apply them to the spatio-temporal world. We saw that the justification of this possibility (deduction) rests on the postulate of pure practical reason with regard to rights, which says that, on pain of our 'outer freedom' coming into a practical contradiction with itself, we must postulate that 'it *is* possible for [us] to have any external object of [our] choice as [ours]' (*MS* 6: 246). The postulate itself, Kant holds, rests on the commands of pure practical reason (as Kant interprets them in his critical works). In short, Kant believes he has shown that *his* ethical theory can adequately demonstrate the possibility of applying the a priori concepts to empirical objects.

But in addition to being able to apply concepts of private right to the spatio-temporal world, we are in need of guidelines concerning their *rightful* application. The key to applying these concepts rightfully lies in bringing them under concepts of public right. We saw that claims of possession (understood in the broad sense) involve *universal legislation* in that they contain claims concerning *everyone's* duty to respect the agent's right. In other words, every claim of possession involves making a claim upon the wills of others. According to Kant, the only *rightful* way to make a claim of possession is to do so in accordance with the Universal Principle of Right, which says that 'an action is right if it can coexist *with everyone's freedom* in accordance with a universal law'. We also saw that for Kant, any instance of a unilateral volition necessarily violates the freedom of others and it is only the omnilateral will (or the 'will of all united a priori') that can ground rightful claims of possession.

The 'will of all united a priori', we saw, is an *idea of reason* since it serves as a regulative principle for the legitimate application of concepts of private right. Taken jointly, ideas of reason constitute the necessary condition for the rightful application of concepts of private right. In other words, concepts of public right closely resemble Kant's transcendental ideas in the first *Critique*. On the one hand, 'civil union' and other similar ideas are concepts that have no congruent objects in experience, but they are instrumental for bringing into systematic unity concepts of private right. The task of *Rechtslehre*, Kant says, is to determine 'what belongs to each', and to do so 'with mathematical exactitude'. That is, at the very least, *all* claims of possession ought to be made reconcilable with each other in accordance with the Universal Principle of Right. This task can be accomplished only if we bring concepts of private right under concepts of public right, or, in Kant's language, if we 'subsume' concepts of private right under concepts of public right. We saw that the transcendental ideas of reason bring concepts of understanding into a systematic unity, and that they thereby provide us with the 'sufficient mark of *empirical* truth' (*KrV* A651/

B679). Similarly, we can now say, concepts of public right make the rightful use of concepts of private right possible. They make possible the coherent application of *all* the claims involving possession, and thus provide us with the mark of *political* truth.

Notes

1 All references to Kant correspond to the Prussian Academy Edition. Unless otherwise indicated, I am using the Cambridge translations of the *Critique of Pure Reason*, of the 'The Doctrine of Right', and of the *Critique of Practical Reason*.

2 Here, I follow Werner Pluhar's translation of A320/B376–7: 'By the idea *of* a necessary concept of reason . . .' (my emphasis).

3 For extensive and insightful discussion of Kant's view on knowledge and truth, see Ido Geiger, 'Is the assumption of a systematic whole of empirical concepts a necessary condition of knowledge?', *Kant-Studien*, 94/3 (2003), 273–98. According to Geiger, 'the assumption of systematic unity is a necessary condition for determining the correspondence of concepts and objects' (291).

4 Together with Kant, I will be talking about *possession* (*Besitz* or *possessio*), not property (*Eigentum* or *dominium*).

5 In *Rechtslehre*, the references for these are the following: civil constitution (RL 6: 362–3; 6: 371; 6: 372); original contract (RL 6: 315; 6: 340; 6: 344); original community of land (RL 6: n. 251); right of nations (RL 6: 311; 6: 347; 6: 350; 6: 351); state (RL 6: 313; 6: 315); civil union (RL 6: 323); community of all nations (RL 6: 352); head of state or of the sovereign (RL 6: 338; 6: 371); original possession in common (RL 6: 262); peaceful community of nations (RL 6: 352; 6: 350 for 'perpetual peace'); punitive justice (RL 6: 363); will of all united (RL 6: 264) and *choice* of all united a priori (RL 6: 274); right (RL 6: 249; 6: 253).

6 Kant's account in the first *Critique* implies a stronger claim. Though in B159 (along with A85/B117) Kant says that a deduction 'exhibits' the *possibility* of the a priori categories as '*a priori* cognitions of objects of an intuition in general', e.g. towards the conclusion of the B-deduction, he claims that one of the 'results' of this deduction is the following: 'we *cannot* think any object except through categories' (*KrV*: B165). Similarly, when in *Rechtslehre* Kant talks of 'the theory that it is *possible* to abstract from [the empirical conditions] . . .' (RL 6: 273) he makes a more modest claim than he ends up arguing for.

7 The empirical side of possession involves 'holding' (RL 6: 253); the empirical side of acquisition involves 'taking control' and 'expending

one's labor' (RL 6: 268–9); the empirical side of contract-making involves an 'empirical act of declaration' (RL 6: 272).

8 In RL 6: 252, Kant says that this postulate is a 'theoretical principle'. This is ambiguous, and it might to be helpful to draw a contrast between *postulates* and *regulative (theoretical) principles*. The latter function in theoretical philosophy, and aim at the *unity of reason*. By contrast, the postulates do not seek to expand our theoretical knowledge by aiding speculative reason; rather, the postulates of practical reason are propositions that transgress the boundaries of theoretical thought, but that nonetheless must be accepted for moral reasons. In the context of his discussion of Kant's *Idea for a Universal History with a Cosmopolitan Intent*, David Lindstedt provides a helpful analysis of this distinction: Lindstedt, 'Kant: progress in universal history as a postulate of practical reason', *Kant-Studien*, 90/2 (1999), 129–47. (I would like to thank Sorin Baiasu for pointing out that Kant's claim in RL 6: 252 that postulates are 'theoretical propositions' should not be taken at face value.)

9 Ultimately, and as far as morality goes, *all* willing (unilateral or omnilateral) *in accordance with the imperatives of morality* is universally binding. But in *Rechtslehre*, 'unilateral' refers to a particular willing *as particular willing*. Thus, even if a *particular* volition coincides with the *general* will, this contingent fact does not make the particular willing universally binding. Another sense in which unilateral willing cannot be universally binding is this: all legally binding claims concerning possession et al. must ultimately be supported by a set of institutions (e.g. I cannot declare someone to be *my husband* unilaterally; for this claim to be legitimate, there has to be an *institution* of marriage). This is perhaps what Kant means when he says that only the *general* will is '*powerful*' enough to support the claims of possession. (I would like to thank Garrath Williams for pointing out that unilateral volition in the realm of morality *can* be universally binding, and that the meaning of 'universally binding' in *Rechtslehre* must therefore be in some respects different from that of the *Groundwork* and of the second *Critique*.)

10 Kant usually uses the term *allgemeine Wille* (e.g. in RL 6: 256 he calls it '*kollectiv-allgemeiner* [*gemeinsamer*] *machthabender Wille*'). This term corresponds to Rousseau's notion of the general will (though Rousseau distinguishes between the 'will of all' and the 'general will'). When Kant talks about *allgemeine Wille*, he refers to the latter; in fact, he often adds the crucial 'a priori vereinigter' to it, i.e. 'a will united *a priori*' (RL 6: 264.)

11 Although more often than not Kant uses the term 'unconditioned' to refer to various *types* of unconditioned, A326/B382 (together with Kant's discussion of 'absolute') seems to suggest that, ultimately, the

absolutely unconditioned must be one. 'A transcendental concept of reason always goes to the absolute totality in the synthesis of conditions, and never ends except with the *absolutely unconditioned*, i.e. what is *unconditioned in very relation*" (*KrV* A326/B382; my emphasis).

References

Geiger, I., 'Is the assumption of a systematic whole of empirical concepts a necessary condition of knowledge?', *Kant-Studien*, 94/3 (2003), 273–98.

Kant, I., *Critique of Practical Reason*, in *Kant: Practical Philosophy*, ed. and trans. M. J. Gregor (Cambridge: Cambridge University Press, 1996).

——, *Critique of Pure Reason*, ed. and trans. W. S. Pluhar (Cambridge, MA and Indianopolis: Hackett, 1996).

——, 'The Doctrine of Right', in *The Metaphysics of Morals*, ed. and trans. M. J. Gregor (Cambridge: Cambridge University Press, 1996).

——, *Critique of Pure Reason*, ed. and trans. P. Guyer and A. Wood (Cambridge: Cambridge University Press, 1997).

Lindstedt, D., 'Kant: progress in universal history as a postulate of practical reason', *Kant-Studien*, 90/2 (1999), 129–47.

7 • Practical Agency, Teleology and System in Kant's Architectonic of Pure Reason

Lea Ypi

1. The role of the Architectonic of Pure Reason

The section on the Architectonic of Pure Reason has until recently been among the least read parts of Kant's first *Critique*.[1] Historically, those few authors that thought it worth commenting on these pages seem to agree with Schopenhauer's early judgement that their presence in the *Critique of Pure Reason* is due more to Kant's 'Liebe für architektonische Simmetrie'[2] than it adds anything worth exploring to the rest of this major work. This paper tries to show that, far from being of 'slight scientific importance' or merely satisfying an interest for 'the personality of Kant',[3] the Architectonic of Pure Reason is crucial to understanding the primacy of practical reason and the systematic place of his later political writings.[4] Kant intended the Architectonic to form an essential part of his critical system and refers to it in all the major works (*KpV* 5: 10; *KU* 5: 381; *Anth* 7: 226). As the following pages emphasize, in this section Kant defends for the first time a teleological conception of human reason, addressing an issue of the highest importance for the development of his successive practical and political work.

The Architectonic, significantly defined by Kant as 'the art of constructing a system', faces the challenge of bringing into one systematic perspective the two uses of reason that the *Critique of Pure Reason* has previously divided: the speculative and the practical one. The legislation of human reason, Kant emphasizes at the end of this section, 'has two objects – nature and freedom – and thus contains not only the laws of nature, but also those of ethics, at first in two separate systems, but finally into one philosophical system' (*KrV* A840/B868). The goal of the Architectonic is to reflect upon the principles according to which philosophical cognitions can be ordered so as not to remain in an aggregative state but rather constitute a system, for it is thus alone, Kant stresses, that the practical ends of reason may be promoted (*KrV* A832/B860).

Now the question of the unity between the two objects of reason, nature and freedom, stands at the heart of the Introduction to the *Critique of the Power of Judgment* and of a number of Kant's political writings such as 'Towards Perpetual Peace'.[5] This issue is crucial to understanding the possibility of realizing the highest good in the sensible world as well as the role that Kant's political writings play in the larger philosophical system.[6] Several scholars have emphasized that one of the most difficult points in this respect concerns Kant's assumption of historical progress, the systematic role that the justification of teleological principles plays in understanding such an assumption, and the relationship between teleological principles and the idea of Providence in Kant's political thought.[7] However, until now, almost no attempt has been made to establish conceptual links between the first *Critique* and those other works with regard to the ways in which such questions are conceptualized at an early stage, before the full development of Kant's practical philosophy. Even those authors who touch upon the question have often limited their research to emphasizing the analogies between the Appendix on the regulative employment of the ideas of reason in the first *Critique* and the use of reflective judgement in the *Critique of the Power of Judgment*.[8] Many interpretations, however, tend to overlook the relevance of practical agency in Kant's first *Critique* and fail to consider the role of teleology in supporting a systematic conception of experience which is able to link the theoretical use of reason to the realization of its supreme moral ends.

The Architectonic of Pure Reason, I argue in this paper, is devoted to precisely this question. In a way similar to the *Critique of the Power of Judgment*, it relies on teleological principles to illustrate the links between the theoretical demand for systematic unity in science and the imperative of promoting the realization of the highest good as the supreme end of practical reason. However, as I will try to show, the status of such principles in the first *Critique* remains ambiguous and the tensions that their use produces, both from a theoretical and practical perspective, ultimately threaten to weaken some of Kant's main achievements with regard to natural teleology and the physico-theological proof for the existence of an intelligent designer of the universe. Moreover, a similar ambiguity runs the risk of undermining the practical/political rationale with which the Architectonic starts. The following pages aim to shed light on these tensions and reconstruct the conceptual background against which Kant's return to such *problématiques* in the *Critique of the Power of Judgment* and in successive political writings needs to be assessed.

2. Two definitions of philosophy

In the Architectonic of Pure Reason Kant offers two definitions of philosophy, the analysis of which helps to clear the ground of one of the most common assumptions about the first *Critique*: the idea that its main goal is to clarify the conditions of possibility of synthetic a priori judgments. The first is what Kant calls the 'scholastic' definition, according to which philosophy constitutes 'the system of all philosophical cognition' and aims to achieve the logical perfection of knowledge (*KrV* A838/B866). Kant introduces this definition only to undermine it by suggesting that it is an incomplete one, failing as it does to take into account that part of philosophy which attempts to promote the moral ends of humanity. 'The mathematician, the natural philosopher, and the logician' – he stresses – 'however far the first may have advanced in rational, and the two latter in philosophical knowledge – are merely artists, engaged in the arrangement and formation of conceptions; they cannot be termed philosophers' (*KrV* A839/B867). It is only the second definition of philosophy, Kant emphasizes, 'which has always formed the true basis of this term'. According to it, 'philosophy is the science of the relation of all cognition to the ultimate and essential aims of human reason (*teleologia rationis humanae*), and the philosopher is not merely an artist – who occupies himself with conceptions – but a lawgiver, legislating for human reason' (*KrV* A839/B867).

This second definition of philosophy is introduced in the first *Critique* as philosophy in its 'cosmic' sense (*Weltbegriff*). It is interesting to notice that in several lectures on logic and metaphysics Kant also refers to the same definition as the 'cosmopolitical' (*Weltbürgerlich*) conception of philosophy, or philosophy '*in sensu cosmopoliticu*', thus making more explicit the link between the practical task of philosophy and the need to promote a specific political and moral order, the scope of which expands worldwide (*Log* 9: 24). Of course, Kant's essay on universal history and the successive political writings articulate in greater detail this 'cosmopolitical' conception of philosophy, linking it to the postulate of humanity's progress in the realization of its moral ends. What is interesting to notice here is the attempt to integrate systematically, as early as in the *Critique of Pure Reason*, the 'scholastic' acquisitions of the Transcendental Doctrine of Elements with the moral ends outlined in the Transcendental Doctrine of Method, in particular the Canon of Pure Reason. In Kant's own words, while the Transcendental Doctrine of Elements has provided the material with which the edifice of the *Critique of Pure Reason* ought to be constructed, the Transcendental Doctrine of Method has an architectonic task: to design the 'plan' of such edifice according to the material gathered but 'at the same time sufficient for all our wants' (*KrV* A707/B735).[9]

In the concluding pages of his first major work Kant is not merely interested in the epistemological question which starts with the facts of Newtonian science to investigate the conditions of possibility of objective knowledge. The project of the first *Critique* here is parallel to that of the essay on universal history; Kant investigates the practical significance of reason's speculative knowledge and the question of how the variety of human cognitions could be put at the service of its moral ends. The philosopher, 'the ideal teacher', Kant emphasizes, is not merely engaged in the formation of concepts: he 'employs them as instruments for the advancement of the essential aims of human reason' (*KrV* A838/B866). The philosopher's task is therefore an eminently practical and political one; it needs to be understood in the context of the necessity for all human agents to realize the highest good in the world.

It is in the light of this renovated conception of philosophy, understood not merely as the ability to expand theoretical knowledge by means of a critique of dogmatic metaphysics but also as a concrete action-directing discipline, that the project of the Architectonic of Pure Reason should be investigated. The theoretical and practical interests of reason do not run parallel to each other, but need to be considered in a systematic way. Yet it is precisely when the question of the unity of the system is raised that the tensions in Kant's first *Critique* emerge most clearly. When the Architectonic inquires on how to conceptualize the principles that allow us to link the spheres of nature and freedom, it hits a considerable difficulty – a difficulty that arises from an underdeveloped conception of reason's spontaneous capacity to set moral ends, and from an analysis of nature as a teleologically subordinated whole. Let us first examine why.

3. The Architectonic of Pure Reason and the problem of the system

The term 'architectonic' in Kant defines 'the art of the system'. Since, as he points out, 'without systematic unity, our knowledge cannot become science . . . architectonic is the doctrine of the scientific in cognition, and therefore necessarily belongs to the doctrine of method' (*KrV* A832/B860).

As the opening passage of the section on the Architectonic of Pure Reason suggests, the main purpose of these pages relates to the need to distinguish between rhapsodic knowledge and system. Kant emphasizes here that 'reason cannot permit our knowledge to remain in an unconnected and rhapsodic state, but requires that the sum of our cognitions should constitute a system'. This is not just a theoretical requirement, it is a practical one. For only in this way, Kant stresses, 'is [it] possible to promote the essential ends (*wesentliche Zwecke*) of reason' (*KrV* A832/B860). The central task of the Architectonic is not exhausted in discovering a set of universal rules serving the systematic use of understanding in its reflection upon experience in general. Far from involving merely the theoretical conditions of the possibility of experience in general, the crucial question here relates to the possibility of a unitary and comprehensive conception of reason in both its speculative and practical use. This means that it is simply not enough to reflect theoretically on the transcendental laws of the understanding and on the theoretical use of the ideas of reason. It is necessary to integrate this knowledge with the capacity of human agents to act practically in the sensible world in order to transform it according to reason's own essential ends. The need for systematicity arises because the sphere in which reason ought to exercise its practical activity and attempt to realize its moral ends should be in harmony with the body of knowledge that its speculative use has previously examined.

Analysing The Architectonic of Pure Reason means exploring the way in which sensitive and rational human beings comprehend as a whole a reality that depends on the understanding for its epistemic conditions of possibility, and on reason's ability to transform the world according to essential ends. Kant does not merely intend to emphasize here that that the rules grounding the use of understanding do not contradict the practical function of reason, as has so often been suggested. The Architectonic tries to identify a set of principles according to which nature and freedom could be considered part of the same system, and the need for such principles is determined by the necessity to 'support and promote' ('*unterstützen und befördern*') reason's moral ends.

It is thus not from the point of view of the causes but from that of the consequences of practical agency that Kant intends to explore the issue of the system. He is less interested in the conditions of possibility of moral agency than in the guarantees for its effective realization in the sensible world. Human beings must pose their moral ends in the phenomenal world assuming that at least the possibility of a harmonic unity between such ends and the laws of nature is given. Without postulating a similar guarantee there would be no visible effect of our exercise of practical agency, no possibility of knowing that the world can be successfully transformed to be compatible with reason's moral ends. This is a question that it is possible to find, *mutatis mutandis*, in all of Kant's political writings when they address the questions of natural teleology and of the possibility of progress for the human species. In these writings Kant wrestles with the need to show that reason has an effective possibility of achieving its moral ends, that its continuous attempts to realize the categorical imperative throughout human history are not vain, and that the realization of a political order through which the freedom of each can coexist with that of every other is possible to obtain (*IaG* 9: 27–8; *ZeF* 8: 360–3 ff; *MS* 6: 353–4). It is therefore unsurprising to find the Architectonic of Pure Reason raising a similar problem. But where does Kant find evidence of the possibility of harmonizing nature and freedom in the *Critique of Pure Reason*? And how does the Architectonic provide conceptual tools for resolving the issue of the coherent mediation between theoretical and practical philosophy?

It is possible to answer this question by emphasizing the mediating role and teleological nature of ideas in the *Critique of Pure*

Reason. Kant first mentions the kind of concepts necessary to the architectonic unity of experience in the section introducing the epistemological status of 'ideas' in the Transcendental Dialectic. Here, discussing the role of Plato's conception of the idea in bridging the gap between theoretical and practical knowledge, he emphasizes that 'this ascent from the ectypal mode of regarding the physical world to the architectonic connection of it according to ends, that is, ideas, is an effort which deserves imitation and claims respect' (*KrV* A318/B375). However, some more clear reasons for linking 'ideas' and 'ends' in reflecting upon the systematic unity of reason are provided in the section on the Architectonic. Kant emphasizes here that a necessary condition for distinguishing between an aggregate and a system is the ability to take into account the 'form of a whole, in so far as the conception determines a priori not only the limits of its content, but the place which each of its parts is to occupy'. The very definition of a system as 'the unity of various cognitions under one idea' (*KrV* A832/B860) entails a rational redescription of the concept of totality as both anticipating a priori the role of each part in a systematic whole and constituting a concrete unity to which the parts themselves tend. As Kant emphasizes here, the scientific 'idea' of a system contains 'the end and the form of the whole which is in accordance with that end' (*KrV* A832/B860).

It is interesting to notice that in these passages the idea of an 'end' anticipates the role that reflective judgement plays in the third *Critique* in order to bring systematic unity to the speculative and practical use of reason. Here too, Kant refers both to the pure concept of reason or the idea (*Vernunftbegriff*) as conferring systematic unity on the multiplicity of particular cognitions, and to the notion of 'end' clarifying the system's internal process of development.[10] The unity of an end is what makes it possible for the parties, which refer to it as their organizing principle, also to be linked to each other in a way such that 'the absence of any part can be immediately detected from our knowledge of the rest' and that 'determines a priori the limits of the system, thus excluding all contingent or arbitrary additions' (*KrV* A833/B861).

However, the absence of the faculty of reflective judgement, which in the third *Critique* determines the subjective possibility of linking teleological principles to the idea of the whole without ever admitting that nature as such constitutes a system of ends, has significant consequences for Kant's project. In the absence of such a faculty, it is necessary to explain how the idea of the whole is necessarily linked to the ends of reason, and also why in the first *Critique* we find no warning of the merely subjective necessity of conferring to the system a teleological character serving reason's practical ends (as Kant often points out in the *Critique of the Power of Judgment*). In order to clarify this problematic point it is necessary to explore the teleological role of ideas in the first *Critique*, their ability to link the theoretical and the practical use of reason, and the consequences of this relation for the status of the principle guaranteeing the possibility of systematic unity at this stage.

4. The systematic principle of the Architectonic and the theoretical use of ideas

As we have already noted, there is no mention in Kant's first *Critique* either of a separate faculty with specific teleological principles (like the faculty of judgement in the third *Critique*) or of the merely reflective status of such principles in supporting a teleological understanding of nature that serves reason's essential aims. There is nevertheless an attempt to justify the legitimacy in the use of such principles by linking the theoretical idea of the whole to the capacity of reason to set ends in the practical domain.

Kant emphasizes the following:

> We require, for the execution of the idea of a system, a schema, that is, a content and an arrangement of parts determined a priori by the principle which the aim of the system prescribes. A schema which is not projected in accordance with an idea, that is, from the standpoint of the highest aim of reason, but merely empirically, in accordance with accidental aims and purposes (the number of which cannot be predetermined), can give us nothing more than technical unity. But the schema which is originated from an idea (in which case reason presents us with aims a priori, and does not look for them to experience), forms the basis of architectonical unity. (*KrV* A833/B861)

The use of the term 'schema' to clarify the relationship between the principle of conformity to ends and the architectonic idea of an all-encompassing system of cognitions is extremely interesting here.

The discussion of the schema appears slightly modified from the one that we find in the famous pages of the Transcendental Analytic, yet it is not the first time that the hypothesis of a schematism of reason (besides that of the understanding) appears in the first *Critique*.[11] Kant also employs it in the Appendix of the Transcendental Dialectic while inquiring on a similar problem, that of the manifold empirical laws and the need to postulate a teleological order of nature which grounds the possibility of the systematic use of the understanding. As Kant puts it here: 'it cannot be seen how there could be a logical principle of rational unity among rules, unless a transcendental principle is presupposed through which such a systematic unity, as pertaining to the object itself, is assumed a priori as necessary' (*KrV* A651/B679). A thorough analysis of the role of ideas in the Appendix and in the Architectonic falls outside the scope of this paper.[12] Here it suffices to notice that in both sections the issue of schematism arises from the need to mediate between two different faculties (understanding and reason) by an attempt to render homogeneous their respective principles and use. Just as in the case of the Analytic Kant recurs to the concept of a 'schema' in order to confer uniformity to the materials of sensation and of the understanding, from the Transcendental Dialectic onwards the issue becomes that of making compatible the spheres of application of understanding and reason. The Appendix eventually succeeds in justifying a positive, if only hypothetical, use of the pure concepts of reason. Ideas act here as heuristic devices guaranteeing the possibility of inferring from a variety of particular empirical laws of nature those universal properties that would guarantee their unity. Yet Kant claims that this inference is made possible only by postulating the possibility of systematic unity in science and by 'giving its idea an object' conceived as a 'being of reason' (*ens rationis ratiocinatae*) (*KrV* A681/B709).

The transcendental deduction of ideas thus emphasizes the necessity of problematically accepting the existence of a supreme designer of nature, without reference to which there could be no possibility of rationally understanding systematic unity between the speculative and the practical use of reason. The concept of a higher intelligence, Kant emphasizes, is a mere idea, that is 'a schema, ordered in accordance with the conditions of the greatest unity of reason' and in so far as 'one derives the object of experience, as it were, from the imagined object of this idea as its ground or cause' (*KrV* A670/B698). When we talk about such a being, Kant further clarifies, we refer to nothing other than the 'rational concept of God' (*KrV* A685/B713).

Ideas open new perspectives in 'relating according to teleological laws' objects of the universe, thus obtaining their maximal systematic unity (*KrV* A687/B715). It is however interesting to notice that here, unlike in the third *Critique*, instead of explaining in what way reason justifies those *teleologischen Gesetze* and how their use could be grounded in the idea of a supreme author of the world, Kant simply postulates the existence of the latter. Indeed, if in nature we fail to presuppose a priori – that is 'almost inhering to its essence' – 'a supreme conformity to ends' (*die höchste Zweckmäßigkeit*), how else could we rely on nature in searching for 'the highest perfection of a creator as one that is absolutely necessary and could be cognized a priori'? The principle of conformity to an end requires here that 'systematic unity as unity of nature' be conceived as 'absolutely deriving from the essence of things' (*KrV* A693/B721).

Interestingly, the *Critique of the Power of Judgment* and the successive political writings make use of an almost opposite argument in a very similar context. While discussing the link between nature and freedom, the idea of a supreme intelligence acting as a guarantee for the realization of moral ends in the sensible world is here perceived in analogy with the way in which reason proceeds in the practical domain. Even if we were able empirically to grasp the whole system with regard to the functioning of nature, 'experience could never lead us as far as to the determined concept of that supreme intelligence', Kant claims (*KU* 5: 438). No matter how important it may be, the teleological unity of freedom and nature cannot be guaranteed a priori but only in analogy with the causality according to ends that reason deploys in the practical or in the artistic domain.

In the Appendix, on the other hand, the concept of conformity to ends does not precede but rather follows the postulate of the idea of God, thus inverting the order of the demonstration. To be sure, Kant affirms here as well that the 'maximal systematic unity, and therefore the teleological unity of nature is the school and even the foundation of the possibility of the maximal use of human reason', but he never really proves the validity of this observation and is certainly far from establishing a link between reason's capacity to posit ends in the practical domain and the idea of an intelligent designer of the universe.

A similar interpretation is confirmed by the analysis of the link between the theoretical and practical uses of reason in the section on the Architectonic of Pure Reason. Here, systematic unity and the postulate of an intelligent designer of the world are especially required in order to promote and realize reason's essential ends. A schema for the idea of totality is not needed merely to guarantee the transcendental foundation of the logical use of reason but also to ensure that everything works to the benefit of its practical ends. However, while raising one of the most crucial issues for the whole critical system (the passage from the idea of freedom to that of nature), the Architectonic of Pure Reason does not mention the reflective status of an analysis of nature as a system of ends. But without the distinction between determinate and reflective judgement, the idea of God, schematized through the application of teleological principles, threatens to weaken some major achievements of the first *Critique*. Some of these issues are explored in the following section.

5. Systematic unity and practical teleology

In the Architectonic of Pure Reason, while discussing the way in which the idea of the whole is represented in a 'schema', Kant repeats some of the remarks made with regard to schematism in the Appendix but with a further interesting addition. He emphasizes that 'a schema that is not outlined in accordance with an idea, i.e. from the chief end of reason' (*aus dem Hauptzwecke der Vernunft*), but rather 'empirically, in accordance with aims occurring contingently' only produces 'technical unity' (*KrV* A833/B861). Here, he warns against a mere scholastic understanding of philosophy according to which what matters is the logical perfection of cognitions regardless of the ends that reason furthers by means of it. Only the schema that is executed according to an idea 'where reason provides the ends a priori and does not await them empirically', he emphasizes, grounds architectonic unity (*KrV* A833/B861).

But what is the difference between the empirical determination of reason's ends and their architectonic disposition? Kant insists on the distinction between the two because only a priori ends support the correct schematic representation of the idea of the whole. The architectonic schema must in fact mediate between the manifold particular empirical cognitions and an idea of totality given a priori as universal and necessary by means of reason's practical ends. Precisely those practical ends constitute the intermediate concepts according to which reason's particular cognitions are disposed in accordance with the supra-sensible idea of a whole that grounds the systematic unity of reason and contains its 'supreme and internal end'.

The latter is explicitly mentioned by Kant when he emphasizes that what we call 'science' can never arise 'technically', 'from the similarity of the manifold or the contingent use of cognitions in concreto for all sorts of arbitrary and external ends'. It must arise 'architectonically', 'for the sake of its affinity and its derivation from a supreme and inner end (*einigen obersten und inneren Zwecke*) which first makes possible the whole (*der das Ganze allererst möglich macht*)' (*KrV* A833/B861). But why is it that only the 'supreme' and 'internal' end of reason may ground architectonic unity? How does it transform a rough aggregate of elements into a coherent, systematic whole?

It is important here to emphasize the difference between the *obersten und inneren Zwecke* – which, Kant believes, ground systematic experience – and those *wesentliche Zwecke* that reason gives a priori to make possible their comprehension. Kant does not clarify the distinction here, referring to it only a few paragraphs after in one of the most mysterious passages of the first *Critique*. As he emphasizes there, essential ends (*wesentliche Zwecke*) 'are not yet the highest (*die höchsten*) of which (in the systematic unity of reason) there can be only a single one'. They thus constitute either the 'final end' (*Endzwecke*) or 'subalternate ends' (*subalterne Zwecke*), which necessarily belong to the former as means. This is nothing other than the 'entire vocation of human beings, and the philosophy of it is called moral philosophy' (*KrV* A840/B868).

The reasons for which the moral destination of human beings also constitutes a final end of nature are clarified in the Canon of Pure Reason, and it is not necessary to repeat them here. Suffice it to mention that Kant believes that the unconditional duty to realize the highest good justifies the postulate of a supreme will, necessary in order to give an 'appropriate effect' to moral actions. How else, Kant asks, 'could we find complete unity of purposes under different wills'? The idea of a kingdom of ends inevitably leads here to a teleological order of nature guaranteed by the assumption of an idea, that of God, without which it is impossible to think of the physical and moral world as finding systematic unity and causal efficiency (*KrV* A816/B844).

What is interesting to notice, as far as the Architectonic is concerned, is that Kant repeats here the findings of the Canon of Pure Reason, but is far from linking the possibility of knowing the *Endzweck* of nature only to the moral nature of human beings. On the contrary, he defines it as one of the most important ends that are given a priori to reason, ground the possibility of reflecting upon experience in a systematic way and provide schematic access to its 'supreme' and 'internal' end. A similar teleological principle determines the possibility of knowing the constitution of the whole system of experience according to an 'idea' which is both cause and effect of its own. The *Endzweck* of reason thus acts as the *ratio cognoscendi* of natural teleology, whilst natural teleology constitutes the *ratio essendi* as well as the guarantee of moral teleology in the phenomenal world.

The teleological constitution of practical reason, Kant is emphasizing here, proves the possibility of a teleological order of nature without the existence of which reason could not promote and realize its essential ends in the world of the senses. The final end of practical reason, however, also ultimately allows the system to be considered in an architectonic way, according to both the scholastic and the cosmic definition of philosophy, and guarantees the passage from the realm of nature to that of freedom. Therefore, only after exploring the theoretical and practical use of the concept of a final end of nature does Kant affirm the deeper unity of human legislation whereby nature and freedom, initially forming 'two separate' systems, are ultimately joined in one 'single philosophical system' (*KrV* A840/B868).

The solution of the Architectonic to the question of the *Übergang* from the system of nature to that of freedom anticipates some relevant themes of the *Critique of the Power of Judgment* but is also significantly different. The distinction between 'essential' and 'supreme' ends of reason returns in this latter work too, but the uncritical identification of the moral destination of human beings with the final end (*Endzweck*) of nature is problematized and ultimately dissolved. The third *Critique* defines *Endzweck* as that which does not require any other as its condition of possibility ('Endzweck ist derjenige Zweck, der keines andern als Bedingung seiner Möglichkeit bedarf') and identifies it with the 'supreme objective end of the existence of a world'. However, Kant clarifies that the final end of nature can never be known as such by human beings considered as participants of a natural order; it may only be related to the essential ends of reason and to humanity's moral destination. Thus the moral agent continues to be at the centre of a teleological system, but the causality of this system does not rely on the possibility of proving the existence of an intelligent author of the world. It is grounded on the 'fact' of freedom (which only makes its first appearance in the *Groundwork*) and on the capacity to treat the objects of nature as means of promoting humanity's moral end.

The third *Critique* does not therefore subordinate the kind of teleological principles necessary for the systematic unity of nature and freedom to the *Endzweck* of nature, quite the opposite: the final end of nature is, as such, considered wholly inaccessible. The possibility of practically promoting the ends of reason does not depend on the assumption of the idea of totality but on the exercise of judgement, and Kant continuously warns the reader that further attempts to use teleological principles as grounds for proving the existence of an intelligent author of the world would surpass the limits of reason. In the Architectonic of Pure Reason, however, Kant does not hesitate to use the subjective necessity of a teleological ordering of nature, the practical ends of reason, as a means to schematize the idea of a systematic and teleologically oriented whole. In order to integrate the speculative and practical uses of reason in a common architectonic project, he argues here, the world needs 'to be represented as having arisen out of an idea if it is to be in agreement with that use of reason without which we would hold ourselves unworthy of reason' (*KrV* A815–16/B843–4). Such a purposive unity of all things in nature is necessary, given the need for reason to realize its essential ends in the world. However, through this necessity 'all research into nature is thereby directed toward the form of a system of ends, and becomes, in its fullest extension physico-theology' (*KrV* A816/B844).

But how can reason satisfy its systematic needs simply by postulating an idea and then unilaterally confirming its reality? What justifies the passage from moral teleology to the teleological system of nature and then to the physical-theological proof of the existence of God? Physico-theology can never go beyond a statement of faith in the existence of a wise and good author of the world and in the belief that everything in nature works for the best. Subjective faith in the existence of God might well be enough to persuade single individuals that their good deeds will be rewarded in an indeterminate future, but is it really sufficient to justify that nature is, as such, teleologically oriented? How does physico-theology respond to reason's need for systematic unity? And how does it serve to support the effective fulfilment of the 'cosmopolitan' vocation of philosophy which is so important at the end of the first *Critique*?

The Architectonic of Pure Reason is ultimately unable to account for the consequences of a practical endorsement of transcendental theology on the unity of the system. To the extent to which it does, it runs the risk of weakening some major achievements of the first *Critique*, including the distinction between thinking and knowing, the impossibility of a theoretical proof of the existence of God, and the limitation to the practical domain of Kant's attempt to resurrect metaphysics as a science. It is in the light of these difficulties that Kant's return to these issues in the third *Critique* and in the political writings needs to be assessed. Even if the Architectonic of Pure Reason ultimately provides an unsatisfactory answer to the issue of the guarantee of the highest good in the world, even if it gives a relatively weak account of the unity of nature and freedom, it constitutes an important section of the first *Critique*. Besides anticipating some of the most difficult issues of Kant's entire philosophy, it is important in drawing our attention to an often neglected practical/political reading of Kant's first major work, and for understanding the systematic roots of his later reflections on teleology. Only after examining the limits of Kant's first attempt to conceptualize the necessity of realizing the highest good in the sensible world – a concern that we find unchanged in the third *Critique* and in successive political writings – is it possible to appreciate the genealogy of Kant's analysis of the faculty of judgement and to understand why the postulate of historical progress that defines Kant's later work on perpetual peace can be only subjectively guaranteed.

Notes

1 For references to the historical reception of the Architectonic, emphasizing its neglect in the context of Kant's systematic work, see also Paula Manchester, 'Kant's conception of architectonic in its historical context', *Journal of the History of Philosophy*, 41/2 (2003), 187 n. 2. For recent studies emphasizing the systematic importance of the section within Kant's critical theory, see Hans F. Fulda and Jürgen Stolzenberg (eds), *Architektonik und System in der Philosophie Kants* (Hamburg: Felix Meiner Verlag, 2001); Manchester, 'Kant's conception of architectonic in its philosophical context', *Kant-Studien*, 99/2 (2008), 133–51.

2 Arthur Schopenhauer, 'Kritik der kantischen Philosophie. Anhang', in *Sämtliche Werke*¸ed. P. Deussen (Munich: R. Piper, 1924), pp. 610, 625.

3 Norman Kemp-Smith, *A Commentary to Kant's* Critique of Pure Reason (New Jersey: Humanities Press International, 1962), pp. 579–82.

4 For other studies emphasizing Kant's primacy of practical reason and his interest in political philosophy as manifested in the *Doctrine of Method*, see Onora O'Neill, *Constructions of Reason: Explorations of Kant's Practical Philosophy* (Cambridge: Cambridge University Press, 1989); Richard Velkeley, *Freedom and the End of Reason: on the Moral Foundation of Kant's Critical Philosophy* (Chicago: University of Chicago Press, 1989).

5 See Ypi, '*Natura daedala rerum*? On the justification of historical progress in Kant's Guarantee of Perpetual Peace', *Kantian Review*, 14/2 (2010), 118–48.

6 Yirmiahu Yovel, *Kant and the Philosophy of History* (Princeton, NJ: Princeton University Press, 1980); Pauline Kleingeld, *Fortschritt und Vernunft: Zur Geschichtsphilosophie Kants* (Würzburg: Königshausen, 1995); Paul Guyer, 'Reason and reflective judgment: Kant on the significanc of systematicity', *Noûs*, 24/1 (2005), 17–43.

7 For further discussion and a useful review of the literature see Katrin Flikschuh, 'Reason and nature: Kant's teleological argument in *Perpetual Peace*', in G. Bird (ed.), *A Companion to Kant* (Oxford: Blackwell, 2006).

8 Guyer, 'Reason and reflective judgment'.

9 See for further discussion on this metaphor and how it relates to Kant's political philosophy O'Neill, *Constructions of Reason*, pp. 3–27; 'Vindicating reason', in P. Guyer (ed.), *The Cambridge Companion to Kant* (Cambridge: Cambridge University Press, 1992).

10 Hans Driesch, 'Kant und das Ganze', *Kant-Studien*, 29 (1924), 366–76.

11 The way in which schematism is discussed here would appear to challenge Ernst Cassirer's thesis that the problem of schematism is at the heart only of Kant's theoretical philosophy: Cassirer, 'Kant und das Problem der Metaphysik', *Kant-Studien*, 36 (1931), 1–2.

12 For a further analysis see François Marty, *La naissance de la métaphysique chez Kant: une etude sur la notion kantienne d'analogie* (Paris: Beauchesne, 1980).

References

Cassirer, E., 'Kant und das Problem der Metaphysik', *Kant-Studien*, 36 (1931), 1–2.

Driesch, H., 'Kant und das Ganze', *Kant-Studien*, 29 (1924), 366–76.

Fulda, H. F. and J. Stolzenberg (eds), *Architektonik und System in der Philosophie Kants* (Hamburg: Felix Meiner Verlag, 2001).

Flikschuh, K., 'Reason and nature: Kant's teleological argument in *Perpetual Peace*', in G. Bird (ed.), *A Companion to Kant* (Oxford: Blackwell, 2006).

Guyer, P., *Kant's System of Nature and Freedom* (Oxford: Oxford University Press, 2005).

——, 'Reason and reflective judgment: Kant on the significanc of systematicity', *Noûs*, 24/1 (2005), 17–43.

Kant, I., 'The Jaesche Logic', in *Lectures on Logic*, ed. and trans. J. M. Young (Cambridge: Cambridge University Press, 1992).

——, 'The metaphysics of morals', in *Practical Philosophy*. ed. and trans. M. J. Gregor (Cambridge: Cambridge University Press, 1996).

——, 'Toward perpetual peace', in *Practical Philosophy*, ed. and trans. M. J. Gregor (Cambridge: Cambridge University Press, 1996).

——, *Critique of Pure Reason*, ed. and trans. P. Guyer and A. Wood (Cambridge: Cambridge University Press, 1998).

——, 'Critique of Practical Reason', in *Practical Philosophy*, ed. and trans. M. J. Gregor (Cambridge: Cambridge University Press, 1999).

——, *Critique of the Power of Judgment*, ed. P. Guyer, trans. P. Guyer and E. Matthews (Cambridge: Cambridge University Press, 2000).

——, 'Anthropology from a pragmatic point of view', in *Anthropology, History, and Education*, ed. and trans. G. Zoller and R. B. Louden (Cambridge: Cambridge University Press, 2007).

——, 'Idea for a universal history with a cosmopolitan aim', in *Anthropology, history, and education*, ed. and trans. G. Zoller and R. B. Louden. (Cambridge: Cambridge University Press, 2007).

Kemp-Smith, N., *A Commentary to Kant's* Critique of Pure Reason (New Jersey: Humanities Press International, 1962).

Kleingeld, P., *Fortschritt und Vernunft: Zur Geschichtsphilosophie Kants* (Würzburg: Königshausen, 1995).

Manchester, P., 'Kant's conception of architectonic in its historical context', *Journal of the History of Philosophy*, 41/2 (2003).

——, 'Kant's conception of architectonic in its philosophical context', *Kant-Studien*, 99/2 (2008), 133–51.

Marty, F., *La naissance de la métaphysique chez Kant: une étude sur la notion kantienne d'analogie* (Paris: Beauchesne, 1980).

O'Neill, O., *Constructions of Reason: Explorations of Kant's Practical Philosophy* (Cambridge: Cambridge University Press, 1989)

——, 'Vindicating reason', in P. Guyer (ed.), *The Cambridge Companion to Kant* (Cambridge: Cambridge University Press, 1992).

Schopenhauer, A., 'Kritik der kantischen Philosophie. Anhang', in *Sämtliche Werke*, ed. P. Deussen (Munich: R. Piper, 1924).

Velkeley, R. L., *Freedom and the End of Reason: on the Moral Foundation of Kant's Critical Philosophy* (Chicago: University of Chicago Press, 1989).

Yovel, Y., *Kant and the Philosophy of History* (Princeton, NJ: Princeton University Press, 1980).

Ypi, L., '*Natura daedala rerum*? On the justification of historical progress in Kant's Guarantee of Perpetual Peace', *Kantian Review*, 14/2 (2010), 118–48.

8 • What a Kantian Can Know A Priori: An Argument for Moral Cognitivism

Katerina Deligiorgi

From a meta-ethical perspective, the Kantian position appears straightforwardly cognitivist: the moral law is a genuine piece of knowledge.[1] However, speaking of moral knowledge sounds un-Kantian. For Kant, epistemic questions concern mainly the domain of 'theoretical knowledge', which is restricted to putative objects of experience. Moral questions are 'practical' and arise within the domain of practical reason. The former address what is, the latter what ought to be.[2] In pressing this distinction, Kant explicitly contrasts knowledge and practice. When, for instance, he discusses the ideas of freedom, God and immortality, he explains that these 'are not in any way necessary for knowledge . . . their importance, properly regarded, must concern only the practical' (*KrV* A800/B828). The sharp demarcation between the cognitive and the practical, however, does not commit Kant to anything like a modern non-cognitivist, let alone a sceptical, position.[3] Though reticent in his use of the term 'knowledge' in the practical realm,[4] he makes clear that we are capable of moral knowledge and that such knowledge as we may obtain in moral matters is a priori. It is these two claims that concern us here.

One difficulty with the Kantian position is that it does not fit neatly into the available meta-ethical categories. Questions of moral epistemology, including evidential support and justification, and those of moral psychology, including what matters to us or is 'normative' for us and how this informs our practical reasonings, are tightly connected in Kant's writings. Accordingly, recent vindications of the soundness of the moral law focus on how we, finite rational beings, are in fact *subject* to the law and recognize its authority because of commitments we already have, for instance to rationality or to freedom.[5] Certainly, if the moral law lacks justification, we may doubt its authority; if it lacks authority, it cannot be said to be binding; and if it is not binding, it cannot be said to specify any actual moral commitments. But there is a difference between our getting a grip on something and something having a grip on us. Focusing on the former allows us to evaluate a central contention of Kantian ethics and a key presupposition of the morality of autonomy, namely that we are able to judge right and wrong because we are in a position to know what morality demands of us. The aim of this paper, then, is to examine the epistemic and metaphysical commitments that sustain this contention and to outline a Kantian answer to the question 'how is moral knowledge possible?'

Here a further obstacle arises. In contemporary arguments for or against cognitivism, how one goes about evaluating the truth of moral propositions is seen to depend directly on whether one affirms or denies the existence of moral facts. Such facts may be 'irreducibly' moral, properties we intuit or perceive, or reducible to natural facts, about the desirability or usefulness of an action, or supernatural facts concerning God's will.[6] The underlying assumption is that (some version of) correspondence theory of truth is as good in moral matters as in matters relating to grass and snow, with the minimal condition that the relation between truth and fact be preserved. This gives us what we might call the propositional interpretation of moral statements: when we say '*x* is right', we assert a moral proposition (or we intend so to do) and we evaluate it as true or false with reference to some fact. This approach could not be further from Kant's. Kant states explicitly that we find ourselves confronting a paradox: we do not issue moral laws on the basis of prior knowledge of facts about the good, but rather the concept of good 'must be defined after and by means of the law' (*KpV* 5: 62). Secondly, it is essential to the idea of an ethics of autonomy that we do not act in obeisance to facts – which is precisely what has encouraged critics to think of Kantian ethics as 'arbitrary self-launching'.[7] Finally, Kant emphasizes the spontaneity of practical reason, which suggests that whatever moral knowledge we possess it is not a matter of conformity with pregiven moral facts. Of course, we do encounter in Kant's ethics the notorious 'fact of reason' but this obscure item further complicates the issue.

Still, why not just accept that the Kantian position is simply irreconcilable with contemporary positions and leave it at that? Because focusing on facts has a distorting effect: it creates expectations that do not permit a proper appreciation of the distinctiveness of the Kantian position. Whilst a full-blown defence of this position is outside the scope of the present paper, a start can be made by showing how cognitivist demands can be satisfied without recourse to a realist metaphysics and without ignoring Kant's warning about the limitations of the theoretical approach to ethics. Section 1 gives the Kantian answer to the question of moral truth, while sections 2 and 3 examine what evidential support and justification we are given for it.

1. Moral truths without moral facts

The idea that claims to moral knowledge cannot be sustained unless we can adduce facts in their support seems plausible. Grammatically, propositions such as '*x* is right' do seem to behave like propositions such as '*y* is square', and this would appear to warrant the thought that, like the latter, the former can be judged because they are factual. Moral sceptics joining forces with non-cognitivists have easy work drawing a wedge between the two, pointing at the diversity of moral beliefs and the prevalence of moral disagreement.[8] Though they do not deny the existence of scientific disagreement, they claim that it stems from insufficient evidence. Once all the relevant facts are available, the issue is decided one way or another. Moral appraisal, by contrast, is thought to depend on moral sensibilities, ways of life and pre-existing commitments. So, it is argued, when we are asked to account for our judgements there is no 'obvious reason to assume anything about "moral facts"'.[9] The aim of this type of argument is to disabuse us of expectations of objectivity and truth in moral propositions. Puzzlement when disagreements arise or when we encounter unexpected and unfamiliar perspectives can indeed motivate doubt about our ability to get 'right' right. Just as plausibly, though, such an experience can motivate the search for moral knowledge. So we need to consider why, on the sceptical side, such a search is fruitless.

The most familiar argument is Mackie's epistemological queerness argument. This is a companion to the metaphysical queerness argument, which targets the motivational inertness of moral facts.[10] Epistemological queerness concerns access to moral facts. Mackie's basic premise is that objective valuation, and also truth evaluation, of moral propositions requires reference to moral facts, 'entities, qualities, or relations'.[11] Such facts are unlike any others we come across. So to know that they exist and to know what they are, we need a special faculty. We have no reason to believe that we have such a faculty. Therefore we have no reason to believe that we are in position to establish that such facts exist and what they are; so meta-ethical scepticism is justified. The context of Mackie's argument is provided by his commitment to an empiricist epistemology and also possibly an empiricist theory of mind, both of which can and have been challenged.[12] It is not the context that concerns us here but the basic premise. In the remainder of this section, I want to show how it is possible to evaluate the truth of moral propositions without recourse to facts.

Because there are no facts to uncover, truth is to be understood minimally: to say '"*x* is right" is true' is to assert our moral cognitive competence, that is, to underscore that we are in a position to know and show what is right.[13] So the propositional interpretation is correct to the extent that it accurately describes what we do (we assert a proposition) and our epistemic expectations of what we do (truth evaluation, justification of belief). It is incorrect when it directs us to the search for facts, and prescribes the ways in which we might proceed in assessing the epistemic propriety of our truth-evaluating practices.[14]

Truth evaluation on the Kantian model amounts to conformity with the moral law: 'So act that the maxim of your will could always hold at the same time as a principle establishing universal law' (*KpV* 5: 30). In Kant's terminology, an action that conforms to this law is a duty, and an action is right if it is a duty (*MS* 6: 224). To assert correctly that '*x* is right', we need to establish that *x* conforms to the conditions specified by the law, that it can be held as a principle establishing a universal law. The formula for rightness, then, is universalizability. Universalizability is not a property we pick out (as is 'good' for Moore). The formula rather describes a test which works as follows. If we satisfy ourselves that we can assert *x* without contradiction as a principle establishing a universal law, we can only claim that the action is permissible. 'Permissible' is morally neither right nor wrong, because wrongness can be absent without rightness being present. To obtain 'right', we are interested in actions that *fail* the test. Failure indicates what is contrary to duty and so wrong; 'right' is simply the opposite of this.

'Right', 'wrong' and 'permissible' do not exhaust the moral categories used by Kant. The most important, 'morally worthy', requires in addition to conformity with the law knowledge of psychological facts about the agent's motivation: whether, that is, the agent acts out of 'reverence for the moral law'. Because there is no reliable way of establishing such facts, Kant acknowledges that we are not generally in a position reliably to estimate moral worth. So an accurate characterization of Kant's position is cognitivism about moral propositions (right and wrong) and scepticism about propositions concerning moral motivation (moral worth).

There are open and interesting interpretative issues both about the nature of the contradiction that yields non-universalizable maxims and the application of the test to particular cases. What is more urgent, however, for our present purposes is to examine what reasons we might have for accepting the universalizability formula itself as a piece of knowledge. It is worth considering here that in his criticisms of rival consequentialist and sentimentalist theories, Kant argues that they base moral distinctions on some fact, which provides a merely contingent basis for moral distinctions. So unlike contemporary critics, Kant is not concerned with accessibility or the motivational force of moral facts, but with their contingency – and also their heteronomy. What motivates the move to pure reason in ethics is the need to identify an unconditional ground for moral determinations and also for moral obligations. Even to begin to defend a position along those lines, we need an account of why universalizability captures right and why it expresses rationality in ethics. The rest of the paper is an attempt to do this. In the next section I show the importance of moral experience to the presentation of the concept of universalizability, and in the final section I show how Kant's conception of practical reason enters into the justification of universalizability.

2. '. . . All our knowledge begins with experience'

The examination of beliefs, moral as well as theoretical, tends to focus either on their causal origin or on their epistemic propriety. Kant's approach to such matters is not so clear-cut. Let us consider the claim that 'all our knowledge begins with experience' but that 'it does not follow that it all arises from experience' (*KrV* B1). That all our knowledge begins with – literally 'is lifted out of' ('anhebt') – experience appears to be a claim about causal origin. The same can be said about the claim that not all of it arises from – or 'has its source in' ('entspringt aus') – experience. But both cannot be the case (either 'all' is, or 'some' is not). Now it is possible to interpret the claim that some knowledge does not have its 'source' in experience as a claim about the criteria that must be satisfied if something is to be called knowledge. Kant addresses the issue of epistemic propriety when he defends the aprioricity of the principles that should guide our understanding. Proper epistemic conduct requires that we know and respect the boundaries of the domain within which knowledge claims are exclusively redeemable. But this is not what he is saying in the opening page of the *Critique*. For a start it would be simply too much anticipatory and complex argument packed into too few words. So we need a third interpretation that is neither about causal origin nor about epistemic propriety. That knowledge is 'lifted out of experience' may mean that there is knowledge to be gained by making evident that which is contained in experience. 'Beginning in experience' does not refer to causal origin. This is because experience for Kant is not just the provision of raw material for knowledge, it is itself knowledge. Kant's 'analysis' of experience thus aims to show precisely what I already 'know' when I know, for instance, that the leaves on the tree outside my window are turning yellow: namely that a unified spatio-temporal world is necessary for experience of discrete entities, that causality is necessary for the experience of change and so forth. These necessary presuppositions, which are available on reflection but on which we rely effortlessly when we observe things about our world, are not empirical. I want to argue that something similar is the case in the moral domain.

Speaking of 'moral experience' in the context of Kantian ethics is likely to cause concern: if Kant rarely uses 'moral knowledge', he certainly never uses 'moral experience'. What he does use a great deal, in both the *Groundwork* and the *Critique of Practical Reason*, is reference to 'shared' 'common' ideas (*GMS* 4: 389, 392; *KpV* 5: 5–11). Collectively, these common ideas constitute pre-philosophical moral cognitions. Such cognitions are expressible in the form of judgements. Although no reference is made to moral experience, it is not too far-fetched to say that these basic judgements are the stuff of our everyday moral experience. This commits us to no particular philosophical thesis, certainly not to a search for moral perceptions or intuitions. All it says is that our ordinary moral interactions are 'unified' in judgements that use these 'shared' or 'common' ideas. It also says that we have a basic familiarity with moral terms, that we have uses for them in our daily lives before philosophy steps in. This pre-philosophical familiarity is *also* 'moral experience'. Kant assumes that we are not innocent of the demands of morality, just that we do not have their measure aright.

Kant presents the universalizability formula as emerging out of careful examination of the 'common' or 'shared' concepts used in ordinary moral judgements. Ordinary moral knowledge has two functions in Kant's argument. Firstly, it matters for Kant's philosophical affirmation of our moral cognitive competence; it is important that the ordinary and the philosophical hook up with one another. Secondly, ordinary knowledge provides evidential support for the universalizability formula. Though not derived from common ideas, the universalizability formula is nonetheless shown to be compatible with them (*a* can count as evidence for *b*, but *b* is not derived from *a*). Kant thus affirms our moral cognitive competence, philosophical and ordinary, whilst at the same time providing us with a genuinely new way of judging what we know morally.

In the *Critique of Practical Reason*, Kant insists on the importance of ordinary moral knowledge, arguing that he brings nothing new to morality: 'Who would want to introduce a new principle of morality and, as it were, be its inventor, as if the world had hitherto been ignorant of what duty is or had been thoroughly wrong about it?' (*KpV* 5: 8) But although he does not add substantively to the 'knowledge we have already gained', he does give a 'definite formula', he says, of the principle of duty (*KpV* 5: 8). He compares this formula to mathematical formulae as being similarly useful 'in determining what is to be done in solving a problem' (*KpV* 5: 8). The difficulty with this parallel is that the relation between mathematical concepts and mathematically analysable reality is not significant enough to help us understand the relation between *moral* concepts and *morally* evaluable reality. Another parallel Kant draws may be more helpful. He says that his aim is to give our common, pre-philosophical knowledge a more 'philosophical and architectonic character' (*KpV* 5: 10).

Ordinarily, we have experience of a building without knowledge of its structure; we do not know, for instance, which walls are load-bearing. Lack of technical knowledge does not mean ignorance. Our experience of a building entitles us to say that we know it, we know how to use it, we can describe it, appraise it, be at home in it. When this ordinary knowledge does not suffice, when we decide to extend or mend our building, *then* we find ourselves posing the technical questions. The analogy suggests that just as we have ordinary experience of buildings but can also legitimately and usefully inquire after technical knowledge, so we have ordinary moral experience and can also legitimately and usefully inquire after systematic moral knowledge.

The analogy with architecture is, of course, illustrative not probative. It may be objected that with buildings we know that there is a structure, while with moral knowledge we do not know this. The objection is not disabling. It suffices that we avoid thinking of Kant's endeavour – to give ordinary knowledge a philosophical character – as a process of discovery by which we are led to uncover some hitherto hidden moral facts. Indeed, it is important that we do not understand Kant as saying that inspection of what is common knowledge will allow moral patterns to emerge, and so somehow vindicate the universalizability test as an interpretation of 'right'.

If we are not embarking on a process of discovery, then what are we doing? Kant uses the term 'analysis' (*GMS* 4: 388; *KpV* 5: 7 n. 9). Now, it is tempting to dismiss this as mere rhetoric. A comparison could be drawn with Descartes's 'analytical' method, which aims to compel the reader's participation 'so that if the reader is willing to follow it, he will make the thing his own and understand it as perfectly as if he had discovered it himself'.[15] There is, however, more to Kant's 'analysis' than rhetoric. We can distinguish the following progression in his argument. Beginning with 'knowledge we have already gained', we seek to obtain 'exact and . . . complete delineation of its parts', and then we 'see all these parts in their reciprocal interrelations' in light of their 'derivation from the concept of the whole' (*KpV* 5: 10).[16] So the first step is identification of the basic moral concepts used in pre-philosophical knowledge ('delineation'), the second is exposition of how they fit together ('interrelation'), and the third connection with the 'idea' or 'concept' of the whole ('derivation').

Although Kant uses 'analysis' to describe the first two parts of this procedure, the term does not provide an accurate characterization because the relations he establishes between concepts are not in the nature of logical entailments. A brief example from early on in the *Groundwork* shows this. Kant makes the case for a pure moral philosophy 'completely cleansed of everything . . . empirical', by appealing to the shared idea (*gemeine Idee*) of duty (*GMS* 4: 389).[17] The reasoning seems to be that if there is a shared idea of duty, then we have use of the notion of necessity that is itself necessary for morality. Kant denies that such necessity can be established a posteriori and concludes that the right approach to morality is through pure moral philosophy (*KpV* 5: 12). This 'analysis' amounts to no more than the claim that our ordinary understanding of duty uses a notion of necessity that exceeds what can be established empirically. The 'feet' of the argument are in ordinary knowledge, but the lead-up to pure morality is not analytical (in the sense of analysis of logical relations that obtain between concepts): the link between duty and necessity is assumed to be implicit in our ordinary sense of duty.What we need to begin the Kantian analysis is the expectation that the phenomenon we examine, morality, forms a consistent whole that contains all the moral concepts we currently use, with their current or revised content, and also a means for showing why they have the content they do. These concepts are shown to be related through a set of connective steps that depend on *specific* interpretations of these concepts. If we ask 'what overall idea controls the interpretation?', 'what are the constraints of this reflective assessment of our moral knowledge?' or, more bluntly, 'why are precisely *these* connections made and not others?', we discover that the 'whole' from which these 'interrelations' are 'derived' is a conception of morality encoded in the moral law and which stipulates that morality is a matter of universalizable laws (rather than, say, God's will, maximal desire satisfaction etc.). It is this conception that controls the 'analysis' of the common moral concepts. The idea of universalizability has a formal function – to establish consistency in our moral experience – and universalizability is as such a test for reflection upon our moral knowledge. However, it is also a test that directs our moral reflection and enables us to identify what is right. To show that universalizability is a plausible candidate for these functions, Kant devotes a significant portion of his argument to showing that universalizability fits with ordinary moral knowledge.

Kant's argument in the *Groundwork* begins with an answer to an unarticulated question. The question is: what is *unconditionally* good, good without qualification? This is already an interpretation of the question we pose when we find ourselves in a situation of moral perplexity. The assumption is that when we seek guidance, this is what we want to know. But an alternative interpretation also seems plausible, namely that we seek to find out what is good or right *in the circumstances*. There are caricatures of moral particularism in which the notion of right is entirely emptied of meaning (no overlap of use is allowed), and of moral absolutism in which the question does not make sense (it is cut off from any recognizable moral context in which we might care for it). For the present purposes all we need to say is that 'unqualified goodness' is a plausible interpretation of ordinary requests for moral guidance and advice, because it flags the idea that we look for an objective take on our situation. It may turn out that we find nothing. Also, this search does not signify forgetfulness of our rootedness in the specific situation in which the moral puzzle first arises for us. Awareness of the contextual limits of goods is perfectly compatible with wondering about the possibility of an unconditional good.[18]

The closest we come in ordinary thought to the idea of a good in itself, Kant claims, is the concept of the good will. As an ordinary moral concept, good will has a range of uses, but as an answer to the question of 'good without qualification' it identifies a will whose goodness is not dependent on anything external to it, such as inducements or consequences. This 'delineation' of the concept of the good will through its 'interrelation' with the concept of the unconditionally good produces an entirely negative definition of good will. The 'interrelation' of 'good will' and 'duty', another concept abstracted from common knowledge, adds some substance to the former and identifies the latter as good will 'exposed . . . to certain subjective limitations and obstacles' (*KpV* 5: 12). So whilst there are no external conditions for the will's goodness, there are external conditions for the good will's existence. When these are adverse, as they generally are for finite creatures like ourselves, we speak of duty.

The idea of duty is crucial because it allows Kant to pursue two different sides of the argument. The side concerning motivation takes us from the limitations that ordinarily affect moral agents (disinclination, fatigue) to ideas of moral worth: because duty is a type of willing, a willing that is good in itself, it is also a type of motive, that is, a motive for actions performed out of duty. The side that is of relevance to us concerns the form of dutiful willing, that is, knowledge of what is good without qualification under conditions of finitude. Kant relates the dutiful will to the notion of 'law', another ordinary concept, arguing that a dutiful will is a lawful will. This 'law' must be such that the mere thought of it suffices to determine the will (*GMS* 4: 402). Sufficiency is not a psychological but a semantic requirement here, that is, the law must capture what we know already about the will's goodness, and must relate to the original demand for unconditionality. The notion of 'law' captures the idea of a bare moral ought; for the idea of 'good without qualification', we then need to specify the meaning of this bare 'ought' further, and this yields 'universal law as such' (*GMS* 4: 402). This interpretation of 'universal law' emerges from a process of 'analysis' that leads from good will, to duty and law, and finally to the universalizability formula of right. Its purpose is to show that ordinary moral concepts can provide support for the universalizablity formula. They cannot, however, justify it. For this we need to look to pure practical reason.

3. Cognition without objects

Kant claims that our knowledge of the moral law is 'knowledge through reason' (*KpV* 5: 12). To understand what he means by this I begin by testing his arguments against three standard a priori justification procedures, appeals to self-evidence, to inference and to intuitive knowledge.

(1) Self-evidence. Assuming that there are some beliefs that are self-evident, is the moral law one of them? Whether we take the marker of self-evidence to be that a belief is understood to be true just by being understood, or that its contrary is contradictory, the link between universalizability and right does not appear to be of this sort for at least two reasons.[19] First, universalizability enables us to identify what is right only by reference to what fails the test, so the connection is not a straightforward one; we would be abusing the notion of self-evidence were we to apply it here.

Secondly, the relation of universalizability to ordinary moral concepts, concepts that are *protera pros hemas*, can be identified only after considerable interpretation ('analysis') of common moral knowledge.

(2) Inference. If the moral law is not self-evident then the links between the elements that make it up must be some other a priori propositions. Note that Kant says that the a priori has the marks of universality and necessity. It is therefore tempting to try to connect universalizability with universality and argue that something can be morally necessary if it is universally commanded. However, the search for propositions that could be used to justify the moral law is cut short by Kant's unambiguous claim that the moral law is underived. Justification of the law cannot be 'ferreted out from antecedent data of reason' (*KpV* 5: 31), and cannot be proved through 'exertion of the theoretical, speculative, or empirically supported reason' (*KpV* 5: 47). The moral law is not an instance of inferential knowledge and so not an instance of a priori inference.

(3) Intuition. It is possible to think of the moral law as the object of a basic moral intuition, a basic underived 'datum' of reason. Although I argued that the truth of moral propositions is not dependent on moral facts, there is limited textual evidence supporting the existence of at least one fact: the moral law itself, known in a direct way by a special 'intuition'. That Kant speaks of a 'fact of reason', which he describes as a bare 'thought' that is available to us immediately (*KpV* 5: 31; 5: 47), makes it natural to interpret knowledge of the moral law intuitionistically. There are two ways of understanding a priori intuition. The first is in terms of self-evidence, and we have already discarded this. The second requires the positing of an object to which we have direct access through an act of intellection (we can designate both faculty and object as 'intellectual intuition'). This is the most serious candidate position so far, which, if applicable to Kant, it would commit him to a non-naturalist realism. I will argue that though tempting, the position is not applicable.

This line of interpretation is cut short by Kant's explicit *denial* that we should understand a priori 'consciousness' of the moral law in those terms. This is not merely a restatement of the familiar general thesis that we are incapable of intellectual intuition. In the *Critique of Practical Reason*, he gives the following description of the tasks and powers of practical reason: 'practical reason is concerned not with objects in order to know them but with its own capacity to make them real . . . consequently it does not have to furnish an object of intuition, but as practical reason has only to give a law of intuition' (*KpV* 5: 90; 5: 92).[20]

What Kant seems to be saying here is that we do have 'consciousness' of a fact, but also that we do *not* intuit or apprehend anything thereby. Consciousness of the law is a cognition, but not a cognition of a pre-existing object. This negative result is important, because it reminds us that it is expectations of theoretical or speculative reason that lead us to this 'vacant place'.[21] We are led in the sphere of metaphysics but are guided to a vacant place. We are thus introduced to an idea that gives Kantian critical metaphysics its distinctive shape: reason is not a discoverer of facts. Reason is productive, it is a priori practical and it makes real its own objects. The question is how?

A clue can be found in the contrast Kant draws between theoretical and moral knowledge: in the former I represent 'what there is', in the latter 'I represent what there ought to be (*was da sein soll*)' (*KrV* A633/B661, also A802/B830). Why call 'knowledge' a representation of something that is so far defined simply as what is not? Of course, it cannot be a representation of the mere absence of an object, which we establish simply by knowing what there was before and what is now missing, counting on our general knowledge of how natural things tend to behave. But the representation of what there ought to be 'has no meaning whatsoever', Kant insists, when we have the 'course of nature' alone in view (*KrV* A547/B575). In the moral case, he says, 'reason does not follow the order of things as they present themselves in appearance, but frames for itself with perfect spontaneity an order ['eine eigene Ordnung'] of its own according to ideas' (*KrV* A548/B576). This is the core Kantian position. What stands in the way of grasping its full import is the opacity of the notion of 'perfect spontaneity', which can mislead us into thinking that the moral law is an arbitrary invention. Clearly this is not what Kant means, since he is speaking here not just of a power of reason but also of an *order* that is rational, that is, in accordance with reason's ideas. How then is spontaneity to be reconciled with the idea of an order, and how, given reason's production of its object, can we persist with our attempt to treat this object as knowledge?

We can interpret the claim that practical reason is spontaneous to mean that moral knowledge is not based on antecedent representations or relations between representations (no inference), and that it is not itself an act of intellection (no intellectual intuition). The negative meaning of spontaneity blocks the regressive search for prior cognitions. This negative interpretation cannot satisfy us, however, because it leaves undetermined the productive function of reason. One option is to say that reason directs us to be rational without attaching further content to the designation 'rational'. But that seems odd. After all, we do in the end get hold of an object, albeit a formal one, namely the universalizability formula for right. Another option is to say that the moral law springs out of practical reason. But this does not help either, because what we want is to get to grips with this process. A way out is presented if we think of spontaneity as directing us to conceive of a rational function that is productive of 'order' (order here does not carry the sense of command but rather of orderly arrangement, *Ordnung*). Read in full, the spontaneity claim tells us that reason frames *an order* for itself. What I want to argue is that the formula of universalizability represents the spontaneous order of reason.

Reason's production is not a random guess or an inscrutable given, it is something we must be able to recognize as orderly. Because such order is underived, it is no good trying to find the ideas that connect the elements of the proposition that expresses the moral law. Further, although we turn to reason for objective guidance, we are repeatedly warned not to expect that reason will provide us with knowledge of an object. If the order of reason does not correspond to an object, its objectivity can be only formal. The requirement for formal objectivity is fulfilled by the idea of universal validity, and thus through a test that specifies conditions of universal validity.[22] But we have such a test precisely in the universalizability test. We can then say that the moral law represents an order that pure reason frames in accordance with its own ideas.

We can now link the ordinary and the philosophical as follows. Rather than seeking to make a start from the a priori downwards, we can start with the question 'what is right?' In the absence of facts that would provide an answer to this question and so give meaning to the concept 'right', we can look for objectivity in the judgement of right itself. If we do not think of objectivity as a feature of a judgement that appropriately refers to a given object (say as a fact, natural, unnatural, supernatural), then we are left with objectivity as a feature of a judgement itself. Objectivity as a feature of a judgement itself can be formal only (because it does not refer to what the judgement is about). Formal objectivity, this time from the perspective of putative judges or agents, is validity for the will of everyone. Validity for the will of everyone is a representation of an 'order' framed by practical reason, which is none other than the moral law.[23]

The idea of a rationally instituted order brings the theoretical analysis of practical reason to an end: this is as far as we may go within the constraints imposed by Kant's argument. Kant vindicates his claim that we are in a position to know what morality demands of us. He answers the question 'what is right?' by offering a new formula of right, which he believes fits much of what we already know about right and wrong and so links up with the substantive moral concepts we ordinarily use in our moral judgements. Finally, he shows how this formula is rationally defensible without being based on rational intuitions of any sort.[24]

Notes

1 I use 'cognitivist' to refer to aptness of truth evaluation of particular moral propositions; I also use it specifically in relation to Kant to refer to the aptness of epistemic evaluation, i.e. justification, of the moral law itself in its 'universalizability' interpretation. There is a further non-technical sense in which Kant is a cognitivist: he holds human beings to be morally cognitively capable, see Jerome B. Schneewind, *The Invention of Autonomy: a History of Modern Moral Philosophy* (Cambridge: Cambridge University Press, 1998), p. 523. Non-cognitivists deny that moral claims are truth-evaluable; meta-ethical sceptics accept that moral claims are truth-evaluable but hold that they are false.

2 'Reason', Kant argues, 'provides laws which are imperatives, that is, *objective laws of freedom*, which tell us *what ought to happen* . . . therein differing from *laws of nature*, which relate only to *that which happens*' (*KrV* A802/B830).

3 The development of contemporary expressivist cognitivism, by Mark Timmons and Terry Horgan, complicates the usual meta-ethical categories of what James Dreier calls the 'good old days' in 'Metaethics and the problem of creeping minimalism', *Philosophical Perspectives*,

18 (2004), 23–44. Timmons and Horgan's cognitivism is essentially a linguistic claim, however, whereas Kant's is not.

4 See *KrV* A633/B661; *KpV* 5: 4, 12.

5 See Christine Korsgaard, *Sources of Normativity* (Cambridge: Cambridge University Press, 1996); 'Motivation, metaphysics, and the value of self: a reply to Ginsborg, Guyer, and Schneewind', *Ethics*, 109/1 (1998), 49–66; Paul Guyer, *Kant on Freedom, Law, and Happiness* (Cambridge: Cambridge University Press, 2000); Onora O'Neill, 'Constructivisms in ethics', in *Constructions of Reason: Explorations of Kant's Practical Philosophy* (Cambridge: Cambridge University Press, 1989); 'Constructivism vs. Contractualism', *Ratio*, 16/4(2003), 319–31. For critical discussion of Korsgaard and Guyer see Donald H. Regan, 'The value of rational nature', *Ethics*, 112 (2002), 267–91. See also Andrews Reath, 'Value and law in Kant's moral theory', *Ethics*, 114 (2003), 127–55. A rare contemporary treatment of moral knowledge can be found in Stephen Engstrom, 'Kant's distinction between theoretical and practical knowledge', *The Harvard Review of Philosophy*, 10/1 (2002), 49–63.

6 For a contemporary defence of intuitionism see Michael Huemer, *Moral Knowledge* (London: Macmillan, 2005); for naturalist realist positions see David Brink, *Moral Realism and the Foundations of Ethics* (Cambridge: Cambridge University Press, 1989); Peter Railton, *Facts, Values and Norms* (Cambridge: Cambridge University Press, 2003); Michael Smith, *Ethics and the A Priori* (Cambridge: Cambridge University Press, 2004). For recent defences of supernaturalism see Phillip Quinn, 'The recent revival of divine command ethics', *Philosophy and Phenomenological Research*, 50/supplement (1990), 345–65; 'The primacy of God's will in Christian ethics', *Philosophical Perspectives*, 6 (1992), 460–503.

7 Regan, 'The value of rational nature', 278.

8 An early philosophical use of moral disagreement in arguments against moral objectivism can be found in Denis Diderot. The argument is examined in Stephen Toulmin, *The Place of Reason in Ethics* (Cambridge: Cambridge University Press, 1950), p. 33, and provides the context for John Mackie's argument on relativity in *Ethics: Inventing Right and Wrong* (Harmondsworth: Penguin,, 1977), pp. 36–8. For a response to Mackie, see David Wiggins, 'Objectivity in ethics: two difficulties, two responses', *Ratio*, 17/1 (2005), 1–26.

9 Gilbert Harman, *The Nature of Morality: an Introduction to Ethics* (Princeton, NJ: Princeton University Press, 1977). Harman appears to use a 'direction of fit' argument – which is usually thought to support a Humean account of motivation, see Smith, *Ethics and the A Priori*, pp. 5–15 – to explain the diversity of moral views and so to prop up relativity arguments such as Mackie's.

10 Although the argument is 'metaphysical', it does not concern us at this juncture because its main focus is normativity and action, and so conative impotence of realist positions. Facts fail what Philippa Foot calls 'Hume's practicality requirement': they do not have 'to-be-pursuedness' built into them, see Foot, *Natural Goodness* (Oxford: Clarendon Press, 2003), p. 9; also Mackie, *Ethics*, p. 40. Brink, *Moral Realism*, argues that Mackie's unargued assumption of the truth of internalism is what underpins his queerness argument. For a dissenting view on Mackie, see Terry Horgan and Mark Timmons, 'Troubles on moral twin earth: moral queerness revived', *Synthese* 92 (1992), 221–69. For a dissenting view on Hume, see Kieran Setiya, 'Hume on practical reason', *Philosophical Perspectives*, 18 (2004), 365–90. For a useful classification of the varieties of internalism, see Stephen Darwall, 'Autonomist internalism and the justification of morals', *Noûs*, 24 (1990), 257–68.

11 Mackie, *Ethics*, p. 38.

12 Considering a possible intuitionist reply to the argument on epistemological queerness, Mackie admits that the 'only adequate reply' would be to show how empiricist foundations suffice to provide us with an account of all ideas, beliefs and knowledge we have (*Ethics*, p. 39). Intuitionism is not Mackie's only target: he also finds 'supervenience', which is a feature of various naturalist positions, mysterious (p. 41).

13 Here I focus on the right-hand side of '*x* is right'. What is troublesome for sceptics are *moral* facts that would make '*x* is right' true or false, not facts about killing and lying, or about how we use language, or about how communities behave in particular contexts. But arguably, for the meta-ethical sceptic who has no trouble agreeing to the existence of the full range of moral items that make up the left-hand side ('lying', 'helping others who are in need', 'being cruel' etc.), access to the range of evaluative practices that yield these items must at some level be blocked. The issue of getting the '*x*' right opens a whole set of problems about descriptions that exceed the scope of this paper.

14 Kant presents his argument from the perspective of the agent, the practical perspective signalled in the question 'what ought I to do?' This is why constructivists treat moral knowledge as knowledge of what is *required* of us as rational agents, that is, as agents who are already confronted by categorical moral demands. So the effort goes to show that such demands are reasonable or universally acceptable (see O'Neill, *Towards Justice and Virtue: a Constructive Account of Practical Reasoning* (Cambridge: Cambridge University Press, 1996). That the practical reasoning position absorbs cognition into justification is not surprising because it responds directly to the 'practicality requirement' (see Thomas Nagel, *The Possibility of Altruism* (Oxford:

Oxford University Press, 1970), p. 8. A similar line is taken in Alan Donagan, *The Theory of Morality* (Chicago: University of Chicago Press, 1977). This response, which is formulated at least in part to address doubts about the categorical nature of moral imperatives, can be seen as vulnerable to doubts about the model of practical reasoning employed (see Rosalind Hursthouse, 'Practical wisdom: a mundane account', *Proceedings of the Aristotelian Society*, 106/3 (2006), 283–307 (citation 288).

15 John Cottingham, Robert Stoothoff and Dugald Murdoch (eds), *The Philosophical Writings of Descartes*, vol. 2 (Cambridge: Cambridge University Press, 1985).

16 See also: 'this concept which is already present in a sound natural understanding requires not so much to be taught as merely to be clarified' (*GMS* 4: 397); or 'we have at hand examples of the morally judging reason' (*KpV* 5: 163). In the Preface to the *Critique of Practical Reason*, Kant insists that he need introduce no 'new language', or 'make up new words for accepted concepts', assures his audience that his thinking is 'very close to the popular way of thinking' and that 'common expressions' are perfectly adequate for his argument. So concerned is he to maintain this link that when he departs from accepted usage, he adds a footnote to explain his reasons (*KpV* 5: 11 and notes).

17 It is worth considering briefly G. E. M. Anscombe's criticism in 'Modern moral philosophy', *Philosophy*, 33 (1958), 1–19, that duty is a currency without cover (in God's will). Anscombe's aim is philosophically *and* socially revisionist. By contrast, Kant seeks to identify a new 'formula' for duty which does not require the traditional 'cover', by building onto our shared moral experience. Central to this for Kant is the common idea of bindingness which he considers essential to the very concept of moral laws: see *MS* 6: 215.

18 Kant is willing to entertain the idea that the search for the unconditional can lead in some contexts to nonsense. In moral matters, the need to think of morality as a coherent system – that is, as a system that does not on reflection contain contradictory demands – guides the 'analysis' but is not a given (certainly not an empirical given). The thought is that architectural order *can* be established in moral matters, or that there is a basic principle that holds the basic structure together. Authors who have dealt with this, especially Harman and Nussbaum, take it that this is just a historical or psychological accident that commits some to the idea of a single homogeneous morality. But something less artificial can be the case: the idea that if we come to different moral judgements in appraising situation *x* and situation *y*, then we must be able to recognize salient similarities and differences in

situation *x* and situation *y*. This demand for consistency across cases is deeply rooted in our common ideas of fairness. To say this is *not* to vindicate the principle. This is why it remains to be shown that it is right that we hold the idea of a moral law as a unifying moral principle. To paraphrase Kant, we can say that all our moral knowledge *begins* with experience but it does not all arise from experience. However, this makes more urgent the issue of epistemic propriety of the moral law that we put to one side in order to follow Kant's analysis of experience. See Harman, *The Nature of Morality* on absolutism and Martha Nussbaum, 'The discernment of perception: an Aristotelian conception of private and public morality', in *Love's Knowledge: Essays in Philosophy and Literature* (Oxford: Oxford University Press, 1992) on metricity and singleness.

19 The self-evidence notion is usually illustrated with non-moral examples: e.g. something cannot be green all over and red all over at the same time. In moral philosophy, self-evidence takes a more readily intuitionistic character. Robert Audi, *Practical Reasoning and Ethical Decision* (London: Routledge, 2006) identifies no fewer than nine self-evident moral obligations (justice, non-injury, fidelity, reparation, beneficence, self-improvement, gratitude, liberty and respectfulness). For an intuitionistic interpretation of Kant see Audi, *The Good in the Right: a Theory of Intuition and Intrinsic Value* (Princeton, NJ: Princeton University Press, 2004), pp. 90ff.

20 One way of understanding this is to say that moral knowledge is not like geometrical knowledge (which for Kant requires the a priori form of intuition). But this does not take us very far. It is a telling point of reception history that the 'fact of reason' doctrine was early on discarded as untenable fiction; see Franz Brentano, *The Origin of the Knowledge of Right and Wrong* (London: Routledge and Kegan Paul,1969) p. 49. Kant's rejection of self-evidence and of intuitionism more broadly shows that non-naturalist realism, which is one of the available meta-ethical descriptors that could be used to characterize his position, does not in fact apply (despite affinities with current neo-Moorean positions).

21 'Pure practical reason now fills this vacant ['leer'] place with a definite law of causality in an intelligible world (causality through freedom). This is the moral law' (*KpV* 5: 49).

22 See especially *KpV* 5: 43–4; also *Reflection* 6864 (*Refl* 19: 184).

23 As Sami Pihlström commented in discussion, the procedure I outline here resembles the transcendental procedure. However, the difference is that there is no moral equivalent to the leaves of the tree turning yellow outside my window. The latter is not something I can opt out of, it is an experience we all – Humeans, Kantians or non-philosophical

tree-watchers – have qua human experiencers. For Kant there is nothing like this in moral matters, where we come with expectations of coherence which on reflection we find are satisfied through the employment of pure practical reason alone. The advantage of a fully transcendental vindication of the universalizability formula is that it answers the question of why this formula is a formula for morality (see Sorin Baiasu's paper in this collection). A difficulty with this approach is the modal status of the starting premise 'there is moral experience'. Another transcendental approach, recommended by Stephen Houlgate in discussion, focuses on the distinction between hypothetical and categorical imperatives: if we take as our primary datum this aspect of language use, then we arrive at something like the a priori commitment I propose here. The difficulty with this is the need to provide a separate defence of categoricity (against Foot-style arguments).

24 I thank Sorin Baiasu for extensive comments on the piece; also Jason Gaiger, Seiriol Morgan, Stephen Houlgate, Howard Williams and the organizers and participants of the Kant panel at the 4th ECPR General Conference (Pisa 2007), especially Sami Pihlström, Sharon Anderson-Gold and Mark Timmons.

References

Anscombe, G. E. M., 'Modern moral philosophy', *Philosophy*, 33 (1958), 1–19.

Audi, R., *The Good in the Right: a Theory of Intuition and Intrinsic Value* (Princeton, NJ: Princeton University Press, 2004).

——, *Practical Reasoning and Ethical Decision* (London: Routledge, 2006).

Brentano, F., *The Origin of the Knowledge of Right and Wrong* (London: Routledge and Kegan Paul,1969).

Brink, D., *Moral Realism and the Foundations of Ethics* (Cambridge: Cambridge University Press, 1989).

Cottingham, J., R. Stoothoff and D. Murdoch (eds), *The Philosophical Writings of Descartes*, vol. 2 (Cambridge: Cambridge University Press, 1985).

Darwall, S. L., 'Autonomist internalism and the justification of morals', *Noûs*, 24 (1990), 257–68.

Donagan, A., *The Theory of Morality* (Chicago: University of Chicago Press, 1977).

Dreier, J., 'Metaethics and the problem of creeping minimalism', *Philosophical Perspectives*, 18 (2004), 23–44.

Engstrom, S., 'Kant's distinction between theoretical and practical knowledge', *The Harvard Review of Philosophy*, 10/1 (2002), 49–63.

Foot, P. *Natural Goodness* (Oxford: Clarendon Press, 2003).

Guyer, P., *Kant on Freedom, Law, and Happiness* (Cambridge: Cambridge University Press, 2000).

Harman, G., *The Nature of Morality: an Introduction to Ethics* (Princeton, NJ: Princeton University Press, 1977).

Horgan, T. and Timmons, M., 'Troubles on moral twin earth: moral queerness revived', *Synthese*, 92 (1992), 221–69.

Huemer, M., *Moral Knowledge* (London: Macmillan, 2005).

Hursthouse, R., 'Practical wisdom: a mundane account', in *Proceedings of the Aristotelian Society*, 106/3 (2006), 283–307.

Kant, I., *Critique of Pure Reason*, trans. N. K. Smith (Basingstoke: Macmillan, 1985).

——, *Critique of Practical Reason*, trans. L. W. Beck (New York: Macmillan, 1989).

——, *Groundwork of the Metaphysics of Morals*, trans. H. J. Paton (London: Unwin Hyman, 1989).

——, *The Metaphysics of Morals*, trans. M. J. Gregor (Cambridge: Cambridge University Press, 1995).

——, *Critique of the Power of Judgment*, trans. P. Guyer and E. Matthews (Cambridge: Cambridge University Press, 2001).

Korsgaard, C., *Sources of Normativity* (Cambridge: Cambridge University Press, 1996).

——, 'Motivation, metaphysics, and the value of self: a reply to Ginsborg, Guyer, and Schneewind', *Ethics*, 109/1 (1998), 49–66.

Mackie, J., *Ethics: Inventing Right and Wrong* (Harmondsworth: Penguin, 1977).

Nagel, T., *The Possibility of Altruism* (Oxford: Oxford University Press, 1970).

Nussbaum, M., 'The discernment of perception: an Aristotelian conception of private and public morality', in *Love's Knowledge: Essays in Philosophy and Literature* (Oxford: Oxford University Press, 1992).

O'Neill, O., 'Constructivisms in ethics', in *Constructions of Reason: Explorations of Kant's Practical Philosophy* (Cambridge: Cambridge University Press, 1989).

——, *Towards Justice and Virtue: a Constructive Account of Practical Reasoning* (Cambridge: Cambridge University Press, 1996).

——, 'Constructivism vs. Contractualism', *Ratio*, 16/4(2003), 319–31.

Quinn, P., 'The recent revival of divine command ethics', *Philosophy and Phenomenological Research*, 50/supplement (1990), 345–65.

——, 'The primacy of God's will in Christian ethics', *Philosophical Perspectives*, 6 (1992), 460–503.

Railton, P., *Facts, Values and Norms* (Cambridge: Cambridge University Press, 2003).
Reath, A., 'Value and law in Kant's moral theory', *Ethics*, 114 (2003), 127–55.
Regan, D. H., 'The value of rational nature', *Ethics*, 112 (2002), 267–91.
Schneewind, J. B., *The Invention of Autonomy: a History of Modern Moral Philosophy* (Cambridge: Cambridge University Press, 1998).
Setiya, K., 'Hume on practical reason', *Philosophical Perspectives*, 18 (2004), 365–90.
Smith, M., *The Moral Problem* (Oxford: Blackwell, 1994).
——, *Ethics and the A Priori* (Cambridge: Cambridge University Press, 2004).
Toulmin, S., *The Place of Reason in Ethics* (Cambridge: Cambridge University Press, 1950).
Wiggins, D., 'Objectivity in ethics: two difficulties, two responses', *Ratio*, 17/1 (2005), 1–26.

9 • Metaphysics and Moral Judgement

Sorin Baiasu

1. Introduction

Nowadays, Kantians seem to make little progress in the attempt to offer guidance for our decisions concerning right and wrong. Every time some principle of moral judgement is suggested, Kantian ethical theories seem happy to accept that 'there is much more tinkering we can do', and they seem to embrace, rather than try to avoid, a 'permanent fix-it situation'.[1]

I think the main reason for the proliferation of this approach is that commentators misidentify the source or nature of moral normativity. This is, I think, a consequence of the current tendency in much ethical and political theory to avoid metaphysics and to account for the unconditional, necessary character of Kantian moral claims in non-metaphysical terms. Consequently, the test for the moral permissibility or impermissibility of maxims, a test which Kant regards as bound up with transcendental logic, is reduced to a logical contradiction in the traditional sense or to other types of contradiction based on contingent, empirical factors.

In this paper, I am trying to do precisely the opposite, namely to retrieve some of the Kantian metaphysics which is usually left behind and to explain why this is essential if Kant's ethics is to have any chance of being a guiding theory. Needless to say, by 'Kantian metaphysics' I mean the critical, transcendental approach offered by Kant, rather than the traditional metaphysics that Kant himself criticizes.

Recall the Universal Law Formulation of the categorical imperative: 'Act only in accordance with that maxim through which you can at the same time will that it become a universal law' (*GMS* 4: 421). The test presupposed by the Universal Law Formulation would prove its guiding force if it could identify at least one maxim through which I cannot at the same time will that it become a universal law. This would happen precisely when it was contradictory to will through my maxim that it become a universal law. So one question at this point refers to the kind of contradiction that can arise when I think of myself as acting on a maxim in a world in which that maxim is universalized.

The dominant interpretations of this universalizability test are the 'Logical' and 'Practical' interpretations.[2] On these interpretations, I am supposed to imagine a world in which the maxim of my action is universalized, and I am also supposed to imagine myself in that world as intending to act on my maxim. According to the Logical Interpretation, a contradiction emerges when I intend to act on a maxim which only makes sense by reference to a certain conceptual framework, a framework which is destroyed by the maxim's universalization. For instance, when universalized, the maxim of making false promises will lead to a world without the institution of promising, that is, a world without the conceptual resources for making sense of a maxim of making false promises. I cannot even make sense of a maxim of making false promises in a world where promising does not exist, let alone try to perform such an act.

The second interpretation, the Practical one, identifies a contradiction in the intention of performing a certain action in a world where the conditions for its performance are undermined by its universalization. So, taking as an example the maxim of killing my successful rival, in a world in which this maxim was universalized, I could not act on it without contradiction: any action requires that the agent be alive, and this is a condition undermined by the univerzalisation of the maxim of murdering a successful rival. Here the issue is not that of making sense of the maxim (which, in this case, unlike the case of false promising, does not depend on the persistence of a social practice, or so Korsgaard claims;[3] the issue is that of successfully performing an action on the basis of a maxim.

According to the Standard View[4] of the categorical imperative, the evaluation of actions is supposed to work in the following way:

> It asks whether we can simultaneously intend to do *x* (assuming that we must intend some set of conditions sufficient for the successful carrying out of our intentions and the normal and predictable results of successful execution) and intend everyone else to do *x* (assuming again that we must intend some conditions sufficient for the successful execution of their intentions and the normal and predictable results of such execution).[5]

For instance, by making a false promise the agent must intend both the set of conditions necessary for the successful performance of the act, and the normal and predictable results of the maxim's universalization. The Practical Interpretation relates in an obvious way to this Standard View: it examines precisely whether the universalization of the maxim does not have results which undermine the possibility of performing actions based on that maxim. Moreover, the set of necessary conditions for the successful performance of the act includes the existence of the institution of trust and its corresponding conceptual framework. Hence, the Logical Interpretation can also be derived as a particular version of the Standard View. The Practical Interpretation focuses on the conditions for the successful performance of an action on a particular maxim, whereas the Logical Interpretation examines the conditions of the required conceptual framework.

Elsewhere, I presented some of the difficulties of using the Logical and Practical Interpretations in the evaluation of specific maxims.[6] I also formulated the general problems faced by these two accounts and traced the problems back to their root, the Standard View. Finally, I raised several objections to the Standard View, examined possible replies, and concluded that although the objections and replies were not wholly conclusive, several of Kant's comments suggested a distinct account of moral normativity which contrasted quite strongly with the standard view.

In this chapter, my aim is to reconstruct this distinct account of practical judgement and to make evident the role and importance of metaphysics for practical judgement. I think this account will not only offer a more accurate interpretation of Kant's texts, but will also be an improvement in philosophical terms. Let me start from some of Kant's claims.

2. Kant's account of practical judgement

Kant discusses the question of practical judgement in a condensed but explicit manner in the *Critique of Practical Reason*, in the Section 'Of the Typic of Pure Practical Judgement'. Thus, for Kant,

> the concepts of good and evil first determine an object for the will. They themselves, however, fall under a practical rule of reason which, if

> the reason is pure, determines the will a priori with regard to its object. Now, whether an action possible for us in sensibility is or is not a case that falls under the rule requires practical power of judgement, by which what was said universally (*in abstracto*) in the rule is applied *in concreto* to an action. (*KpV* 5: 67)

Here, 'practical judgement' refers to what Kant calls, in the *Critique of Judgement*, a 'determinative' type of judgement (*KU* 6: 179). Practical judgement is determinative or subsumptive, because it starts from the rule of practical reason and tries to determine the instances which fall under the rule. By contrast, a reflective judgement starts from an instance and tries to find the rule corresponding to it. For determinative practical judgement, the rule is the moral law, and this rule also determines the application of the concepts of good and evil.

Practical judgement determines which actions fall under the rule of practical reason and can thus be seen as subsuming actions under this rule. But importantly, for Kant, practical judgement is not merely about determining whether a particular action is possible:

> In the subsumption of an action possible for me in the world of sense under a *pure practical law* the concern is not with the possibility of the *action* as an event in the world of sense; for this possibility pertains to the judging of the theoretical use of reason according to the law of causality. (*KpV* 5: 68)

Hence, practical judgement has to do with the application of a rule to an action *in so far as the action is possible for us in the world of sense*. In other words, the object of practical judgement is an action which can exist in the world for us to perceive. An action which, say, is presented in terms that do not make sense to us, or an action which requires for its successful performance conditions that cannot be met in our world is not an action which can exist for us to perceive; or, as Kant puts it, it is not an action possible for us in the world of sense.

Moreover, Kant explicitly states that the possibility of an action in sensibility is to be accounted for by the 'theoretical' use of reason. Therefore, in order for practical judgement to evaluate the ethical worth of an action, it must do something other than merely test whether the action can exist for us to perceive. Practical judgement is supposed to determine whether the will was, or is to be, determined by a maxim which can be subsumed under the moral law. This confirms that in Kant's view too, an interpretation such as the Logical or Practical one, or more generally a view of the categorical imperative like the Standard View, cannot provide a test for the ethical worth of actions or maxims.

2.1. The problem of practical judgement

How, according to Kant, can one determine whether the will was, or is to be, determined by a maxim which can be subsumed under the moral law? This is a particularly difficult problem for Kant:

> A practical rule of pure reason, *first*, as *practical*, concerns the existence of an object, and *second*, as a *practical rule* of pure reason, carries with it necessity with regard to the existence of an action and hence is a practical law, and specifically not a law of nature [concerning action] through empirical determining bases but a law of freedom according to which the will is to be determinable independently of everything empirical (merely through the presentation of a law as such and of its form); yet, all occurring cases of possible actions can only be empirical, i.e., can belong only to experience and nature. Therefore, it seems paradoxical to want to find in the world of sense a case which, while to this extent it always falls only under the law of nature, nonetheless permits the application of a law of freedom to it, and to which the suprasensible idea of the morally good to be exhibited in that world *in concreto* can be applied. (*KpV* 5: 67–8)

The difficulty to which Kant points here is generated precisely by the fact that an ethically good action is more than an action which is possible in the world as an object of experience; moreover, an ethically good action is only contingently an existing action which we perceive in the world and for which, as an object of experience, we account by appeal to laws of nature. For in certain situations, ethically good actions are not performed although they ought to have been. What is essential for such actions is that they ought to be performed, not whether they actually are performed. To reduce ethically good actions to objects which can or do exist in the world is to miss what is specific to them, namely their ethically necessary character.

In so far as the necessity of ethically good actions is independent of the actuality of past, present or future objects, ethically good actions are beyond experience and nature. It is in this sense that Kant talks about the 'suprasensible' idea of the ethically good. The condition that Kant states in relation to ethically good actions and which bridges the sensible and the suprasensible is the requirement that ethically good actions be *possible* objects of experience. In this way, a theoretical account of an action can tell us something about the action as a *candidate* for the status of ethically good action. If the action is theoretically possible then it is such a candidate, but it cannot be a candidate if the action is not a possible object of experience.

The difficulty is that of judging whether an existing action is ethically good, for an existing action is actually determined by laws of nature, whereas an ethically good action, in so far as it is ethically good, need not be so determined (although it should of course be possible to determine it in this way). The problem of practical judgement is therefore an implication of the normative character of ethically good actions:

> Hence the power of judgement of pure practical reason is subject to the same difficulties as that of pure theoretical reason, though the latter had a means available to get out of them: namely that, since what counted with regard to the theoretical use were intuitions to which pure concepts of the understanding could be applied, such intuitions (though only of objects of the senses) could yet be given a priori, and hence, as far as the connection of the manifold in them is concerned, could be given (as *schemata*) in a priori conformity with the pure concepts of understanding. By contrast, the morally good is something that, in terms of the object, is suprasensible, so that nothing corresponding to it can be found in any sensible intuition; hence the power of judgment under laws of pure practical reason seems to be subject to special difficulties which are due to [the fact] that a law of freedom is to be applied to actions as events that occur in the world of sense and thus, to this extent, belong to nature. (*KpV* 5: 68)

This long quotation contains several important clues concerning Kant's account of how the categorical imperative is supposed to test maxims. In what follows, I will discuss these clues with a view to clarifying Kant's account of practical judgement. For presentational purposes, I will split the long quotation into smaller parts, which I will discuss in turn.

2.1.1. Similarities between the theoretical and practical problems
First, on Kant's account, '. . . the power of judgment of pure practical reason is subject to the same difficulties as that of pure theoretical reason' (*KpV* 5: 68, 90). Here, Kant points to the similarities between the problem of practical judgement and that of the schematism in his theoretical philosophy. The problem of the schematism is clearly presented in the first *Critique* as follows:

> Whenever an object is subsumed under a concept, the presentation of the object must be *homogenous* with the concept, i.e., the concept must contain what is presented in the object that is to be subsumed under it. For this is precisely what we mean by the expression that an object is contained *under* a concept. Thus, the empirical concept of a *plate* is homogenous with the pure geometrical concept of a *circle*, inasmuch as the roundness thought in the concept of the plate can be intuited [also] in the circle. (*KrV* A137/B176)

The problem of theoretical judgement or of the schematism therefore concerns the possibility of subsuming an object under a concept; more exactly, it is the problem of *appropriately* referring to an object by means of a concept. The answer to this problem, Kant says, is that the presentation of the object displays a feature which is contained in the concept under which the object is to be subsumed. In the case of empirical concepts, like that of a plate, this condition can easily be met, since concepts are defined precisely by including as a distinguishing mark the features displayed by the way objects appear to us.

However, the situation is different in the case of pure concepts of understanding, which are a priori and hence cannot be defined on the basis of the empirical presentations of the object to be subsumed. This makes it unclear how categories or pure concepts of the understanding can capture anything of the objects which they are supposed to subsume. We thus end up with the problem of the schematism. As Kant puts it:

> pure concepts of the understanding, on the other hand, are quite heterogeneous from empirical intuitions (indeed from sensible intuitions generally) and can never be encountered in any intuition. How, then, can an intuition be *subsumed* under a category, and hence how can a category be *applied* to appearances – since surely no one will say that

> a category (e.g., causality) can also be intuited through senses and is contained in appearances? (*KrV* A137–8/B176–7)

If the concept of causality is a priori, then it cannot be defined by reference to those features of the objects which we perceive in experience. The concept of causality, for instance, is not the concept which refers to the fact that so far when I have experienced an occurrence of a certain type (say, smoke), I have also experienced another event which preceded it (say, fire). Such a concept would not be a priori, but would plainly depend on experience. But if the concept of causality is a priori, independent from experience, how can it relate to the empirical intuitions which constitute our experiences? How is it possible for the empirical intuitions of a new experience to present to us any features subsumable under an a priori concept of causality?

This is the problem of the schematism or of the judgement of pure theoretical reason, which Kant sees at work in the judgement of pure practical reason: what guarantees do we have that the concepts of good and evil, with their rules of reason, can refer to any aspect of our actions?

2.1.2. Kant's solution to the problem of theoretical judgement

Let me now move to the second point I wanted to make in relation to the long quote above. Given that in the theoretical realm we already have a solution for the problem of judgement, and given the similarities between this problem and that of practical judgement, this solution might be useful in suggesting an approach in the practical realm. As we have seen, for Kant, reason in the theoretical realm

> had a means available to get out of them [such problems]: namely that, since what counted with regard to the theoretical use were intuitions to which pure concepts of the understanding could be applied, such intuitions (though only of objects of the senses) could yet be given a priori, and hence, as far as the connection of the manifold in them is concerned, could be given (as *schemata*) in a priori conformity with the pure concepts of understanding. (*KpV* 5: 68)

The theoretical solution is that of a third element which bridges a priori concepts and empirical intuitions, an element which Kant calls the 'transcendental schema'. The role of transcendental schemata is to explain how a priori concepts will capture features of the experience – features given by the basic presentation of empirical intuitions – and hence to guarantee that categories will capture features of experience. There are two issues which seem to be raised by the problem of schematism that a transcendental schema must solve: firstly the issue of the connection between a priori elements (categories) and empirical elements (sensible intuitions), and secondly the issue of the connection between the understanding (through its a priori concepts) and sensibility (through its intuitions).[7] There is, then, firstly a question of bridging two epistemic elements which have distinct epistemic statuses (a priori and empirical), and secondly a question of bridging two distinct epistemic faculties (the understanding and sensibility).

The first issue can be explained away by a consideration of the very notion of the schema. The schema of a concept is the 'presentation of a universal procedure of the imagination for providing the concept with its image' (*KrV* A140/B179–80).[8] An image can only be provided in sensibility. If the schema is to be a genuine mediating element between sensibility and the understanding, then it cannot be part of sensibility. In fact, Kant repeatedly warns against this misinterpretation: he stresses that a schema is not an image, but *the procedure* for producing such an image (*KrV* A140/B179; my emphasis).This explains how the schema can connect an a priori concept to empirical intuitions, since what it does is to provide a *method* through which the a priori concept can be presented in sensibility. Since all empirical intuitions occur in sensibility in time, a schema is a procedure for the presentation of the categories in time. For instance, for Kant, the schema of the pure concept of magnitude is the conjoint encompassing of the successive addition of one item to another. The experience of magnitude will occur by the organization of sensible intuitions through the schema under the concept of magnitude. The a priori concept relates a priori to the a priori intuition of time, which guarantees that whenever something occurs, since it occurs in time, if it presents itself as a successive series of intuitions which are conjoint, it has a magnitude.

The connection of a priori concepts to empirical intuitions through schemata is possible when categories are connected to the a priori intuition of time. Given that empirical intuitions will be presented in time, and given that a priori categories are related to time through schemata, it is necessarily the case that empirical intuitions will be subsumed under a priori concepts. But this also explains the second issue – that the understanding and sensibility can relate to each other and that they necessarily do so in our experience. This becomes clearer if we note that a category is nothing other than a rule for the organization in time (through schemata) of empirical intuitions. Hence the understanding and sensibility can be and are necessarily connected through schemata.

2.1.3. Differences between the theoretical and practical problems

Does this suggest anything useful for the problem of practical judgement? The answer is not immediately clear, since the solution to the problem of practical judgement will in certain respects be different from the solution to the problem of theoretical judgement. This is what Kant says in the third and final part of the long quote above:

> The morally good is something that, in terms of the object, is suprasensible, so that nothing corresponding to it can be found in any sensible intuition; hence the power of judgment under laws of pure practical reason seems to be subject to special difficulties which are due to [the fact] that a law of freedom is to be applied to actions as events that occur in the world of sense and thus, to this extent, belong to nature. (*KpV* 5: 68)

Kant explains here that the distinct character of the problem of practical judgement is given by the fact that the concepts of good and evil cannot refer to actions through schemata. This is because the concepts of good and evil refer to the causality of the free will, which does not concern the relationship between objects of sensible intuition, as natural causes and effects.

Hence while the problem of practical judgement, just like the problem of theoretical judgement, concerns the possibility of connecting a priori concepts (good or causality) to events in the world (actions or objects), the solution to the latter problem is not applicable to the former, since the attempt to subsume an event under the concepts of good and evil *brings to the fore as essential* the suprasensible aspects of the event. In other words, the problem is that of connecting a priori concepts to things which happen in the world, but *not to such things as they are given by sensible intuitions*.

So far, I have presented the similarities between the problems of theoretical and practical judgements, the solution to the problem in the theoretical realm and the reason why this solution cannot merely be extrapolated in the practical realm. There is, however, a considerable amount to be learned from the discussion of the problems of practical and theoretical judgement, as can be seen in the next section.

2.2. The solution to the problem of practical judgement

The solution Kant proposes is given by what he calls the 'type' of moral law:

> The moral law has no other cognitive power to mediate its application to objects of nature than the understanding (not the power of imagination). What the understanding can lay at the basis – as a law for the sake of the power of judgement – of the idea of reason is not a *schema* of sensibility but a law, but yet a law that can be exhibited *in concreto* in objects of the senses, and hence a law of nature, though only in terms of its form; therefore we call this law the *type* of the moral law. (*KpV* 5: 69)

Kant responds, therefore, by connecting the a priori concept of the good to actions through the model of a law of nature, that is, through the *type* of the moral law. This type is a general, formal law, a law which represents what is common to all laws of nature: their lawfulness.

The concept of the good can refer to an action through the type. If the principle which determines the will to act in that particular way (that is, by enacting that particular action) could also function in the way in which a law of nature does, namely by universally determining agents' wills, then the action and its corresponding principle could be referred to by means of the concept of the good. Hence the connection between a priori concepts and events in the world is this time given by the type, which as a model of a *law of nature* can connect with events in the world, but as a *formal law* only is also able to connect with the a priori concepts of ethics.

This leads to the rule of practical judgement: 'Ask yourself whether, if the action you propose were to occur according to a law of nature of which you were yourself a part, you could indeed regard it as possible through your will' (*KpV* 5: 69).

How, according to Kant, can we tell whether or not the action I propose could be regarded as possible through my will if it were to take place by a law of nature of which I were a part? The first thing to note is that we have to regard the proposed action as taking place by a law of nature. Hence the maxim which determines the action must be seen as determining the will of every agent who is situated in the relevant context.

This is how laws of nature function too. For instance, the laws of friction will determine the behaviour of all moving objects which are in contact, but they do not apply to stationary objects (although, of course, they will apply to stationary objects which start to move). However, Kant warns us that we can draw on the analogy with the laws of nature only up to a certain point. We should not imagine that the maxim we propose actually starts to determine the actions of agents in the world:

> Everyone knows well that if he secretly permits himself to deceive, it does not follow that everyone else does it too, or that if – without being noticed – he is unloving, everyone would not immediately be so toward him as well; hence, by the same token, this comparison of the maxim of his actions with a universal law of nature is not the determining basis of his will. But this law is nonetheless a *type* for the judging of the maxim according to moral principles. (*KpV* 5: 69)

On Kant's account, the ground of my action should not be given by the way I feel about other people acting on the same maxim towards me as I act towards them. Hence Kant excludes an interpretation of the rule of practical judgement as a version of the Golden Rule. By contrast, he suggests, by sticking to the limits of the analogy between moral maxims and natural laws, I imagine a world in which the maxim functions as a law, but without trying to calculate the sensible impressions such a world would produce in me. Since it may well turn out that I can free-ride for most of the time and enjoy the benefits of this without any adverse consequences, the test must refer strictly to what is common to laws of nature and moral laws, namely to their lawfulness:

> Hence using *the nature of the world of sense* as the *type* of an *intelligible nature* is also permitted, so long as I do not transfer to the latter any

> intuitions and what depends on them, but refer to it merely the *form of lawfulness* as such . . . For to this extent laws, as such, are the same, no matter from where they take their determining bases. (*KpV* 5: 70)

So the test Kant proposes is meant to evaluate the lawfulness of ethical laws. What is important is not the content of such laws, but their very status as laws. By focusing on particular consequences, for instance, I turn the practical investigation of the ethical worth of actions into a theoretical calculation of causes and effects.

The universal determination of the will by the maxim of deceitful promising will bring about deceitful promises whenever the situation is appropriate. This is not a conclusion about the consequences of the universalization of the maxim; a maxim of making deceitful promises when in need, which determines a person's will, will bring about deceitful promises when the person is in the appropriate contexts because this is what it means for a maxim to determine the will of a person. Again, since making deceitful promises implies that there are other persons to whom these promises are being made, we have to include among the implications of the universalization of the maxim of deceitful promises the fact that there will be persons who will be deceived.

Now, beyond the implications mentioned so far, a consideration of possible consequences emerges only when we try to determine whether those who are deceived and deceiving will react in such a way that the institution of trust dies out (that is, whether they will become suspicious and no longer believe any promise). To be sure, according to Kant, we can use the universalized maxim of self-love and the idea of happiness as the type for the morally good, that is as a model of a natural law, in order to test a maxim by the rule of practical judgement. And the maxims of self-love and happiness imply a consideration of consequences. Nevertheless, Kant also warns against using these principles as the criterion of moral goodness, for what is to be taken as a type of the morally good is the form of a law of nature, the lawfulness of a particular natural law, and not that particular law as such:

> Reason is entitled and also required to use nature (in terms of nature's pure form of understanding) as the type of the power of judgement; . . . although happiness and the infinite useful consequences of a will determined by self-love, if this will at the same time turned itself into a

> universal law of nature, can indeed serve as an entirely adequate type for the morally good, it is still not identical with it. (*KpV* 5: 70)

A correct use of nature and its laws in practical judgement leads to the correct position with regard to practical reason, namely 'rationalism':

> Only the rationalism concerning the power of judgement is adequate to the use of moral concepts; it takes from the sensible nature nothing more than what pure reason can also think on its own, i.e., lawfulness, and carries into the suprasensible nothing but what can, conversely, be actually exhibited through actions in the world of sense according to the formal rule of a natural law in general. (*KpV* 5: 71)

If my interpretation so far is correct, then rationalism of judgement should not be understood in accordance with the Standard View of the categorical imperative. It is *not* a matter of imagining a world in which a maxim functioned as a universal law and of trying to determine whether the conditions for willing to act on the maxim would be undermined by the consequences of the maxim's universalization.

The suggestion is that we can draw an analogy with laws of nature and conceive of the maxim as such a law – not in so far as the law is a law of *nature*, but in so far as it is a *law*. We are therefore supposed to focus on its form of lawfulness, and check whether we can will to act on the maxim in a world where the maxim functions as a law. But how can we imagine a world in which all persons acted according to the maxim of deceit if we are not supposed to work out the implications of the universalization of this maxim? It is not all such implications that must be avoided in practical judgement.

Consider now the example of a maxim of making false promises when in need. If universalized, the maxim of making false promises when in need will determine the wills of all persons. All persons who are in need will make a false promise in order to satisfy that need. The consequences will not necessarily be the disappearance of the institution of trust, since in principle there might still be cases of genuine promises when the person who makes the promise is not in need. Moreover, one may in principle conceive of a world in which this maxim determines the wills of the inhabitants universally and yet no person has to have recourse to making a false promise, since circumstances are such that persons in need could not satisfy their needs by making false promises.

But even in such circumstances, the fact remains that persons place their needs above the value of truthfulness. The principle of their acts would imply making a truthful promise when not in need, if making the promise is the appropriate course of action. Even in cases where we deal with a world in which inhabitants have not so far acted on the maxim, since they have not yet encountered a situation in which their needs could be provided for by making false promises, it remains the case that the principle which determines their wills in the relevant circumstances (that is, where a promise is required) is that of making a false promise when in need.

Now, like any promise, a false promise contains a claim about an unconditional commitment to do something, but unlike a genuine promise, the agent makes the claim while at the same time having no intention of keeping the commitment. Of course, such an act is possible, in so far as false promises have been successfully made and, very likely, will continue to be made. There is also no logical contradiction here, since the unconditional commitment is what I express, not what I am committed to – I am committed only to providing for my need by uttering an unconditional commitment. But there is, nevertheless, a contradiction: namely, that in being committed to providing for my need, I try to determine my will to act – that is, I try to commit myself to acting – on a principle which goes against the principle of conditional commitment that is supposed to regulate universally in my world.

To clarify this further, consider a world in which the conditional principle of truthfulness legislates universally. I am thus to provide for my needs through being untruthful, whenever I can in this way provide for my needs. Yet my commitment to this principle must also be conditional – I am to be truthful in my commitment to this principle when being so cannot provide for any existing need I have or when there is no need I can provide for by being untruthful to myself. Things start to become very confusing in this way, since nothing can stop me arguing in the same way about my commitment to the principle that I am to be committed to the principle of conditional commitment, if lying to myself about this commitment will not provide for some need I have. In general, it will become difficult, in fact impossible, to determine what I am committed to.

Note also that such a contradiction is neither practical nor logical. On the standard interpretation, the Practical and Logical Interpretations are made evident by a consideration of the *consequences* of universalization. By contrast, my claim here is not that I am committed to some end the realization of which is undermined by the consequences of a universal pursuit of the end. We can easily imagine a world in which the universal observance of the maxim of false promising when in need has the same consequences as the universal observance of the maxim of truthful promising. Hence the universalization of the maxim would not undermine the realization of any end: on the contrary and paradoxically, it would be more likely for me to find a person to trust me there than it would be in our world, where people sometimes provide for their needs by making false promises.

The contradiction I am pointing to here is that of assuming a world regulated by morally valid principles – and hence by universal principles – without one of its constitutive elements, just as the contradiction involved in thinking about a world without causality is neither logical, nor practical, nor empirical (in so far as this contradiction is meant to prove the necessary character of causation), but is *critical* in the sense that we try to imagine a world – and hence a possible experience – without one of its constitutive elements.

Now, assuming this is correct, to talk about a principle of truthful promising as constitutive of a moral world is to attribute to it an ontological status, and this step that moral theory must take into the realm of metaphysics is currently regarded by many ethical theorists and political philosophers as problematic. I do not think this is necessarily in fact an illegitimate step to take, but an argument for this must await another occasion.

4. Conclusion

On the Standard View, the force of ethically worthy principles is correctly identified as the force of an injunction to avoid contradictions. The problematic aspect is the way in which these contradictions are understood. Thus, to test the ethical status of a maxim, we are supposed to check whether a person could intend to act on that maxim in a system of nature in which the maxim functioned universally as a law of nature.[9] To test this possibility, we are supposed to establish whether a person can intend to act on a maxim and at the same time intend that maxim as a law.

More precisely, since intending the maxim as a law implies also intending the necessary conditions and consequences of its univerzalisation, and since intending to act on the maxim implies also intending the conditions and consequences of so acting, for an impermissible action the contradiction is supposed to arise between the normal and predictable consequences of the maxim's universalization and the necessary conditions for acting on the maxim. Yet there does not seem to be anything *morally* impermissible about an action which relies on conditions that are undermined when more people perform that type of action.

I have discussed in detail Kant's comments on practical judgement with the aim of working out the alternative strategy of justification he seems to propose. I have shown that a strategy of justification which relies on working out the normal and predictable consequences of the maxim's universalization is unsuccessful, because it makes the moral status of the principles depend on such consequences and we can work out these consequences only by making certain assumptions about the interests, inclinations and desires of the agents who act on the maxim. This, however, is nothing but the attempt to employ in the practical realm the solution to the problem of the evaluation of principles from Kant's theoretical philosophy. For what one does in this case is to relate the a priori concepts of good and evil to sensible intuitions concerning what is pleasing or displeasing. And yet, this is precisely what Kant rejects:

> No intuition can be put under the law of freedom (as that of a causality not sensibly conditioned) – and hence under the concept of the unconditioned good as well – and hence no schema on behalf of its application *in concreto*. (*KpV* 5: 69)

The type of necessity which is implicit in morally valid claims ('ought' statements of the type 'A ought not to φ') is independent of the type of necessity which is conferred on events in the world by laws of nature. It is because of this specific character of moral 'facts' that sensibility plays only a limited role in a practical theory, unlike the case of theoretical philosophy.

Nevertheless, for the purpose of doing practical philosophy, in particular for the issue of practical judgement, there is a lot to be learnt from Kant's theoretical philosophy. This is due to the transcendental or critical character of Kant's philosophy in general. As I argued here, the type of contradiction one should look for is specific to transcendental logic, where concepts are important in their relationships not only to each other but also to their objects. In Kant's theoretical philosophy, when a concept or the rule at the basis of such a concept is denied with regard to an experience to the constitution of which the concept or rule is contributing, we do not simply have a logical or empirical contradiction. The necessary character of the concept within that experience is not given by analysis, but by its constitutive role.

By analogy with the theoretical case, I have argued that a similar contradiction must be found in the practical realm. As Kant tells us, freedom plays the role that sensibility plays in the constitution of synthetic a priori judgements. If we imagine the concept of the good or the rule underlying this concept as independent of a maxim which connects through freedom to the concept of the morally good, then we end up with such a contradiction. The rule of practical judgement applies this strategy in the following way: described in general, it assumes that a certain maxim connects a priori with the concept of the morally good through freedom and, if a contradiction arises, concludes that the maxim is impermissible. In particular, the practical judgement implies the following steps.

First, the moral rule, as the rule of the a priori concept of good, is a synthetic a priori proposition which has a constitutive role for our moral discourse. Secondly, practical judgement is supposed to decide whether particular maxims can be subsumed under the moral law, and hence whether they can be regarded as morally good. By analogy with the problem of the schematism, Kant answers the question of practical judgement by means of the typic of judgement, which identifies the lawfulness of the laws of nature as the element which bridges concrete actions and the moral law. Thirdly, if the maxim of an action is tested for its lawfulness and the maxim is found not to be valid, we end up with a situation similar to that of denying a constitutive concept (and its corresponding rule) of our experience. For instance, by trying to deny the maxim of truthfulness by a maxim of deceitful promising, we attempt to imagine a moral situation without one of its constitutive elements.

I have developed here this case of deceitful promising in order to offer a sketch for the activity of practical judgement. Clearly more needs to be said to support these claims – both in working out the idea of a transcendental practical philosophy and in the applications of such an idea to particular cases for the justification of moral principles. What I have shown is that if an account of the normative force of morally valid principles is to be appropriate, then we need something like this critical approach in practical philosophy. Moreover, I have shown why claims to a non-metaphysical action-guiding practical philosophy represent a blind alley. [10]

Notes

1 Barbara Herman, *The Practice of Moral Judgment* (Cambridge, MA: Harvard University Press, 1993), p. 143.

2 Christine Korsgaard lists a third one, the 'Teleological Contradiction Interpretation': 'Kant's formula of universal law', in *Creating the Kingdom of Ends* (Cambridge: Cambridge University Press, 1996), p. 78. In this article I will focus only on the Logical and Practical Interpretations. First, a consideration of these two interpretations suffices for the purpose of my argument here. Secondly, a proper consideration of the teleological view would imply a more detailed account of the distinction between causal and teleological laws, which would take me too far away from the topic of this paper. Thirdly, at least in the version put forward by H. J. Paton, the teleological interpretation engages more seriously with Kantian metaphysics, and it merits separate attention: Paton, *The Categorical Imperative: a Study in Kant's Moral Philosophy* (Philadelphia: University of Pennsylvania Press, 1971). Whereas Kant would probably have classed the Logical and Practical interpretations as versions of an empiricist position in practical philosophy, he would have considered the teleological view as a version of mysticism (*KU* 5: 70–1). As supporters of the Logical Interpretation, Korsgaard refers to Paul Dietrichson, 'Kant's criteria of universalisability', in R. P. Wolff (ed.), *Kant: Foundations of the Metaphysics of Morals: Text and Critical Essays* (Indianapolis: Bobbs-Merrill, 1969); John Kemp, 'Kant's examples of the categorical imperative', in ibid.; and Allen Wood 'Kant on false promises', in L. W. Beck (ed.), *Proceedings of the Third International Kant Congress* (Dordrecht: D. Reidel, 1972). As supporters of the Practical Interpretation, she mentions Marcus Singer, *Generalisations in Ethics* (New York: Atheneum, 1961) and Onora O'Neill, *Acting on Principle: an Essay on Kantian Ethics* (New

York: Columbia University Press, 1975). Korsgaard herself is also a supporter of the Practical Interpretation.

3 Korsgaard, 'Kant's formula of universal law', 84–5.

4 I use this expression, following Peter Steinberger, not only because this view has become the dominant view of how the categorical imperative can assess maxims, but also because it attempts to reduce a fundamentally metaphysical test to something else, in this case an empirical one: see Steinberger, 'The Standard View of the categorical imperative', *Kant-Studien*, 90/1 (1999), 91–9. As mentioned in the Introduction, I take 'metaphysics' here to refer to what Kant calls critical metaphysics as opposed to the traditional, speculative metaphysics.

5 O'Neill, *Acting on Principle*, p. 73. Steinberger identifies Onora O'Neill as the source of this interpretation, but it is probably the case that Rawls's lectures on ethics and his article on Kant advance a similar line: Rawls, 'Themes in Kant's moral philosophy', in E. Förster (ed.), *Kant's Transcendental Deductions: the Three* Critiques *and the* Opus Postumum (Stanford, CA: Stanford University Press, 1989); *Lectures on the History of Moral Philosophy*, ed. B. Herman (Cambridge, MA: Harvard University Press, 2000).

6 Baiasu, 'Kantian metaphysics and the normative force of practical principles', *Politics and Ethics Review*, 3/1 (2007), 37–56.

7 Kant implicitly distinguishes these two problems when he says that 'pure concepts of the understanding . . . are quite heterogeneous from empirical intuitions (indeed from sensible intuitions generally)' (A137–8/B176–7, 210).

8 A proper discussion and clarification of this passage will require digressions concerning the notion of an image and the faculty of imagination. For the purpose of this paper, however, I will focus only on the function of the schema (which is to provide the concept with its image).

9 In the Appendix to a recent paper, Mark Timmons sorts the interpretations of Kant's universalizability tests along two dimensions: 'The categorical imperative and universalizability', in C. Horn and D. Schoenecker (eds), *Kant's* Groundwork of the Metaphysics of Morals: *New Interpretations* (Berlin: De Gruyter, 2006). First, interpretations differ in respect of the information they allow in the tests. There are austere interpretations which accept only necessary truths knowable a priori. Other interpretations, however, consider that a posteriori information can also play a role in the tests. The second dimension refers to the precise locus of the alleged contradiction. For some interpretations, the contradiction is within the maxim and emerges once the maxim is universalized. For others, the contradiction occurs within a system of nature, where the maxim plays the role of one of the laws

of nature. Finally, other interpretations regard the contradiction as emerging among the intentions involved in the process of raising one's maxim to universal law. For my purpose, the important thing to note is that the a priori necessary truths accepted by the austere interpretations are regarded by Timmons as analytic. Given that the other interpretations will adopt less austere views on the type of information allowed to play a role in the test, it follows that the contradiction will either necessarily reject the maxim as incoherent, or will reject it contingently as involving a contradiction which depends on some empirical assumptions. In the first case, the maxim is not a principle of a *possible* action, and as we have seen, on Kant's account, practical judgement will not apply. In the second case, the normative force contradiction will be contingent on empirical facts, and hence will not manage to account for the normative force of ethical claims.

10 Versions of this paper were presented at the 4th ECPR General Conference (Pisa 2007) and at the Keele Political Philosophy Seminars (2007/8). I would like to thank participants in both events for discussion, questions and suggestions. I am particularly grateful to Mark Timmons, who acted as discussant for my paper in Pisa and offered valuable comments, to Katerina Deligiorgi, who provided me with detailed written comments, and to Kenneth Westphal and Sami Pihlström for discussion. I would also like to thank John Horton, Giuseppina D'Oro and James Tartaglia for very useful feedback.

References

Baiasu, S., 'Kantian metaphysics and the normative force of practical principles', *Politics and Ethics Review*, 3/1 (2007), 37–56.

Dietrichson, P., 'Kant's criteria of universalisability', in R. P. Wolff (ed.), *Kant: Foundations of the Metaphysics of Morals: Text and Critical Essays* (Indianapolis: Bobbs-Merrill, 1969).

Herman, B., *The Practice of Moral Judgment* (Cambridge, MA: Harvard University Press, 1993).

Kant, I., *Critique of Judgement*, trans. W. S. Pluhar (Indianapolis: Hackett, 1987).

——, *Critique of Pure Reason*, trans. W. S. Pluhar (Indianapolis: Hackett 1996).

——, 'Groundwork of the Metaphysics of Morals', in *Practical Philosophy*, ed. and trans. M. J. Gregor (Cambridge: Cambridge University Press, 1996).

——, *Critique of Practical Reason*, trans. W. S. Pluhar (Indianapolis: Hackett, 2002).

Kemp, J., 'Kant's examples of the categorical imperative', in R. P. Wolff (ed.), *Kant: Foundations of the Metaphysics of Morals: Text and Critical Essays* (Indianapolis: Bobbs-Merrill, 1969).

Korsgaard, C., *Creating the Kingdom of Ends* (Cambridge: Cambridge University Press, 1996).

O'Neill, O., *Acting on Principle: an Essay on Kantian Ethics* (New York: Columbia University Press, 1975).

Paton, H. J., *The Categorical Imperative: a Study in Kant's Moral Philosophy* (Philadelphia: University of Pennsylvania Press, 1971).

Rawls, J., 'Themes in Kant's moral philosophy', in E. Förster (ed.), *Kant's Transcendental Deductions: the Three* Critiques *and the* Opus Postumum (Stanford, CA: Stanford University Press, 1989).

——, *Lectures on the History of Moral Philosophy*, ed. B. Herman (Cambridge, MA: Harvard University Press, 2000).

Singer, M., *Generalisations in Ethics* (New York: Atheneum, 1961).

Steinberger, P., 'The Standard View of the categorical imperative', *Kant-Studien*, 90/1 (1999), 91–9.

Timmons, M. 'The categorical imperative and universalizability', in C. Horn and D. Schoenecker (eds), *Kant's* Groundwork of the Metaphysics of Morals*: New Interpretations* (Berlin: De Gruyter, 2006).

Wood, A., 'Kant on false promises', in L. W. Beck (ed.), *Proceedings of the Third International Kant Congress* (Dordrecht: D. Reidel, 1972).

10 • 'Intelligible Facts': Toward a Constructivist Account of Action and Responsibility

Garrath Williams

> An action is called a *deed* insofar as it comes under obligatory laws and hence insofar as the subject, in doing so, is considered in terms of the freedom of his choice. By such an action the agent is regarded as the *author* of its effect, and this, together with the action itself, can be *imputed* to him, if one is previously acquainted with the law by virtue of which an obligation rests on these . . . *Imputation* (*imputatio*) in the moral sense is the *judgment* by which someone is regarded as the author (*causa libera* [free cause]) of an action, which is then called a *deed* (*factum*) and stands under laws. (*MS* 6: 223, 226)

Fifty years ago, one writer on responsibility made the famous claim that 'we are all Kantians now'.[1] This chapter argues that facts about who did what and who is responsible for what can best be analysed using terms familiar from Kant's philosophy – as 'intelligible' or 'noumenal' realities. For paid-up Kantians, this is a matter of course: the questions would be how to cash out this claim, and how it relates to the metaphysical commitments of Kantian theory. For the rest of us, however, it would be truer to say that 'we are all naturalists now' – at least in a broad sense of naturalism which holds that the acts and interactions of human beings always remain part of the natural world. From this perspective, any turn to Kantian noumena is likely to attract scepticism. Why can't we be satisfied with a more empiricist analysis of action and of responsibility? Can Kantian lines of thought illuminate their nature without making dubious metaphysical claims?

I share this broad naturalism, and am sceptical about much that Kant himself says. So I will not be concerned with textual exposition and will not claim that the position sketched here is wholly Kantian. It might be labelled constructivist; and in the final part of the chapter I briefly try to allay some concerns – about contingency or relativism – that we often associate with constructivist positions.

To approach the issues at stake, I begin by noting three fairly simple reasons why we should not want to tie our understanding of action and responsibility too closely to empirical facts about agency, before proceeding to my main business: how it may be illuminating to invoke Kant's category of the intelligible in the understanding of action and responsibility. I mean these points to have a certain naïve quality, although they come with whole cargoes of philosophical baggage.

First, facts about moral responsibility are intrinsically normative, unlike most other facts, including facts about the causality of actions (qua events). When we say someone did something under some morally relevant description, and is thus answerable for certain consequences, we are plainly dealing with a claim that is meant to guide future actions. If we try to analyse culpability in terms of psychological and causal facts, or in terms of supposed facts about a person's psychological or causal capacities, then we must be trying to derive a normative claim from a set of factual claims. It remains unclear how we are meant to do this.

Second, there can be facts about responsibility in the *absence* of empirical (psychological, causal) facts. The obvious cases are those of laudable or culpable omissions. There may be no positive fact to which we can trace someone's praiseworthiness or culpability. Nor, in many cases, will it do to offer a story about her capacities: for example, that she could appreciate the force of moral criticism for her failure to act. This may be empirically false, so far as we can tell. Moreover, to attribute to someone a standing incapacity to, say, regard the needs of strangers is not to mitigate blame but rather to offer a powerful moral condemnation. Evidently facts about what is *not* the case are as empirically true as any others. But we need to account for how, out of all the infinity of things a person does not or could not do, a handful may be singled out as relevant to a person's responsibilities.

Third, facts about action and responsibility have a certain timelessness. Actions are, as Hume once noted, 'temporary and perishing'.[2] But they stick to their doer as stubbornly as any empirical characteristic we might care to name. The acts remain *his* even when he does not remember them, even when they do not reflect his character, even when he thinks of them in quite different terms than others may do, even when the deed no longer has any tangible impact. So it is not facts about a person's psychology or make-up, nor about causality, that make his actions remain his over time. Note, too, that if one were inclined to think that facts about action or agency were not normative (an issue I skirted in stating my first point), the language of *ownership* that we rely on when speaking of deeds might give us pause for thought.

This is to say both too little (to convince) and too much (raising issues that I cannot properly address in one chapter). All I want to do is to motivate a starting-point that seems difficult to square with naturalistic commitments: that an analysis of claims about action and responsibility is likely to founder if its sole resource consists in causal or psychological facts, or supposed empirical facts concerning individual capacities to think or act. My question is then: what resources can we find in the Kantian idea of intelligible facts? These are facts that plainly have a normative force, that go beyond what can be revealed by empirical investigation, that even have – as Kant notoriously claims – the quality of timelessness.[3] These are certainly 'queer' facts. But it seems we need this sort of queerness to accommodate our familiar claims about action and responsibility.

In pursuing this question, I will resist – in the name of broadly naturalistic commitments – one Kantian line of thought. I do not think that the category of the intelligible should be understood as a domain of more or less metaphysical facts about individual agency. Consider, for instance, Kant's insistence that everyone has a capacity to discern moral truths and to act on them regardless of what others do – a claim that our experience of human beings provides absolutely no warrant for. Or consider his claim that we can link act to actor in terms of an individual capacity of will, even in the absence of lingering empirical or psychological ties. Instead of supposing that the category of the intelligible concerns the capacities of individual human beings, I want to follow another path, one also attested to by Kant's texts. This is to interpret the intelligible as a domain of intersubjectivity.

In doing so I partly follow a line of naturalistic analysis made famous by Peter Strawson. 'Freedom and Resentment' attempts to vindicate claims about responsibility in the light of our tendency to respond to one another in particular ways.[4] The argument is based, first, on facts about what we usually feel and do. This gains normative purchase, second, from the claim that the alternatives are scarcely imaginable and would involve grave costs to human interaction. Although I will not discuss Strawson's own account, I will rely on a similar, two-pronged strategy. First, I use John Searle's category of 'institutional facts' to suggest how facts about what someone did or is responsible for may emerge from our shared beliefs and practices.[5] This account is empiricist and naturalistic, although the resulting institutional facts are distinctly queer. Second, we need to vindicate these beliefs about action and responsibility. I suggest that practices of responsibility can be thought of as a fundamental, practical realization of *critique*, whether one adopts a Kantian or any other plausible critical standard for actions. In sum, I propose an intersubjective analysis of Kant's intelligible facts, where 'intelligible' equals 'institutional' plus 'normatively justified'.

1. Kant on property and Searle on institutional facts

There is a clear analogy between claims about action and responsibility and property claims. Both Arthur Ripstein and Tamar Schapiro have already suggested that since our acts are *ours*, in some sense that is intelligible rather than empirical, Kant's analysis of property as an intelligible relation ought to be informative for our thinking about action and responsibility.[6]

The force of Kant's analysis is to emphasize that property relations are first of all relations between persons, and not – as Locke's well-known 'labour' account so temptingly suggests – relations between a person and a thing. Locke's account is empiricist and individualistic. It is based on facts about what a given person has caused through her labour; it denies that facts about others play a constitutive role in founding rights to property. Kant's critique is devastating. He refers to 'the tacit prevalent deception of personifying things and of thinking of a right to things as being a right *directly* against them, as if someone could . . . put things under an obligation to serve him and no one else' (*MS* 6: 269). Given that property is meant to represent a relation between a person and a thing that persists even when the thing is not in a person's hand, he argues that an extravagant metaphysics must enter the scene: 'a *guardian spirit* accompan[ies] the thing, always pointing me out to whoever else wanted to take possession of it' (*MS* 6: 260).

Kant, by contrast, does not need very much metaphysics if he is to answer the puzzles that arise on Locke's account. I am thinking, among other things, of three difficulties that parallel those I mentioned in my introduction for any account of responsibility that rests on psychological or causal facts: (1) the slide from 'is' to 'ought' – between the fact of labouring on an object and a supposed right over it; (2) the fact that I may well own something without having done anything at all; (3) the fact that I continue to own something even where there is no empirical connection between me and the object, despite the fact that the world contains no such thing as 'guardian spirits' – nor even (for any Kantian, *contradictio in adjecto*) 'natural rights' to property.

We can see Kant's intelligible account of property as having two sides to it – as I am calling them, the institutional and the normative. The normative side is well-known. Kant points out that human beings rely on means to pursue their ends, beyond their own bodies. Only a system of property rights ensures that our use of such means is compatible with a like freedom for others.[7] So too – to be even briefer – a legislative and coercive state is needed to specify, adjudicate and enforce specific property rights, norms of exchange, and so forth.[8] When I claim that property has an *institutional* as well as a normative status, it would be natural to think of the state as the relevant institution. But there is no role for the state in specifying or adjudicating moral responsibility, so this would be rather embarrassing for the parallel I wish to develop. Instead, I use 'institution' more abstractly, in the sociological sense by which promising or dating are institutions. This use corresponds to John Searle's account of 'institutional facts' in *The Construction of Social Reality*.

On Searle's account, an institutional fact obtains just in virtue of the fact that we all believe it to be so. Sounds and symbols mean what they do because we regard them as having this meaning: thus norms of spoken and written language. Certain pieces of paper have monetary value, just because everyone in a certain jurisdiction regards them as having this value: thus norms of money and exchange. We have willed these things into being; if our shared knowledge of them were to evaporate so too would the things themselves. (There might be noises but not meanings, bits of paper but not money.) Differently put: our practice enacts certain norms, by which certain entities are made to *count* for something beyond their empirical qualities. It is a fact – an intrinsically normative fact, yet one plainer than most empirical facts – that such and such noises have a certain meaning, and that you ought to understand this meaning. It is a fact as plain as the nose on your face that the owner of a ten-pound note has a right to buy goods to that value. These facts *empower* and *entitle* people in myriad ways.[9]

Something similar is true of property. My flat is mine, whether or not I am in it, just because (nearly) all of us accept that flats are owned and lots of people know that this particular flat is owned by me. Evidently property rights do not rest merely on our shared belief that people may own things, since (as Kant reminds us) authoritative institutions also play an important role. For my purposes, however, the important point is that in most everyday contexts, it is the sheer fact of shared belief that establishes my ownership as a fact. Even when I am absent, even when workmen are 'mixing their labour' with it, my flat belongs to me more surely than the apple I have just picked up at random off the ground. We may even say that here, the empirical is less real than the intelligible. The intelligible reality obtains because most people will not interfere, and some people will positively help me to make use of the flat, precisely because they believe it to be mine. Other people's beliefs provide no such guarantee in the case of the apple.

There is therefore nothing metaphysically mysterious about the category of the 'intelligible' as it applies to property, even though Kant explicitly contrasts this with 'empirical' possession. An object is mine because we all believe this to be the case. This 'belief' is above all practical in nature: everyone else behaves as if my possessions were not theirs; should anyone fail to do so, we will challenge his behaviour. (This is still in a certain sense an empirical fact, of course; but it is of a peculiar and very complex sort, depending as it does on our collective beliefs.)[10] This institutional fact is normatively warranted by the claim that human coexistence and cooperation requires the institution of property, and by the further judgement that my ownership is in accordance with the norms of property we have instituted. I will suggest that we can think about human action in a parallel way.

2. Two senses of action

It is easy to object to the idea that action – as opposed, perhaps, to ideas of moral responsibility – is an intrinsically normative category. Animals act: birds of prey hunt, sheep herd together, and so on. Although the human being is obviously a distinctive sort of animal, it is not clear that much of our activity is so different to that of other animals. Similarly, when we use the metaphor of ownership to connect actor and deed, it is not obvious that this involves any normative commitments. Since we readily identify an animal with 'its' actions, the language of ownership hardly contradicts a straightforward, empirical picture of the relation between an agent and its deeds.

Here, I follow Tamar Schapiro in distinguishing two senses of action.[11] This distinction corresponds to the two senses of ownership just discussed: the *empirical*, whereby the bird in my hand is mine (even though I poached it, say), and the *intelligible*, whereby the birds in the bush are mine (since I own the estate, say). In applying this distinction to action, Schapiro distinguishes the empirical 'production' of actions from the normative relation of *authorship*. I quote at length her account of these two relations:

> An action can be 'mine' in either an empirical or a normative sense . . . the idea is that I can either cause my actions, or I can claim representation by them . . . Production is a causal relation which holds between a subject and an action, where both are construed empirically. Insofar as an action is my production, I am the locus of certain psychological processes . . . through which the action is produced as an effect. *By contrast, authorship is a normative relation which holds among a plurality of subjects with respect to a certain action.* To author an action is to identify myself with it, in the sense of claiming representation by it[12] and taking responsibility for it. One who identifies herself with an action in this sense thereby makes a claim on others to take the action to be representative of her, and to hold her responsible for it. Hence the 'I' that stands behind an authored action is not in the first instance a locus of psychological processes, but rather a source of normatively binding interpersonal claims.[13]

Action as production is exhibited by all agents, animal or human. In this case, actions 'belong' to agents in the empirical sense that they perform them. Even 'action as production' is susceptible to normative evaluation, in the sense that it might fulfil or fail some particular criterion of success. We can make this sort of evaluation about the conduct of animals, infants or even the insane. However, this is not enough to generate claims of responsibility.

For many philosophers of responsibility, it has been plausible to trace the normative significance of the act-agent relation to the nature of the individual agent who performs a deed. This means turning to the peculiar complexity of sane, adult human beings. We might refer to this line of thought as 'action as very complex production'. On such accounts the act-actor relation retains a factual, perhaps psychological or possibly even metaphysical basis – rather as Locke wanted to trace our possession of objects to our labour upon them, or as Plato pictured the soul as tarnished by a person's misdeeds and cleansed by punishment.

To view action in terms of authorship is to take a distinct perspective. As in Kant's account of property, we look beyond the individual agent and take explicit account of relations between persons. The person is the author of her action, not because of psychological or metaphysical facts about her, but because others regard her as such. That is, authorship represents a *status* recognized by others (and, in most cases, also by the self). A person is not only, as science tells us, a particularly complex bundle of causal connections, nor only, as our experience of both animals and human beings testifies, inclined to behave in some ways rather than others. Instead, we believe – and more importantly, we enact the belief – that each person is the author of her deeds.

This is likely to sound very odd. We naturally think of authorship as a fact about a person. He is the author of the book, she did that, and so forth. To common sense, these are obviously *not* facts about other people. They look like simple empirical facts, about who 'produced' what. It is also perplexing from the point of view of responsibility, because authorship seems to be about someone's status as the independent source of her action. Yet judgements of responsibility show no respect for a person's 'independence' as such – no more, indeed, than facts about causality distinguish a person as 'first cause.' Judgements of responsibility involve demands for mutual accountability. How, then, might a person's authorship also be a fact about other people? And how might authorship relate to responsibility?

3. Authorship and responsibility

I already cited Schapiro's claim: 'The "I" that stands behind an authored action is . . . a source of normatively binding interpersonal claims'.[14] One way of interpreting this is to think of that 'I' as having moral status or intrinsic worth, and so deserving respect. We all know that Kantian story. But we might give the claim another interpretation. People who are authors of their actions *make* 'normatively binding interpersonal claims' on one another. They 'can' do so, because they are participants in an institution by which they authorize one another to do so. Let me try to elucidate this rather compressed set of claims.

To see someone as the author of her action is (by definition) not simply to see her as a causal nexus in a chain of events. This would tell us nothing about how we *should* respond to her. To see someone as the author of a deed is, instead, to see her as claiming an *entitlement* to act in that way.[15] Although this may sound surprising, it is a corollary of the idea that the act represents an exercise of *her authority* to decide how she should act.

We might think of this authority as a form of freedom. It emerges where others are prepared to join with a person in agreeing that their interaction should be governed by norms of entitlement and obligation. In this case, the ability to make claims on others is not a psychological or causal fact about the person, but rather an institutional – or even intelligible – capacity. Kant's conviction that each person is free *qua* intelligible entity has perplexed his readers for generations, and discouraged many more from even engaging with his account. His idea is made more puzzling – yet also more intriguing to anyone with broadly naturalistic commitments – by the fact that this is *not* the capacity for contra-causal freedom of some incompatibilists. As Kant insists, morality 'exist[s] in the sensible world but without infringing on its laws'.[16] But what sort of freedom is it, that does not infringe on natural causality?

As both Searle and Schapiro stress, institutions call new capacities into being. Schapiro offers the analogy of a judge.[17] This role is evidently an institutional status; it would collapse if we ceased to take legal institutions seriously. Where people do believe in the institution of law, the person who becomes a judge thereby acquires – as if by magic, yet with no metaphysical mystery – a new ability: to decide cases. At the same time, she acquires a very particular set of institutional obligations, not least as to how she should deliberate and pronounce on those cases. This is no matter of her individual abilities. However highly trained (for example), she is not a judge unless other people recognize her as one. Once they do, however, there is no doubting her ability: it is, so to speak, as real as anything. In terms of my operative formula, '"intelligible" equals "institutional" plus "normatively justified"': assuming that we were morally justified in instituting such a legal order, and that the judge were properly appointed by its norms, her ability would be not merely an *institutional* fact, but also an *intelligible* one.

The idea, then, is that an institution can create an ability by investing a person with an authority: in our case, authorship of one's actions, where actions are understood as claims to a normative entitlement so to act. If this were so, action-as-authorship would represent a fundamental human institution, one with a more basic status than almost every institution we might think of. (Much more basic than basketball, more basic than money or property, as basic as language.) By our shared belief – or rather, our fundamental assumption – that people are the authors of actions that speak to the norms we will share, we call into being intelligible abilities and statuses where before there were only mere, sheer empirical facts. We do this, moreover, without 'infringing' on the laws of the 'sensible world'.

This authority – 'to make normatively binding interpersonal claims' – is obviously not a fact about the person in so far as we consider her empirically, no matter how complex her psychology or causal powers. Nor, on a broadly naturalistic understanding, can it be a metaphysical fact about her as a particular sort of being. Instead, it is a fact that we institute. Our shared belief that a person belongs among us as one whose conduct contributes to shared norms of entitlement and obligation affords her the status of author. We thereby grant her all sorts of freedoms and opportunities. Some of these freedoms are empirical (we have not imprisoned her, we have not fenced off such and such land, and so on). But most of them are institutional. Such freedoms arise when we can depend on others acting in particular ways: thus freedoms from interference, or to cooperate. (We often call such freedoms *rights* – with nothing 'natural' about them at all.) These freedoms come about precisely because of the entitlement that we have accorded someone: to exercise her initiative amongst us, to count on our acting and responding in certain ways. Just as a property right is not primarily a relation between a person and a thing, so too is this a fact about a person's relations to everyone else. It is a claim upon others that obtains its reality from their ongoing consent, that is, their continued belief that the person is so entitled.

To see the internal connection between action as authorship and claims of responsibility, we need only observe that a wrongful action is equally an exercise of a person's authorship. To say that a person has authority to act on her own behalf is to say that she may make corresponding claims on others to permit her to act in such ways or to facilitate her doing so. Our entitlement to challenge wrongdoing is therefore intrinsic to action as authorship. Authorship depends on authority. This authority is the freedom – or normative power – to make claims on others. Such authority arises because others authorize the person as one among others who may make 'normatively binding interpersonal claims'. Where those claims become *impositions* – illegitimate exercises of authority, claims to entitlements that we are not prepared to grant – there can be no question that we may countermand the authority that we granted in the first place.

To the eyes of empiricist and individualistic common sense, 'authorship' looks like a set of psychological or metaphysical facts concerning individual agency. In fact, it is granted by others. Our capacity to act 'independently' is an *intelligible fact* that emerges from our mutual dependence, from our will to live together on shared terms. Hence the terms on which we may exercise that independence – or autonomy, if you like – are necessarily set by others. 'Intelligible' – that is, at once institutional and normatively justified. Institutional because, as I have said, it is distributed across a plurality of persons whose mutual recognition is constitutive of each person's agency qua authorship. But also normatively justified: morally speaking, we have no choice but to recognize self and others as authors of their actions.

Before turning to that second aspect, let me re-emphasize that the intelligible reality is – if I may be permitted to speak of degrees of reality – much more real than the empirical one, at least so long as decent social relations are intact. Empirically speaking, deeds are 'temporary and perishing'. Views based on 'action as production' must struggle to locate any reliable, ongoing empirical connection between act and actor. We might try to trace a chain of (empirical) effects from the action that provides a continuing tie to the actor; or we might argue that the actor is connected to the action by virtue of lasting psychological or character traits revealed by the action.[18] But neither option is very plausible. The first makes for a terribly equivocal account, because every effect can be traced to a plethora of causes, most of which had nothing to do with any particular doer and many of which result from other people's (moralized) perceptions of, and responses to, the deed in question. The second is problematic because we may not recall our deeds or we may have a misplaced sense of their moral import. Likewise, our deeds may not reflect our character (certainly many of their effects do not),[19] while the stability of character traits is itself open to doubt.

On the 'action as authorship' view, by contrast, deeds endure because the act-actor relation is an intersubjective reality – intelligible rather than empirical. So deeds acquire a certain *timeless* quality, so that they subsist beyond any physical effects they may have and transcend the actor's own subjective sense of them. Because we believe that each person should be identified in terms of his deeds, past deeds obtain an enduring existence in people's minds, which gives them a peculiar *tenacity*: despite their naturally fleeting quality, they do not disappear and cannot be destroyed. However, this also gives past deeds a peculiar sort of *changeability*. Other people may release us from our deeds – by forgiveness or acceptance of reparation, perhaps by the infliction of punishment. In every decent society, people weave a stable fabric of knowledge about who did what and who is responsible for what, so that we do indeed become the *authors* of our actions. Equally, they create ways in which people may, by taking responsibility for their past deeds, also *disown* them by disavowing the entitlements they had appeared to claim.

4. From the institutional to the normatively justified

I have briefly sketched responsible action as an institutional reality: one that is created by our shared belief that people are the authors of their actions and thereby – by virtue of the process of mutual authorization involved – have obligations to act wisely and well. But even if people everywhere were to share such a belief, the 'mere fact' of shared beliefs or practices hardly suffices for the Kantian category of an intelligible fact. To see facts about agency and responsibility as *constructed* seems to imply their contingency.

What sort of argument might show the moral necessity of this institution?

One sort of strategy has been suggested by Christine Korsgaard and Arthur Ripstein.[20] They argue that claims of responsibility allow us to relate to one another on an equal and reciprocal basis. I will not say anything about that large project here. Instead, I would like to point to another way of looking at the matter, which is more practical in spirit and which has (perhaps for this reason) escaped philosophers' attention. I suggest that, under conditions of relative freedom and equality, we can see practices of responsibility as the practical manifestation of *critique*. As such, they actually contain the resources for their own vindication.

Practices of responsibility attribution are ubiquitous, in that no social order operates without signals and sanctions for disapproved conduct. Naturally, this is not to say that everyone is equally exposed to those practices, or is granted an equal right to engage in them. We can hardly assume that the norms instituted by a society are always fair or otherwise justified. A society may have an elite that is able to act with impunity, or an underclass that is denied possibilities to act on its own behalf, including rights of protest at the treatment it receives. We are also familiar with schemas for attributing responsibility that seem arbitrary or unjust in the way in which they link agents with outcomes – for instance, if they deny the relevance of a person's intentions. The injustice of such arrangements is a truth we hold (albeit with poor grounds for our trust) to be self-evident.

Consider, however, happier conditions of relative freedom and equality. In such circumstances, everyone is able to respond to social practices and to individual actions – and to the responses that others engage in. Under these conditions, my suggestion is that our holding one another responsible exposes people's thought and conduct – the entitlements that we interpret them to be claiming – to ongoing critique. To see this, we may recall, briefly and approximately, some of the criteria that philosophers have proposed for deciding whether a norm or practice is justified: (1) whether it conduces to human welfare or prevents suffering; (2) whether it would or could be adopted by all; (3) whether it is, or would be, agreed on by people under conditions of non-domination.[21] In each case, practices of responsibility attribution must be essential to our realizing the proposed criterion.

For how do we know whether actions or omissions (1) conduce to human welfare or prevent suffering? We attend to those who are affected by them. What form does our voice naturally take, when our welfare is damaged or we are made to suffer? Complaint, to be sure; but so far as we trace the damage to human hand – or to the failure of human hand to intervene – it is the voice of resentment, accusation, blame. Such protests are accompanied, of course, by the various forms of pressure that lie within our power, which we apply to those we hold culpable. More abstractly, we hold people responsible; we contest the normative basis of their action or failure to act. Or (2): how do we learn whether a norm can be shared? Partly, perhaps, by asking how we would feel if someone treated us in a particular way, or by the thought experiment of universalization. But given that our thought and foresight are so often faulty, given that others have perspectives on the world that are distinct from our own, given that others have rights to speak for themselves – given all these, we also depend on the responses of others. We find out when we get it wrong, to the extent that others hold us responsible. Or again, (3): how do we know what people would agree to if they were trying to choose together, as equals? It hardly needs saying: we try to ensure that they have the freedom to protest and to assert their rights, while taking account of the fact that their claims are not incorrigible.

In other words, practices of responsibility represent the critique of individual actions and social practices: not as a matter of abstract debate, but as a matter of everyday social intercourse. To the extent that these practices are mutual, they enable people to voice their complaints against others, without dominating those others in their turn. These objections take practical form: not just abstract reasoning, nor even complaint, but all the forms of protest and pressure involved in practices of responsibility. Blame, demands for recompense and decisions about the terms on which we will cooperate with others – these naturally pass between people under conditions of non-domination. So too, all the mechanisms by which we endorse and promote activity we approve of. Among the actions and norms that we respond to in these ways are, of course, practices of responsibility themselves: we hold people responsible for how they respond to others' actions.

Strawson claimed that our commitment to practices of responsibility 'is part of the general framework of human life, not something that can come up for review as particular cases can come up for review within this general framework'.[22] In pointing out the connection between these practices and some plausible criteria of critique, I am suggesting a different view. The institution of responsibility is *continually* up for review – and continually vindicated by our practices. Every time we go along with the norms of an institution, we help to maintain its existence. Every time we respect other people's property, we help to stabilise that institution; every time we use language we re-establish its meanings. This is because an institution *just is* people's settled tendency to act and think in certain ways, aware that others are likely to do the same. Just so: every time we respond to one another as entitled to act in particular ways, or every time we dispute such an entitlement, we reinvigorate the institution of action as authorship. In a certain sense, we do not need to do this: it is possible to turn the other cheek (but is it possible to signal no reproach at all?); to treat some as 'above (or below) the law'; or to deny persons – *authors* – a fair opportunity to define the nature of their actions. Nevertheless, to the extent that people continue to recur to practices of responsibility under conditions of relative equality, they are practices that withstand the most practical form that critique can take.

5. Conclusion

Intelligible facts obtain just to the extent that a plurality of persons interprets its interactions in a particular way. These facts have the peculiar, self-reflexive quality of being instituted by our shared belief in them. Because their reality is a matter of shared belief, rather than brute or empirical fact, these facts have a different sort of stability. Up to a point, they are immune to the causal processes that govern normal empirical facts. But they also have a different sort of changeability: one that obtains by virtue of our being able to persuade one another that we should interpret our action and experience in different terms. Hence institutional facts are open to change by *critique*. To the extent that they withstand that critique, however, they gain another peculiar quality: the normative warrant that is the second component of an intelligible fact. Their institutionalization in our shared beliefs represents the actual construction, the living realization of all normative phenomena – property, language, responsibility and so on.

There is no doubt that responsibility – on this account as any other – depends upon many complicated capacities on the part of the individuals who interact with one another. The 'naturalism' of this account consists, however, in its *not* requiring us to think of people as possessing capacities that they do not in fact manifest. We need not think of the wrongdoer as undetermined in his noumenal causality – whatever that might mean. Nor need we think of him as capable of attaining moral truth independently of others' guidance and correction, if he is to be responsible for his actions. Kant thought morality required both, and that he was therefore entitled to postulate them. On a naturalistic worldview, both would be too surprising by half. Instead, we need only suppose that the wrongdoer broke an important norm, probably to the cost of others, and that his authority to act extends only so far as he does not transgress upon the entitlements of others.

Nonetheless, human interaction hides something almost as surprising as any inflationary metaphysics of the self – nearly as surprising, too, as the many inflationary accounts of individual capacities for moral reasoning that often replace such metaphysics in contemporary ethics. This is the fundamental condition of our moral agency, something that we institute together without giving the matter a second thought. I have suggested that responsible agency should be understood in terms of the intelligible order that emerges out of the interaction of a plurality of persons on mutual terms. This order is a domain of status relations: where people *count* as the authors of their actions; where we grant one another the authority to judge and enact the norms we ought to share; where we dispute the initiative of anyone who acts on – and hence claims authority to act on – faulty moral standards. We thereby create a domain of intelligible facts – 'queer' facts that slide between 'is' and 'ought', that are not revealed through empirical investigation alone, and that have the timeless quality which 'temporary and perishing' deeds so conspicuously lack.[23]

Notes

1 Arthur W. H. Adkins, *Merit and Responsibility* (Oxford: Clarendon Press, 1960), p. 2.

2 David Hume, *A Treatise of Human Nature*, ed. D. F. Norton and M. J. Norton (Oxford: Oxford University Press, 2000 [1740]): Book II, Part III §II.

3 *KpV* 5: 99; *KrV* A551ff.; cp. Allison 1990: chs 2 §4, 7 §2.

4 Peter F. Strawson, 'Freedom and resentment', *Proceedings of the British Academy*, 48 (1962), 1–25, reprinted in G. Watson (ed.), *Free Will* (Oxford: Oxford University Press, 1982).

5 John Searle, *The Construction of Social Reality* (New York: Free Press, 1995).

6 Arthur Ripstein, *Equality, Responsibility and the Law* (Cambridge: Cambridge University Press, 1999); Tamar Schapiro, 'Childhood and personhood', *Arizona Law Review*, 45/3 (2003), 575–94.

7 This justification refers to the practice as a whole. There is, of course, another story to be told about the justification of particular property claims.

8 I am being brutally brief: for some more detail, see Kenneth Westphal, 'A Kantian justification of possession', in M. Timmons (ed.), *Kant's Metaphysics of Morals: Interpretative Essays* (New York: Oxford University Press, 2002).

9 Searle, *The Construction of Social Reality*, p. 100.

10 I am drawing deliberately simple contrasts between 'empirical', 'institutional' and 'intelligible' facts. Just as one might say (with Searle) that institutional facts are a special subclass of empirical facts, one might also argue that intelligible facts represent a further, specific subclass of these. This would be true if normative claims were ultimately reducible to empirical facts, as more ambitious versions of naturalism in meta-ethics claim.

11 Schapiro, 'Childhood and personhood'; 'What is a child?', *Ethics*, 109 (1999), 715–38; 'Three conceptions of action in moral theory', *Noûs*, 35/1 (2001), 93–117.

12 Note that this claim to representation or identity must be intelligible rather than empirical, as we can see by recalling all the ways in which a person may *fail* to identify with her deed, or *mis*represent it.

13 'Childhood and personhood', 586.

14 Ibid.

15 Cp. the communicative analysis of action in Garrath Williams, 'Judges in our own case: Kantian legislation and responsibility attribution', *Politics and Ethics Review*, 3/1 (2007), 8–23.

16 *KpV* 5: 43.

17 Schapiro, 'Three concepts of action', 107ff.

18 Thus Humean accounts of responsibility such as Nicola Lacey, *State Punishment* (London: Routledge,1988) and Paul Russell, *Freedom and*

Moral Sentiment: Hume's Way of Naturalizing Responsibility (New York: Oxford University Press, 1995).

19 For a distinguished attempt to overcome this difficulty, see George Sher, *In Praise of Blame* (Oxford: Oxford University Press, 2006).

20 Christine Korsgaard, 'Creating the Kingdom of Ends', in *Creating the Kingdom of Ends* (Cambridge: Cambridge University Press, 1996); Ripstein, *Equality, Responsibility and the Law.*

21 That is, the criteria of (1) utilitarianism, (2) the golden rule and Kantian universalism and (3) discourse ethics or contractarianism.

22 Strawson, 'Freedom and resentment', 70.

23 For comments on versions of this paper, my thanks to participants in a workshop on 'Politics and Metaphysics in Kant', organized by Sorin Baiasu and Howard Williams (Pisa, September 2007), to colleagues in the Department of Philosophy, Lancaster University, and to Tamar Schapiro and Tatiana Patrone.

References

Adkins, A. W. H. *Merit and Responsibility* (Oxford: Clarendon Press, 1960).

Allison, H., *Kant's Theory of Freedom* (Cambridge: Cambridge University Press, 1990).

Hume, D., *A Treatise of Human Nature*, ed. D. F. Norton and M. J. Norton (Oxford: Oxford University Press, 2000 [1740]).

Kant, I., *Practical Philosophy*, ed. and trans. M. J. Gregor (Cambridge: Cambridge University Press, 1996).

——, *Critique of Pure Reason*, trans. P. Guyer and A. Wood (Cambridge: Cambridge University Press, 1998).

Korsgaard, C., 'Creating the Kingdom of Ends', in *Creating the Kingdom of Ends* (Cambridge: Cambridge University Press, 1996).

Lacey, N., *State Punishment* (London: Routledge, 1988).

Ripstein, A., *Equality, Responsibility and the Law* (Cambridge: Cambridge University Press, 1999).

——, 'Justice and Responsibility', *Canadian Journal of Law and Jurisprudence*, 17/2 (2004), 361–86.

Russell, P., *Freedom and Moral Sentiment: Hume's Way of Naturalizing Responsibility* (New York: Oxford University Press, 1995).

Schapiro, T., 'What is a child?', *Ethics*, 109 (1999), 715–38.

——, 'Three conceptions of action in moral theory', *Noûs*, 35/1 (2001), 93–117.

——, 'Childhood and personhood', *Arizona Law Review*, 45/3 (2003), 575–94.

Searle, J., *The Construction of Social Reality* (New York: Free Press, 1995).

Sher, G., *In Praise of Blame* (Oxford: Oxford University Press, 2006).

Strawson, P. F., 'Freedom and resentment', *Proceedings of the British Academy*, 48 (1962), 1–25, reprinted in G. Watson (ed.), *Free Will* (Oxford: Oxford University Press, 1982).

Westphal, K., 'A Kantian justification of possession', in M. Timmons (ed.), *Kant's Metaphysics of Morals: Interpretative Essays* (New York: Oxford University Press, 2002).

Williams, G., 'Judges in our own case: Kantian legislation and responsibility attribution', *Politics and Ethics Review*, 3/1 (2007), 8–23.

11 • Metaphysical and not just Political

Howard Williams

1. Introduction: Rawls's reservations about metaphysics

This chapter examines Kant's method in political philosophy. It looks closely at the understanding of metaphysics the method presupposes and the use to which a legitimate metaphysics is put in Kant. The role of a priori principles in political philosophy will accordingly be considered and I will seek to express Kant's use of these terms in a contemporary idiom accessible to philosophers in the twenty-first century. Although there will be some comparison with the ideas of Rawls and Habermas, the emphasis will be primarily upon reappraising Kant's critical approach to political theory. I illustrate this approach with reference to Kant's account of property, his theory of the state and his evaluation of war. Although political leaders and their subjects may not reflect a great deal on metaphysics from a Kantian perspective, the effective use of their respective positions depends on a general acceptance of certain key metaphysical principles. I argue that modern representative political leaders and the citizens of their states are the carriers and the embodiment of a critically delimited metaphysics.

Kant's modest approval for and use of metaphysics has to be contrasted with the reservations John Rawls shows about its use in ethics and political philosophy. In bringing metaphysics into political philosophy, he argues, the aims of that inquiry will be vitiated. Today's political philosopher cannot afford to be a metaphysician as well:

> The religious doctrines that in previous centuries were the professed basis of society have given way to principles of constitutional government that all citizens, whatever their religious views, can endorse. Comprehensive philosophical and moral doctrines likewise cannot be endorsed by citizens generally, and they also no longer can, if they ever could, serve as the professed basis of society.[1]

Here it seems that what is meant by 'comprehensive philosophical and moral doctrines' overlaps with metaphysics. Metaphysics, which we are 'wont to use in debating fundamental political issues, should give way in public life'. It is inappropriate for Rawls to seek to ground political cooperation in a unified view of knowledge, which is morality of an unrestricted metaphysical variety. What is needed instead is 'a political conception the principles and values of which all citizens can endorse'. Metaphysics cannot be sufficiently reformed to meet the needs of the current age. In the political arena metaphysics must be eschewed altogether. The principles under which we unite must banish all trace of comprehensive inquiries. 'That political conception is to be, so to speak, political and not metaphysical'.[2] According to Idil Boran, Rawls shows how moral and political philosophy can be done without metaphysics: for Rawls, 'normative moral and political philosophy can be genuinely workable if and only if metaphysical questions are avoided'.[3]

At one level the contemporary Rawls-inspired debate about metaphysics and politics is simply about the application of names. In so far as Kant might like to call his approach to politics metaphysical and Rawls does not, we might simply be looking at a dispute about how one or other philosopher prefers to describe his method. Arguably both Rawls and Kant are engaged in the same kind of activity in spelling out the basic concepts of their political philosophies, but Rawls – for reasons he gives when talking about his 'Kantian constructivism' – does not want to use the term 'metaphysics' for his procedure. From a Kantian perspective we can respect and adhere to the terms that Rawls himself wants to deploy when describing the outlook developed in *A Theory of Justice* and *Political Liberalism*, but we might still like to look upon it as 'metaphysical'. This is one amicable way of resolving the conflict between Rawls and Kant: Kant adheres to an old-fashioned term for philosophical reflection on justice, while Rawls wants to demarcate a sphere of distinctively political philosophical reflection on justice by distancing his approach from metaphysics.

However, it might plausibly be claimed that there is something deeper afoot here that a mere dispute about names. Put more polemically, it could be argued that Rawlsians want to use a different name (or abandon the use of the term 'metaphysics') because they wish to distinguish their procedure from one that they think to be indefensible and illegitimate. In this respect Hegel represents perhaps the paradigm of the philosopher-metaphysician. In his *Lectures on the History of Moral Philosophy* Rawls determines to 'say almost nothing about' Hegel's metaphysics, suggesting controversially that 'most of his moral and political philosophy can stand on its own'. For Rawls, however, Hegel is the 'true metaphysician' in that 'he believes that *reality is fully intelligible* – which is the thesis of absolute idealism – and so it must answer to the ideas and concepts of a reasonable and coherent categorical system'.[4] Rawls is fully aware that there is a distinct difference between Kant's transcendental idealism and Hegel's absolute idealism; but there seems to be the strong implication that Kant does not escape entirely the objection that he, like Hegel, is in some respects aiming to make reality fully intelligible. In his Kantian constructivism Rawls sees himself as presupposing less than Kant (he presents himself as a Kantian minus Kant's *comprehensive doctrine*), and suggests that Kant brings too much baggage to the philosophical discussion of politics. Here I think there are grounds for dissent, and there is worth in investigating Kant's metaphysical procedure to see whether or not the comprehensive doctrine of which his metaphysical method is part does damage his account of politics.

Kant's metaphysical baggage is the critical metaphysics outlined in the *Critique of Pure Reason*. I believe that Kant's thinking on politics derives a great deal that is positive from the approach set out in the *Critique*. And indeed there are elements of Kant's argument in this work that have met with strong approval from twentieth-century philosophers who have not been of a metaphysical bent. As Karl Ameriks puts it, 'in general, mainline twentieth-century philosophers have tended to praise rather than lament Kant's attack on transcendent metaphysics and to endorse a relatively modest "descriptive version" of his immanent metaphysics of experience'.[5] When Kant's view of what is legitimate in metaphysics is compared with the original project as set out by Aristotle we see a remarkable lessening of ambition. Indeed, a great deal of what is presented in the *Critique* is destructive of traditional metaphysics. For example the section on the Antimonies attempts to undermine many of the key debates about final causes. Kant presents it as an objective of the work thoroughly to curb comprehensive metaphysical speculation. For Kant there is no ultimate substance towards which a critical metaphysics can reach. Indeed, we cannot go beyond appearances to final essences.

The critical metaphysics of Kant shows a deep respect towards the empirical world. Our knowledge cannot extend beyond what appears to our senses. If so much of the programme of traditional metaphysics is taken away by the critical philosophy, what is left for the new metaphysics to contribute? Reason in its practical capacity (something which Rawls himself exploits in his constructivism as presented in *Political Liberalism*) is vindicated: 'Kant distinguishes two fundamental uses of reason, practical and theoretical (or "speculative"), and it can never be emphasized enough how often he stresses that our reason can establish practically all the important claims it *cannot* establish theoretically'.[6] Because practical philosophy is concerned with our inner mental condition – our maxims, intentions, aims and objectives and their ordering – we can reflect upon these elements comprehensively and seek to draw them into systematic unity. Practical philosophy represents the positive outcome of the critical metaphysics of Kant, and it is to that sphere Kant's political philosophy belongs.

2. The metaphysics of right

One of Kant's major concerns in his political philosophy is to demonstrate how metaphysics impinges on politics and how this important connection can be plausibly presented and understood. He sees that he needs to get over the commonly held idea that 'when one goes from school into the world one becomes aware that one has been pursuing empty ideals and philosophic dreams' (*TP* 8: 277). He regards this as a general problem of trying to distinguish theory from practice in order to discriminate in favour of a theoretically impoverished or deprived practice. The man of the world sees himself as already sufficiently well informed about the nature and aims of human life and believes that social life is simply a matter of determining the best means of achieving self-evident aims. But in Kant's political theory the self-evident aims of the present (the man of the world) have always to be open to question. The man of the world goes by what is done, but what is done is not necessarily the best guide to what should be done. As well as this 'ignorant man' who 'declares that theory is unnecessary and dispensable in his supposed practice', there is also to be dealt with the so-called expert who believes the world is a very different place from that envisaged by the academic. And since the theory that should underlie politics is the metaphysics of right, Kant is very much aware that both the practical politician and the person in the street take the view that what 'sounds good in theory has no validity for practice' (*TP* 8: 277). This attitude has to be challenged. Philosophical reflection is essential in everyday life. Despite his reservations about past metaphysics no one should doubt Kant's commitment to a reformed, critical metaphysics in dealing with law and politics. At the beginning of the *Doctrine of Virtue* he stresses that 'a philosophy of any subject (a system of rational cognition from concepts) requires a system of pure rational concepts independent of any conditions of intuition, that is, metaphysics'. So 'no one will doubt that the pure doctrine of right needs metaphysical first principles' (*MS* 6: 375).

How then does Kant try to overcome this scepticism to show that metaphysics is central to the workings of social and political institutions? Arguably, he does so with a method of reasoning along the following lines. As with the pure moral philosophy, he begins with the reflections of the ordinary individual about our responsibilities to one another and our evaluations of others. Even the most matter-of-fact of individuals will acknowledge that the success of political arrangements depends upon those subject to them accepting obligations both to one another and to the prevailing authorities. In seeking to bring their own projects to fruition they will expect some cooperation from their fellow subjects and expect also that their fellow subjects will not seek wilfully to frustrate their ends. In seeking happiness, even the narrowest of hedonists is likely to accept that there are some duties to be observed towards others. In politics we are concerned primarily with duties of right, for which external lawgiving is possible, and not duties of virtue which concern our internal frame of mind and are not subject to external coercion. For Kant such duties and their corresponding rights are at the centre of political life. This gets us on the trail of metaphysics:

> In the doctrine of duties a human being can and should be represented in terms of his capacity for freedom, which is wholly supersensible, and so too merely in terms of his humanity, his personality independent of physical attributes (*homo noumenon*), as distinguished from the same subject represented as affected by physical attributes, *a human being* (*homo phaenomenon*). (*MS* 6: 239)

Although the doctrine of law does not require that our actions should demonstrate moral worth, it nonetheless relies on a core feature of pure morality or virtue, which is the assumption of freedom. Law, like ethics, assumes we can make our own choices so that our actions can be seen as the product of our will. From a legal perspective it is indeed a matter of indifference how we are motivated to do what is right, but it nonetheless attributes responsibility for an action to the individual: we are all culpable under the law.

3. Property

Kant puts property at the centre of social life. The existence of property is conclusive evidence of a settled social condition. He describes this condition, in keeping with Hobbes and Locke, as a civil society. In a civil society there are dependable social relations that are governed by juridical law. With juridical law a failure to comply on the part of an individual is met with legitimate punishment. But it is possible for property to come into existence with such a system not solely because an individual can be punished if there is a failure to comply with the rules. Property comes into existence also because of a common and shared attitude of mind amongst individuals as to what the institution of property implies and how the institution should be realized. Without individuals having in their heads the idea that an external object can be owned even though the person claiming possession is not physically present at the time and freely complying with this idea, property would not emerge. This is a metaphysical comprehension that seems indispensable to the ownership of property. Property ownership based solely on coercion is a plutocratic tyranny. In settled civil societies most property rights are observed without coercion coming into operation. The possibility of coercion remains, of course, in the background, but the main basis of the respect for property is to be found in the moral consent given to ownership through embracing the metaphysical concept of ownership. Realizing property in a civil society requires that we go beyond the empirical awareness of a need to have an object as our own to the metaphysical comprehension of mutual undertakings that bind us in a society. As Kant puts it, 'something external is mine if

I would be wronged by being disturbed in my use of it even though I am not in possession of it (not holding the object)'. This is a 'synthetic proposition about right' which requires practical reason for its realization (*MS* 6: 249).

Kant is clearly aware that the philosophical recognition that subjects have to accept a synthetic proposition about right is not in itself sufficient to bring property into being as a social institution. Certain historical, social and political arrangements also have to be in place to realize property as a fact. The sum of those external conditions Kant describes as a civil society. So indeed

> the rational title of acquisition can lie only in the idea of a general will united a priori (necessarily to be united), which is here tacitly assumed as a necessary condition (*conditio sine qua non*); for a unilateral will cannot put others under an obligation they would not otherwise have. But the condition where there is a united general will for legislation is the civil condition. Therefore something external can be originally acquired only in conformity with the idea of a civil condition, that is, with a view to it and to its being brought about, but prior to its realisation (for otherwise acquisition would be derived) something external can thus only be acquired provisionally. Peremptory acquisition takes place only in the civil condition.[7] (*MS* 6: 264)

The metaphysics of property ownership and the idea of a social contract associated with it are essential to the actual realization of property but, as can be seen, the metaphysics does not fully determine the reality of the institution. In a striking sense the historical creation of a civil society is the key outward step that gives the metaphysics its reality and substantive content.

The founding of a civil society is, however, not without its own metaphysical underpinning. Not every social formation that comes into existence can be described as a civil society or condition. A dictatorial regime can produce outward order and calm, and indeed certain slave societies can have institutions that resemble modern property relations. The touchstone by which a civil condition can be judged is neither stability nor order, but goes beyond appearances to the application of a metaphysical rule:

> The act by which a people form themselves into a state is the original contract. Properly speaking, the original contract is only the idea

> of this act, in terms of which alone we can think of the legitimacy of a state. In accordance with the original contract, everyone (*omnes et singuli*) within a people gives up their external freedom in order to take it up again immediately as a members of a commonwealth, that is, of a people considered as a state (*universi*). (*MS* 6: 315)

The acceptance by individuals of the metaphysical idea of a social contract is a prime underpinning for the existence of a civil society. However a civil society may have been historically realized – through conquest, war, the ascendancy of one class over others or by agreement amongst its members – the idea of a social contract uniting the will of all the parties is essential to its success. In accepting this intellectual framework for a civil society we should set to one side any romantic hankerings we might have for an unregulated natural condition, because giving into them would make the realization of external law impossible. You 'cannot say: the human being in a state has sacrificed a part of his innate outer freedom for a purpose, but, rather, he has relinquished entirely his wild, lawless freedom in order to find his freedom in general in a legal dependence, that is undiminished in a condition of right; since this dependence arises from his own lawgiving will' (*MS* 6: 315–6).

4. Contract

Kant's account of contract in the *Metaphysics of Morals* brings out very strongly the need for a metaphysical dimension to the philosophy of law and politics. As with property in general, ownership through contract cannot be grasped *without going beyond what we sense and observe*. We cannot deduce the right to have a service carried out for us that has been promised under contract merely from physical considerations. There are certain observed acts such as the meeting of two or more parties, the shaking of hands, the exchange of objects and the execution of certain tasks that we can watch; but none of these are sufficient legally to ground a contract. In comprehending contract as a legal form there is no alternative to going beyond the physical to a metaphysical explanation or derivation. Metaphysics, when it is used positively in his writings, is of course Kant's term for a critically limited metaphysics compatible with his own Copernican revolution in philosophy. Thus when he insists that property and contract right can only be founded metaphysically he is not invoking an extravagant metaphysics that involves theology, cosmology or a complex ontology. For him, metaphysics is a process of the self-examination and limitation of reason. 'Here reason has the sources of its knowledge in itself, not in objects and their observation (*Anschauung*)' (*Prol* 4: 366).

Contract right is conceivable only through human practical reason and its deployment. It is a form of social cooperation that presupposes the existence of civil society and so a system of laws: 'My possession of another's choice, in the sense of my capacity to determine it by my own choice to a certain deed in accordance with laws of freedom (what is externally mine or yours with respect to the causality of another), is a right (of which I can have several against the same person or against others); there is only a single sum (system) of laws, *contract right*, with which I can be in this sort of possession' (*MS* 6: 271). There is an empirical difficulty with contract, in that it is impossible for the undertaking to carry out a task and the carrying out of the task to take place at the very same moment. Thus from an empirical perspective there is always the possibility that a contract can be broken even after it is made. Understanding a contract solely at an empirical level makes any contract a very risky prospect, and if left at that level contract as a social form would never be realized. This is where metaphysics has to step in:

> Only a transcendental deduction of the concept of acquisition by contract can remove all these difficulties. It is true that in an external relation of *rights* my taking possession of another's choice (and his taking possession of mine in turn), as the basis for determining it to a deed, is first thought of empirically, by means of a declaration and counter-declaration of the choice of each in time; this is the sensible condition of taking possession, in which both acts required for establishing the right can only follow one upon another. Since, however, that relation (as a rightful relation) is purely intellectual, that possession is represented through the will which is a rational capacity for giving laws, as intelligible possession (*possessio noumenon*) in abstraction from those empirical conditions, as what is mine or yours. (*MS* 6: 272)

There is only one possible path to get from the desire to bind another person, and the desire to be bound by another person to complete a task, to the reliable completion of that task under a system of law, and this is through an imaginative reflective feat of rational minds. This is where critical metaphysics has a role to play: 'Here both acts, promise and acceptance, are represented not as following upon another but (as if it were *pactum re initum*) as proceeding from a single *common* will (this is expressed by the word simultaneously); and the object (*promissum*) is represented, by omitting empirical conditions, as acquired in accordance with a principle of pure practical reason' (*MS* 6: 273).

The key to the success of a contractual partnership is that the object or service being exchanged should be conceived as belonging to both parties for the period of time of its transfer. 'Transfer (*Die Translation*) is therefore an act in which an object belongs, for a moment, to both together, just as when a stone that has been thrown reaches the apex of its parabolic path it can be regarded as, just for a moment, simultaneously rising and falling, and so first passing from its rising motion to its falling' (*MS* 6: 274). This can occur only as an act of reflection within the minds of the contracting parties. *This is a metaphysical precondition of the success of the transaction.* Arguably, this act of reflection is not one that the participants see as engaging in metaphysics – indeed their minds are most likely to be set firmly on their purposes in initiating the exchange – yet without framing their transaction as involving at some point joint ownership of the good or service being exchanged, it could not occur. Contract is a social institution which is upheld by a framework of law, and as with other social institutions those taking advantage of it do not necessarily have to be clear on the preconditions that make the institution possible. Not everyone needs to know what underlying economic principles make the lending and borrowing practices of banks possible to be able to use them, but those rational principles have to be respected for the institution to function and be used. Similarly, although the individuals involved in a contract need not be fully aware of the underlying reasoning that enables the transaction to go ahead, they are nonetheless relying on that reasoning.

The metaphysics is thus essential although it may not occur to those experiencing or taking part in a contractual relationship. As Allen Wood puts it: 'Kant understood the term "meta-physics" (etymologically, "beyond nature") in epistemological terms. That is, for the purposes of metaphysics, "nature" is what is known through experience, and so "metaphysics" is a science demarcated not by the set of objects with which it deals but by the *a priori epistemic status* of its principles'.[8] There are certain knowledge conditions that have to pertain if human beings are to be able to participate in contractual relations; in other words, it is not possible for beings without intelligence and very specific types of understanding to enter into them. The crucial knowledge that makes contract possible may not be in the forefront of the minds of the parties but it has to be there. This knowledge can only be articulated fully in metaphysics of right. Analogously, very few individuals know in full the grammatical rules that make a language possible but they nevertheless need to observe them to be properly understood.

Three parties are essential to the working of a contract: 'a promisor, an acceptor, and guarantor' (*MS* 6: 284). The first two are the most prominently involved. The promisor is the party seeking the possible recipient of a good or service and the acceptor is the one seeking a good or service. The promisor needs the transaction and the recipient needs what is transacted. But they cannot go ahead on their own. For a contract to be realized in experience requires the existence of a third party who guarantees the transaction. The agreement that constitutes the contract transfers to the recipient only the promise of a good or service, and the promisor in return becomes obligated to make the transaction. Metaphysics cannot of itself deliver the contract. But what metaphysics can deduce is the possibility of contract. One of the conditions is the need for a means of coercion to ensure that the parties live up to their obligations.[9]

5. Metaphysics and peace

Metaphysics enters into a Kantian consideration of the international condition – the relations amongst states – just as much as it enters into the foundational structures of the nation itself. Property and contract cannot be seen in isolation as being possible only within the one state: they have to be possible amongst individuals in general who find themselves in a plurality of states. 'Hence, under the general concept of public right we are led to think not only of national law (*Staatsrecht*) but also of international law (*ius gentium*). Since the earth's surface is not unlimited but closed, the concepts of the national and international law lead inevitably to the idea of law of a state of nations (*ius gentium*) or cosmopolitan law (*ius cosmopoliticum*)' (*MS* 6: 311; translation amended). Relations amongst states, if they are to conform to law, presuppose not only the idea of internal law within states but also the idea of a wider law that covers a potential world state of states and the relations amongst all individuals on the planet under that law.

At the international level Kant's metaphysical approach takes a path which diverges from the one followed at the domestic level. At the domestic level the metaphysics underpins relations that have come into being (such as property and contract). The metaphysics provides a justification and interpretation of key existing social and political institutions. At the international level the metaphysics provides an underpinning for relationships and institutions (such as a federation of free states) that do not yet exist. However, Kant would argue that these future institutions are presupposed by the same metaphysics which establishes the internal sovereignty of states. Here, an approach that is metaphysical *and* political allows an original and inventive dimension to political philosophy. A strictly political approach would imply that we must always remain focused on the state dimension. Thus far in human history a (legally regulated) politics has occurred largely in the context of the territorially delimited state and the relations of such territorial states with each other. World politics of any kind has appeared as an exotic embellishment on the predominant traditional political structures. Arguably Kant's metaphysical approach, whilst recognizing the historically inherited state-dominated approach to politics, does establish the potential of going beyond it. In Kant's day, of course, much of this must have appeared as dreaming – the visions of a prophet. However, at the beginning of the twenty-first century, the trans-territorial nature of politics and legal relations is becoming apparent to all. His metaphysical conjectures have become the stuff of everyday politics. This is as it should be, for Kant wanted to avoid transcendent metaphysics of any kind. In talking about a state of states that would encompass all peoples he was not speaking of a state that could be expressly observed at that time (or that he simply intuited for the future) but one that was implicit in our relations as rational human beings living under laws of our own making, executed by our own representatives.

The grand metaphysical questions that perennially trouble the human mind – whether or not the universe has a beginning in time, whether freedom is possible, whether the universe is the product of one wise Creator – are unanswerable in theoretical terms. From Kant's critical perspective our knowledge does not extend to the resolution of these problems. However, in terms of our active lives as cohabitants of the one planet subject to the limitations imposed by nature and the presence of other humans like ourselves, the grand questions that metaphysics imposes upon us can be answered more affirmatively. The key metaphysical question imposed upon us by moral philosophy – 'what ought I to do?' – is one we can fruitfully address. Here we can legitimately seek finality. When we speculate about what motives we should adopt to act properly we are not speculating about the wholly unknowable. In so far as this metaphysical reasoning relates to our attitude and frame of mind in acting, this is something we can aspire to control and direct. As Sorin Baiasu aptly notes, 'one of the guiding claims Kant makes' is that 'action should not be regarded as an event in the sensible world, but as a determination of the will through a law without any other determining grounds and from the perspective of a *sui generis* concept of causality distinct from natural causality'.[10]

Metaphysics can provide a framework within which political leaders and citizens should act to accord with right. It also plays a future-oriented role for Kant in international politics by seeking to spell out how the leaders of states should conceive of their relations with each other being regulated and developed. In seeking to present a positive, peaceful view of relations amongst states governed by law, the philosopher may legitimately give a progressive account of history. In the first supplement of *Perpetual Peace* on 'the Guarantee of perpetual peace' Kant gives a sketch of human history that takes us beyond the facts and interprets what is given in a reflective manner. He presents the sketch in a provocatively speculative way, arguing that perpetual peace is guaranteed by 'nothing less than the great artist nature (*natura daedala rerum*)' (*ZeF* 8: 360). The status of the guarantee is not of a factual kind. There can be no assurance that history at any one point in time has, or will have, reached a plateau of success. In an empirical sense there is no 'end of history'. However, from the perspective of practice we are justified in proceeding in a way that assumes that in the large view there is a pattern to human events.

It is legitimate to present a progressive account of human history, in order to prevent despondency and fatalism from taking over our affections, in reflecting on the possibility of avoiding evil now. This is a constructivist view of history but it is one that must square with the facts. Human history cannot be portrayed without depicting the many failures and blemishes that form part of it. However, these atrocities and setbacks should be seen as part of larger picture of the gradual self-education of the human race. Progress occurs both because of and despite human action. Our unsociable sociability drives us both to outdo our fellow human beings and to crave their attention in recognizing our feats. This unsociable sociability is equally evident in relations within states and relations amongst states. Wars are the most striking evidence of the irascibility and propensity for evil of the human race as a whole. Flourishing, impoverishment, conflict and destruction are all part of the human scene. Kant, however, refuses to depict this cycle as sheer chaos or mere blind repetition. Such fatalistic conclusions represent a false metaphysics. Metaphysics must also show that it is not impossible to achieve perpetual peace (in the same ways as metaphysical argument establishes in the *Critique of Pure Reason* that it is permissible, and indeed necessary, to conceive of ourselves as free in practical respects).

On the face of it, Kant appears to be engaging here in the kind of extravagant metaphysics that not only he but also twentieth-century analytical philosophers have found inadmissible if we are to restrict ourselves to truly rational thought. However, it is important to bear in mind that Kant's metaphysics of history offers a guarantee of perpetual peace not as a prediction (or a prophecy, as he terms it) but only as a supplement to our ethical and political thinking about world politics. The guarantee is given only in terms of the integrity of our attitude and conduct towards the human race. The guarantee exists only as a dogmatic certainty for practical reason (*ZeF* 8: 362). There is a dialectic in terms of the realization of perpetual peace that Kant draws attention to. First, we can unreservedly advance the thesis that nobody can say that perpetual peace will never occur. Secondly, as an antithesis to that, it can also incontrovertibly be affirmed that nobody can claim that perpetual peace will occur at any given time. As with the antinomies in the *Critique of Pure Reason* the conflict between thesis and antithesis remains unresolved here if one adheres solely to the theoretical perspective. However, if we move to the practical perspective and think in terms of how we ought to act, then we have to acknowledge that whatever the circumstances we have a duty to promote perpetual peace.

It is in this moral dimension that Kant affirms metaphysics. In conceptualizing a non-naturally found condition of perpetual peace (and the advance towards it) we are dealing with more than mere phantoms. We do not 'cognize' progress in 'these artifices of nature or even so much as infer [it] from them but instead (as in all relations of the form of things to ends in general) only can and must add it in thought'. Improvement is not an event that occurs in the world but a 'representation' of the relation to 'and harmony with the end that reason prescribes immediately to us'. This moral end is 'an idea, which is indeed transcendent for theoretical purposes but for practical purposes (e.g. with respect to the concept of the duty of perpetual peace and putting that mechanism of nature to use for it) is dogmatic and well founded as to its reality' (*ZeF* 8: 362/332). The critical deployment of metaphysics requires on the one hand that we take an agnostic view about the empirical assertion that the human race is progressing; yet it demands on the other hand an affirmative, even dogmatic view of an anticipation of progress from a moral and political perspective. The metaphysics Kant brings into politics is exclusively normatively oriented and, as far as ontology is concerned, deliberately inconclusive. Not only is it possible for a delimited, critical metaphysics to coexist with a just theory of politics; it is also, from the Kantian perspective, necessary.

6. Conclusion

In its negative, critical regard I find Kant's interpretation and use of metaphysics most persuasive. Put quite simply, there is a great deal in the Kantian view that there is much we do not and cannot know about nature and the human individual in a final and complete sense. Thus he is correct to stress that we should not be overly assertive about what we suppose we know about the course of the world and the social and political arrangements that are best to deal with it. We can only act *as though* the future might be known to us, not in certain knowledge of its character. And Kant is correct to conclude that this does not leave metaphysics empty or with little to offer us that is of a dependable character. This dependability arises in our moral reasoning, which applies to us as rational beings. Kant's pure moral philosophy – which on his reckoning is wholly metaphysical – is a very fruitful area of philosophical inquiry. And it is this metaphysics of morals that provides an excellent grounding for political philosophy today.

I have one important caveat in recommending Kant's metaphysical approach to politics. Although Kant himself believes our commitment to doing our duty should not be dependent on it, he appears to regard teleological judgement as an important supplement to duty. In his teleological thinking Kant believes we can come to an agreement as rational beings about the final end of nature and the key role of the human species within it. In coming to this agreement, Kant thinks we are driven by reason to presuppose a creator of the universe whose existence we cannot demonstrate, but whom we must nonetheless presuppose to provide a final harmony to our moral lives. Clearly Kant is not talking here about a being with a natural existence.[11] The existence of God has to be one we cannot intuit. But I think there is no need to talk about a supersensible existence of which we know nothing.

It may well be that many experience a need to believe in God which is part of their psychological make-up; indeed, Kant appears to think we all experience such a need. However, I am doubtful that this represents the only possible way of depicting the harmony between the processes of nature and human society, or the harmony of purposes among individuals in society, that are required in order to bring about continuous peace. Since if such a harmony were to come about a great deal would depend on the actions of human individuals, it seems to me that the best chance of success would come from emphasizing this voluntary dimension. In some respects I can agree with Kant that this seems too difficult a task for us to suppose that humans can do it all on their own, but this is perhaps a case for modesty, taking small and gradual steps, rather than handing over the completion of the job to other unknown forces. I think it might be more frank to express uncertainty about the possibilities of bringing about anything resembling Kant's worldwide ethical commonwealth than to invoke grace (albeit in a largely symbolic sense) as a possible facilitator. Unlike Kant I would not place faith in anything outside the agency of the human species.

The evaluation of the metaphysical dimension of Kant's political philosophy thus leads to the conclusion that most attention should be paid to the key legal and political arrangements (highlighted in and by his system) that have to be made to bring about national and international harmony. They are clearly embedded in Kant's critically delimited metaphysics and are nonetheless, in my view, deeply instructive. This means not that we should sideline Kantian practical philosophy or indeed the whole of Kant's metaphysics, but rather that we should aim to amplify it and where necessary reconstruct it. We can of course begin with the wholly positive elements that Kant brings to political philosophy with his critical metaphysics and that are reviewed here: the persuasive grounding of property rights in interpersonal awareness and consciousness; the imaginative grounding of effective contractual relations (in an individually imagined conscious meeting of minds); the novel and subtle account of the social contract; the ingenious grounding of harmony amongst states on the basis of republican constitutions in a worldwide expanding federation; and as a cornerstone of all these, his conception of reason as a shared and homogeneous faculty of the human mind. This list of the positive dimensions of Kant's political metaphysics is of course incomplete. His critically delimited metaphysics is replete with the most profound insights into the human condition and methods for its betterment that we should try to comprehend and to carry further.

Rawls too fully appreciated the fecundity of Kant's thought. However, in his political liberalism he cuts off his appreciation of Kant's metaphysics at too early a point – even before we get to the religious dimension of Kant's philosophy – to take full advantage of Kant's 'constructivism'. In presenting political liberalism 'as a doctrine that falls under the category of the political', Rawls deals less convincingly than Kant with the borderlines between politics and ethics, and politics and history.[12] However politics is interpreted, it necessarily bears a connection to ethics and history. Rawls's attempts to create a 'free-standing' political philosophy are bound to lead to the accusation that his political philosophy implies just as comprehensive a doctrine as those which he attempts to exclude from his political liberalism.[13] Although Jürgen Habermas also raises objections to Kant's metaphysics and finds that Kant was 'a child of his *time* and suffered from a certain colour blindness', he more wholeheartedly subscribes to the 'universalistic programme of Kantian moral and legal theory'. In advocating 'the application of the cognitive procedure of universalisation and mutual perspective-taking which Kant associates with practical reason', Habermas comes very close to recommending the positive, and so still highly germane dimensions of Kant's metaphysical depiction of politics highlighted here.[14]

Notes

1 John Rawls, *Political Liberalism* (New York: Columbia University Press, 1993), p. 10.

2 Ibid.

3 Idil Boran, 'Rawls and Carnap on doing philosophy without metaphysics', *Pacific Philosophical Quarterly*, 86/4 (2005), 459–79.

4 Rawls, *Lectures on the History of Moral Philosophy*, ed. B. Herman (Cambridge, MA: Harvard University Press, 2000). In the same *Lectures* Rawls also refers to Leibniz's 'metaphysical perfectionism' which has the 'following feature: there exists a moral order in the universe fixed and given by the divine nature (in Leibniz's case), an order prior to and independent of us that flows from the divine perfections, and this order specifies the appropriate moral ideals and conceptions for human virtues, as well as the grounds of the principles of right and justice' (Rawls, *Lectures*, p. 109).

5 Karl Ameriks, 'The critique of metaphysics: the structure and fate of Kant's dialectic', in P. Guyer (ed.), *Kant and Modern Philosophy* (Cambridge: Cambridge University Press, 2006), citation pp. 270–1.

6 Ibid., p. 279.

7 This translation is modified.

8 Allen Wood, *Kant* (Oxford: Blackwell, 2005), p. 24.

9 I am grateful to Kerstin Budde for helping me with this formulation of the issue.

10 Sorin Baiasu, 'Kantian metaphysics and the normative force of practical principles', *Politics and Ethics Review*, 3/1 (2007), 37–56 (citation 52).

11 'We must assume a moral cause of the world (an author of the world) in order to set before ourselves a final end, in accordance with the moral law; and insofar as that final end is necessary, to that extent (i.e., in the same degree and for the same reason) is it also necessary to assume the former, namely, that there is a God' (*KU* 5: 450).

12 Rawls, *Political Liberalism*, p. 374. Rawls makes this claim in 'Reply to Habermas', reprinted in *Political Liberalism*. He specifically notes

that political liberalism is distinct from 'the familiar liberalisms of Immanuel Kant and J. S. Mill. Their views clearly go well beyond the political, relying on ideas of autonomy and individuality as moral values belonging to a comprehensive doctrine' (ibid., p. 375).

13 Rawls contrasts his view of political liberalism, which 'works entirely within' the domain of the political, with 'the more familiar view of political philosophy that its concepts, principles and ideals, and other elements are presented as consequences of comprehensive doctrines – religious, metaphysical, and moral' (ibid., 374).

14 Jürgen Habermas, *The Divided West* (Oxford: Polity Press, 2007), pp. 145–6. Arguably, Habermas's differences with Kant are more to do with the deployment of terms than with deep methodological issues. Habermas is clearly not happy with the label 'metaphysics' for the deduction of right he proffers. He prefers to present his political philosophy as arising from his discourse ethics and an imagined direct-democratic procedure amongst citizens. He wants to get away from the a priori dimension of Kant's argument. The discourse ethics provides Habermas with the cooperative individual open to rational persuasion who is swayed only by the power of the better argument, and the deliberative democratic engagement of such individuals provides the appropriate context in which the political bargain is struck: see Robert Fine and Will Smith, 'Jürgen Habermas's theory of cosmopolitanism', *Constellations: an International Journal of Critical and Democratic Theory*, 10/4 (2003), 467–87 (citation 481). This might be seen more as a redescription of Kant's project than an outright rejection of it, for no matter how Habermas conceives his agreement procedure, it is clearly an abstract one.

References

Ameriks, K., 'The critique of metaphysics: the structure and fate of Kant's dialectic', in P. Guyer (ed.), *Kant and Modern Philosophy* (Cambridge: Cambridge University Press, 2006).

Baiasu, S., 'Kantian metaphysics and the normative force of practical principles', *Politics and Ethics Review*, 3/1 (2007), 37–56.

Boran, I., 'Rawls and Carnap on doing philosophy without metaphysics', *Pacific Philosophical Quarterly*, 86/4 (2005), 459–79.

Fine, R. and Smith, W., 'Jürgen Habermas's theory of cosmopolitanism', *Constellations: an International Journal of Critical and Democratic Theory*, 10/4 (2003), 467–87.

Habermas, J., *The Divided West* (Oxford: Polity Press, 2007).

Kant, I., *Prolegomena to any Future Metaphysics*, ed. and trans. L.W. Beck (Indianapolis: Bobbs-Merrill, 1977).
——, 'Metaphysics of Morals', in *Practical Philosophy*, ed. and trans. M. J. Gregor (Cambridge: Cambridge University Press, 1996).
——, *Critique of the Power of Judgment*, ed. P. Guyer, trans. P. Guyer and E. Matthews (Cambridge: Cambridge University Press, 2000).
Rawls, J., *Political Liberalism* (New York: Columbia University Press, 1993).
——, *Lectures on the History of Moral Philosophy*, ed. B. Herman (Cambridge, MA: Harvard University Press, 2000).
Wood, A., *Kant* (Oxford: Blackwell, 2005).

12 • Cosmopolitan Right: State and System in Kant's Political Theory

Sharon Anderson-Gold

It may seem strange to entertain a relationship between political theory and metaphysics since metaphysics is concerned with universal rational principles while politics appears to be composed of particular actions that may have little to do with 'reason'. But in so far as politics claims to be aimed at 'right action', it depends upon a theory of right. Justice, in so far as it provides a universal criterion of right action, cannot take its bearings from positive law since this varies in particular times and places. Therefore, if there is a universal criterion of right action its sources must be in pure reason: there must be a metaphysics of morals.

Kant's *Metaphysics of Morals* contains his theory of right in the form of a comprehensive system of interdependent principles regulating all forms of human interaction. Kant's definition of right, the universal principle of right, is breathtaking in its simplicity. Kant states: 'Any action is *right* if it can coexist with everyone's freedom in accordance with a universal law, or if on its maxim the freedom of choice of each can coexist with everyone's freedom in accordance with a universal law' (*MS* 6: 230). By emphasizing the freedom of the individual as the foundation and purpose of the principle of right, Kant has embedded within this simple formula a comprehensive theory of justice in the form of three interdependent principles: political right, international right and cosmopolitan right. While all three principles are necessary for a universal condition of public right, this paper investigates and defends the foundational character of the third level of public right – cosmopolitan right – in Kant's political theory. I base my argument on the claim that it is cosmopolitan right that ultimately shapes the character of Kant's system of public right, transforming what would otherwise be at best a balance of power among states loosely committed to lawful relations into a cosmopolitan community of states that have internalized principles of right. My argument has three points: that a society of states, by virtue of entering into an explicit juridical condition, has internalized cosmopolitan right; that cosmopolitan right necessarily has universal jurisdiction; and that the implementation of the norms of hospitality required by cosmopolitan right entails global institutions based upon democratic representation.

The systematic character of cosmopolitan right in Kant's political theory is most explicitly expressed in *The Metaphysics of Morals* in the section where Kant defines public right: 'The sum of the laws which need to be promulgated generally in order to bring about a rightful condition is public right. Public right is therefore a system of laws for a people, that is a multitude of human beings, or for a multitude of peoples' (*MS* 6: 311). The three forms of public right are then argued to be interdependent. Kant states: 'So if the principle of outer freedom limited by laws is lacking in any one of these three possible forms of rightful condition, the framework of all the others is unavoidably undermined and must finally collapse' (*MS* 6: 311).

In this passage we are provided with an image of a global system that depends upon a tier of laws much like a complex building. The parts of this system are not independent and cannot attain a correct and stable form outside the system as a whole. While cosmopolitan right is clearly a significant aspect of Kant's theory of right, traditional interpretations of Kant's theory have placed too much emphasis on national or political right without sufficient appreciation for the systematic context in which all law must develop. Given this context, cosmopolitan right must shape both political right and interstate right, thereby affecting the notion of basic personal rights and the conception of sovereignty operating within the federation of free republics that is the ultimate institutional framework in which Kant's system of public law is intended to operate. Kant expresses this systematic interconnection through the image of the earth's spherical shape: 'Since the earth's surface is not unlimited but closed, the concepts of the right of a state and of a right of nations lead inevitably to the idea of right for a state of nations (*ius gentium*) or cosmopolitan right (*ius cosmopoliticum*)' (*MS* 6: 311).

That it is a cosmopolitan system of law that provides the legal foundation of the federation is made clear in *Perpetual Peace*, where cosmopolitan right appears as the 'third definitive article' which must be accepted by all members of the federation. Kant's federation is then a system of interdependent states whose internal governance is structured by the category of community, expressed in the practical sphere by the idea of *commercium* – reciprocal action and reaction. In a cosmopolitan context, domestic and foreign policy are interrelated in a dynamic interchange that continuously transforms both. And as I shall argue further, the resulting conception of international political right provides the basis of global governance without recourse to a world state.

Kant's tripartite juridical system rejects traditional notions of sovereignty built upon 'atomistic' concepts of state independence wherein each state defines and defends its 'rights' in its own terms. According to Kant, in order to pursue its 'rights' a state must accept a public system of law that is intended to define and secure borders under binding rules of arbitration. Independence in a Kantian system is a consequence of reciprocal recognition. But defining and defending borders is not the entire purpose of a public system of law. Law, according to Kant, must capture all possible forms of interaction. Not only must there be civil law to regulate the interaction of citizens within states and interstate law to regulate state-to-state relations; there must also be a form of public law that regulates the relationship of individuals to individuals across states. It is not just that individuals happen to interact across borders as a contingent affair. Their innate right to freedom permits individuals to do anything that does not diminish what belongs to others. Attempts to communicate with others are a primary example of what all are free to do, even if the communications are neither truthful nor valuable, as it is always in the power of others simply to refuse the communication. Censorship on the grounds that people are not able to evaluate such communications is unwarranted paternalism, even if undertaken by the educated elite or the state.

Kant views travel or 'presenting oneself in the society of others' as an extension of the right of communication and itself a residual aspect of original possession of the earth in common.[1] In light of original common possession all actual possessions, including the territory of states, are provisional and depend for their final formations upon a general will that is indefinite (universal) in scope. Kant argues that 'only in an association of states (analogous to that by which a people becomes a state) can rights come to hold conclusively and a true condition of peace come about' (*MS* 6: 350).

Because the rights of individuals simply as human beings are universal or 'cosmopolitan' in nature, civil law and interstate law alone are not adequate to address their scope. For 'rights' in any form to be settled within a system of law with public authority, cosmopolitan rights must be specified at an international level and must be incorporated in both civil and interstate law. Therefore Kant concludes that 'the idea of cosmopolitan right is no fantastic and exaggerated way of representing right; it is, instead, a supplement to the unwritten code of the right of a state and the right of nations necessary for the sake of any public rights of human beings' (*ZeF* 8: 360).

In contrast to the traditional 'atomistic' conception of state sovereignty, I defend Kant's juridical model of a plurality of interacting, interdependent states on the grounds that only such a model captures the requirements for sovereignty understood as autonomy or independence grounded in an intelligible 'community' of nations. Mark Franke puts it this way: 'Kant's republic is free and autonomous insofar as it is able to perpetually contribute to the formation of a partnership of nations. As much as it requires the confidence of a national population within, Kant's republic has no stable existence outside of its relations with the external'.[2] This model requires the universal principle of cosmopolitan right to balance the contrasting forces of interaction and independence (dynamic equilibrium and community) and is the only system of law that can ensure the independence of interdependent states.

Any society of states that has entered into universal juridical relations must acknowledge cosmopolitan right as a condition of their association because in addition to the fact that each state must have its borders recognized by others as a condition of peaceable federation (interstate law), all states must accept the (moral) fact that individuals retain a right of continued association that is not derived from their civic identities. If the right of association were simply confined to one's fellow citizens, states could deny individuals the right to exit their communities. If this were the case then not only could there be no right to travel, but states would in effect 'own' their citizens in the manner of 'things', which Kant claims to be impossible. Civil law according to Kant must reflect the fundamental freedom, equality and independence of moral persons. Positive law that attempted to eradicate a fundamental personal right could never be part of a system of public right. While rights of permanent residence or 'resort' are collectively determined, the right to attempt association with others outside one's civic community appears to remain a fundamentally individual right with universal scope. Kant maintains that this original right of free association is derived from the fact that the earth originally belongs to no one individual. Civic unions can be thought of as provisional collective claims to habitable parts of the 'globe'. While this does not make borders entirely arbitrary since the rights of settlement or first occupancy must be respected by travellers, it is the united general will that confers ultimate legitimacy on these formations. Each specific union is in effect a contingent arrangement that may change over time in keeping with further acts of association or dissociation. At bottom it is individuals who form these unions and it is individuals who retain the rights to reform them. This indicates that there can be no final formation that does not leave open the possibility of future association, and therefore that the principle of hospitality cannot be superseded.

While 'secession' or the claim of a subsection of a population to remove itself from the rule of the whole is not a personal right and will not be discussed further, the minimal and more basic right simply to attempt association without any immediate claim to resort remains the right of each individual. Of course the mere right of attempted association establishes nothing unilaterally. Attempts may be rebuffed or otherwise prove unsuccessful. Offers of commerce can at most establish the conditions for future mutual ventures that can only take shape through specific agreements. What is important here is not the extent of the original right but its function as the juridical instrument of a potential cosmopolitan community in which individuals are the central subjects. As Katrin Flikschuh has expressed it, 'the coming together of peoples in the idea of disjunctive possession in common envisages a gradual dismantling of boundaries that hinder the development of relations of Right between subjects'.[3]

The original community, Kant argues, is not a primitive form of 'communal ownership' from which individual shares can be derived once and for all; rather, it is an individually based 'right to share' derived from a fundamental feature of the human condition, 'reciprocal action' (*commercium*) that occurs in a finite or contained space (a spherical globe). Because they cannot infinitely disperse, individuals' activity puts each individual in 'constant relations with all the rest', and because this remains true even after civil society provides internal rules to determine internal property, the federation has to concern itself both with definitions of borders and with criteria for universal individual-to-individual interactions. 'This right, since it has to do with the possible union of all nations with a view to certain universal laws for their possible commerce, can be called cosmopolitan right (*ius cosmopoliticum*)' (*MS* 6: 352).

It is this right, *ius cosmopoliticum*, that provides the basis for universal laws regulating international intercourse. Kant's insistence on the juridical (a priori) status of cosmopolitan right appears to be neither contingent upon nor subordinate to the recognition of borders. Rather, it is derived from a more fundamental individual right implicit in the universal and innate right to external freedom. Cosmopolitan right shapes the nature of the rightful relation between states and thus places constraints on the form of the federation. The federation is prohibited, by cosmopolitan right as a right of individuals, from becoming a 'closed system' of isolationist communities or communities that trade only on the conditions of nationalist interests. Isolationist communities might be initially non-aggressive, but they would not be committed to cosmopolitan norms of hospitality and could slide into war should foreigners permeate their borders. Nationalist interests might support commerce, but they would do so principally on terms of power, which could result in exploitation leading to conquest and war. Peaceable 'association', then, is intrinsically linked to principles that are universal and rooted in a cosmopolitan community. If this is so, then some form of distributive justice must be at work in the formation of cosmopolitan laws.

A second point of my thesis is that cosmopolitan right is the basis for the formation of public law with universal jurisdiction. The federation, by virtue of forming a juridical association, will need to produce global bodies, public authorities empowered to specify in positive law the norms of hospitality implicit in cosmopolitan right. Therefore some form of global law is entailed by the very condition of a plurality of interacting independent states aspiring to peaceable relations. Given its specification in a global form of positive law, cosmopolitan right opens states to the development of juridical institutions with universal jurisdiction, such as a world court with the authority to determine violations of cosmopolitan right. Judgements from a world court would have to be self-implemented on pain of loss of membership in the (cosmopolitan) society of states and restitution of the state of nature (war) between the federated association and the dissenting state.[4]

As a third point I claim that the public authorities that specify the norms regulating individual and corporate commerce must be founded upon democratic representation and be held accountable to individuals as 'world citizens'. International institutions alone do not make a cosmopolitan community. International institutions as we know them do not fully instantiate the principle of cosmopolitan right because they do not incorporate democratic principles of representation. By providing rich and powerful states with positions of permanent power within most international institutions, these institutions solidify policies of economic exploitation and military dominance of developed states over underdeveloped states in violation of republican values of equality, freedom and independence. Since the ideal of a republic of republics (an ideal espoused at times by Kant) cannot take the form of a universal state under a single ruler, a centralized authority cannot guarantee these values. Rather, the system of positive law, international political right, which must accompany and supplement the development of international right within the federation must be guided by the universal principle of cosmopolitan right; that is, it must be shaped by what is just not merely in the relationship not merely between states as 'powers' but also in that between individuals 'as citizens of the world'. Kant maintains that international right developed under the principle of cosmopolitan right transforms the former and produces international political right as 'a universal right of humanity.' Clearly, the cosmopolitan context within which states are portrayed as constructing global public laws and global public institutions to regulate their interactions is not the former context of power politics but one of respect for the rights of humanity as expressed in the republican values of freedom, equality and independence.[5] The need for global institutions that can secure universal republican values becomes clearer if we investigate the principle of hospitality from the perspective of what type of interactions violate this principle.

Hospitality, Kant insists, is a juridical principle, a legal duty. Here Kant states that 'it is not a question of philanthropy but of right' (*ZeF* 8: 357). Individuals have the right to offer to trade and to communicate as part of the original community of land understood as a community of reciprocal action. Kant did not attempt to provide a detailed legal code for these interactions, but his examples of what constitutes inhospitable interactions provide some guidance on the norms that would be constitutive of rightful interactions. Therefore I will unpack the norms inherent in these examples to explore the possibility that cosmopolitan right must be accompanied by institutional supplements to the federation of free nations, in the form of global institutions based upon democratic representation. Cosmopolitan democratic representation is required so that the form of public law that arises from interstate interactions does not permanently solidify exploitation on the part of dominant states in violation of the norms of cosmopolitan right.

While the principle of hospitality would have no bite without Kant's assumption of a fundamental right to offer to interact with others through trade and travel, Kant's analysis of the ethical limits of expansion into new territories was shaped by his concern about exploitation in the relationship between European states and non-state peoples in the 'New World'. In his concern that Europeans should not take advantage of their superior form of organization to dispossess native peoples, Kant appears to grant to non-state peoples moral standing and rights over the property entailed by their ways of life. In asking whether or not states may create new settlements as a consequence of exploration in the vicinity of a nation (not organized as a state) already settled there, Kant maintains that the right to do so is incontestable with the provision that the new settlement does not interfere with the use of the land of those already settled. He warns that in many cases this will require consideration of the fact that non-state cultures may conceive of rightful possession and use of the land differently from states that have evolved legal standards for permanent title. He says: 'But if these people are shepherds or hunters (like the Hottentots, the Tungusi, or most of the American Indian nations) who depend for their sustenance on great open regions, this settlement may not take place by force but only by contract and indeed by a contract that does not take advantage of the ignorance of those inhabitants with respect to ceding their lands' (*MS* 6: 353). The social organization of non-state peoples may not yet satisfy Kant's definition of civil society, but apparently non-state peoples do have some form of provisional (claim) right in relation to peoples not yet settled, and coercion and exploitation in interactions with the native settlers remain moral evils that cannot be justified. The inhospitable conduct leading to subjugation, Kant maintains, arose because the explorers considered the newly discovered lands as 'countries belonging to no one, since they counted the inhabitants as nothing' (*ZeF* 8: 358).

Even the potential for 'development' (economic and cultural) extending to future generations does not justify dispossession, according to Kant. He states: 'But all these supposedly good intentions cannot wash away the stain of injustice in the means used for them' (*MS* 6: 353). The argument that violence was used in the foundation of states themselves, which Kant accepts to be generally the case, does not move him from the position that cosmopolitan right absolutely forbids the imposition of order by coercion. His comparison of this argument to the so-called right of revolution for the improvement of political organizations (which he soundly rejects) again suggests that the social organization of non-state peoples is not to be regarded as a merely anarchic condition of individuals who can be absorbed into another state. The conditions of right are universal, cannot be annulled, and cover every individual, civilized or not.

Kant subjects commercial interactions as well as settlements to criticism on the grounds of the principle of hospitality. In discussing the inhospitable conduct of the commercial states he goes so far as to equate 'visiting' foreign countries and peoples with 'conquering' them. He states that 'when America, the Negro countries, the Spice Islands, the Cape, and so forth were discovered, they were, to them, countries belonging to one, since they counted the inhabitants as nothing' (*ZeF* 8: 358). Given these experiences Kant concludes that the decisions of China and Japan to restrict the interactions between their states and people with European commerce were both justified and 'wise'. From these examples we can infer that for the principle of hospitality to take effect, all forms of coercion and exploitation must be excluded. Those who accept the offer of interaction must do so not only freely but also with the expectation of fair outcomes (what contemporary cosmopolitans refer to as distributive justice).[6]

But coercion and exploitation are not limited to the eighteenth- and nineteenth-century relations between non-state and state peoples. Exploitation clearly can and does occur in modern state-to-state relationships, particularly between highly developed and underdeveloped states. Such exploitative interactions, I would argue, violate the principle of hospitality and are contrary to cosmopolitan right.

In the twenty-first century, non-state peoples have generally been incorporated into states, and states have been organized in various ways within international organizations. Thus our contemporary political system would seem to approximate more closely the Kantian ideal of a cosmopolitan condition. Yet states do not uniformly represent the interests of their people/s, and within the state the interests of different groups are often given differential weight. Thomas Pogge has analysed underdeveloped states and has demonstrated that a rich store of natural resources is systematically correlated with dictatorships and poverty. He argues that in underdeveloped states the lure of personal power and wealth corrupts political leadership, and that this corruption is supported by the current terms of the international recognition of sovereignty.[7] Since international recognition of sovereignty is currently based on power, the current understanding of international right provides no disincentives to the development of dictatorships, thereby securing continuous access to great personal wealth for those in power at the expense of internal development. Indeed, by conceding that whoever holds power has the right to sell the nation's resources, current international law and practice tends to support this type of political corruption.

This alliance of international recognition of dictatorial power with internal underdevelopment is no mere accident of history. Given the manner in which developed nations tend to use their superior military and economic power to gain advantages in all international forums, it is to the advantage of developed nations to continue to support regimes willing to provide access to natural resources on terms favourable to themselves, regardless of the 'representative' character of the government in power. Thus, the economic gap between developed and underdeveloped countries has grown despite the efforts of some international organizations to provide funds for 'development'. These organizations are not constituted in a manner to offset the effects of the dominance of developed nations and therefore cannot genuinely affect the type of internal development that would systematically reduce global poverty.[8]

Given the negative impact of the policies of these organizations on the most vulnerable, global theorists such as David Held have argued that in addition to international law founded on state-based international organizations, cosmopolitan law must be founded directly upon international democratic institutions whose representatives would be accountable to individuals as 'world citizens'.[9] Such institutions would provide a forum in which ordinary citizens could criticize the policies of their governments and could form alliances with the citizens of other states to address issues of global concern, particularly in the areas of peace, poverty and environmental degradation.

Power politics, Held argues in Kantian fashion, affect the capacity of any and all states to develop their internal values. Internal democracy has little chance to develop where autocrats have the power to offer natural resources on favourable terms to developed nations. Power elites in underdeveloped states thus reflect the overall power differentials between states. While Kant stressed universal republicanism and the equality of states under international law as necessary conditions for the evolution of cosmopolitan law, Held adds to these two conditions the need to establish international democratic institutions. This, I argue, is already implicit in cosmopolitan right as a juridical principle constituting the federation of nations. A level of cosmopolitan democratic law is required if cosmopolitan right is ultimately to be achieved because commerce (at least under the conditions of global capitalist markets) tends to have differential effects across states with respect to individuals or groups, which undermines the ability of those adversely affected to have equal standing (as republicanism requires) in their respective political communities.[10] In a system of interaction shaped by powerful elites, Held argues, democracy (or republican equality) within must be supplemented by democracy without.

Clearly the current organization of international relations does not adequately reflect the principles of a cosmopolitan federation based upon cosmopolitan right, viewed as the right of all individuals to participate in commerce and exchange on fair terms. Structural exploitation, economic and cultural, underlies contemporary struggles for political realignment as well as movements primarily aimed at retribution and destruction.[11] Such struggles undermine respect for and compliance with international law. Systematic democratic reform of the international organizations that produce international law is necessary to bring interstate laws into compliance with cosmopolitan right.[12] In so far as the growing community of interaction can be expected to result in a further development of both national and interstate law, cosmopolitan or world law is a 'necessary supplement' in bringing all forms of law into compliance with cosmopolitan right. Much of this international political law will shape how states articulate the rights of individuals who enter into these exchanges, and thereby influence the formation of domestic law as well.[13]

Global (international) law regulating international exchange, while voluntarily negotiated, will require the development of legal expertise and courts for the exercise of judgement independent of the states that may be a party to particular disputes concerning just implementation of international legal rules. These legal decisions cannot be considered as interference with the sovereignty or freedom of states that are 'associated' in this manner. When international law has become systematized and internalized in domestic law we can expect the decisions of international courts to be self-enforced, since non-compliance would result in the future exclusion of the dissenting state from international exchange. While the principle of hospitality appears to permit such dissociation as long as it remains non-hostile, such a state does others a high degree of 'wrong' because it refuses to allow the exercise of the right of *commercium* and blocks the path to permanent peace and a cosmopolitan community.

Because such a federation, even in its cosmopolitan formation, retains a dynamic character with potential for dissent leading to dissociation and possibly war,[14] it can be objected that it cannot fulfil Kant's imperative of perpetual peace. It has been argued that only the republic of republics, or world state, can fully realize perpetual peace, and that in rejecting the world state Kant violates his own principles. Is there then an inconsistency in Kant's own theory? In her article 'Kant's arguments for a league of states', Pauline Kleingeld provides an interesting and sensible defence of the league. She argues that the republic of republics is best understood as the ideal, which can only be approximated through the use of practical/juridical principles such as cosmopolitan right. She concludes that the cosmopolitan federation is not a 'second best' solution that is substituted for the republic or republics, but the form that the latter takes in the historical world.[15]

We therefore cannot and should not attempt to 'jump over' the federation and coerce nations into a world state. A federated system of states based upon principles of cosmopolitan right can secure the rights of both individuals and nations without recourse to a 'world state', and while such a system would not necessarily be without conflict or dissent I would maintain that because of the nature of its juridical principles it would represent a different international order from that of the 'balance of power', which Kant maintains cannot even approximate to justice in this world. In *Perpetual Peace*, Kant concludes with his strongest endorsement of cosmopolitan right as the foundation of public right when he states that 'cosmopolitan right is no fantastic and exaggerated way of representing right; it is, instead, a supplement to the unwritten code of the right of the state and the right of nations necessary for the sake of *any public rights of human beings* and so for perpetual peace; only under this condition can we flatter ourselves that we are constantly approaching perpetual peace' (*ZeF* 8: 360).

Notes

1 This does not make borders entirely arbitrary or without moral significance. Settlement or first occupancy provides the basis of a provisional right which travellers must clearly respect. But the full force of these claims comes from the same general will that would also support the rights of individuals to associate freely, and so the boundaries of these associations are always placed at the point of 'hospitality'.

2 Mark Franke, *Global Limits: Immanuel Kant, International Relations, and Critique of World Politics* (Albany: State University of New York Press, 2001), p. 109.

3 Katrin Flikschuh, *Kant and Modern Political Philosophy* (Cambridge: Cambridge University Press, 2000).

4 It might be objected that since states may voluntarily terminate their membership in a juridical federation, the traditional conception of sovereignty persists, i.e. that states cannot be coerced to submit to any universal principles. Yet in the context of a juridical federation that has pledged no longer to pursue the 'rights' of states through war, the public repudiation of judgements concerning international justice

would constitute the dissenting state as an 'unjust enemy', a term not applicable in the prior state of nature where unregulated sovereignty was the norm. In the *Metaphysics of Morals* (*MS* 6: 351–2) Kant maintains that unjust enemies constitute a threat to all other states and that states may rightfully unite to deprive the 'offending state' of the power to act in a similar way again.

5 It is arguable that international trade agreements that ignore workers' rights and the health and environmental impacts of trade are exploitative and constitute unfair relations between individuals, not simply unfair relations between states.

6 Kant's references to unjust commercial interactions assume that injustice in these interactions has a universal impact – that is, that the community at stake is not limited to the immediate agents. This is because all have this right to interact with all, and injustice in international dealings is therefore in effect injustice to everyone.

7 Thomas Pogge, *World Poverty and Human Rights* (New York: Polity Press, 2002).

8 Anderson-Gold, *Cosmopolitanism and Human Rights* (Cardiff: University of Wales Press, 2001), ch. 7.

9 David Held, *Democracy and the Global Order* (Stanford, CA: Stanford University Press, 1995), pp. 235–51.

10 Although Kant accepted some degree of economically based political inequality (active vs. passive citizen) even within a justly constituted state, he maintained that it must be possible to work one's way out of dependence. Permanent structural economic inequality violates this principle.

11 Culturally based discriminations must also not be allowed a foothold in law since these will tend to become permanent and structural features of association. This means that in multicultural contexts certain limits on majority rule must be recognized that protect minority interests.

12 The current world 'food crisis' is a good example of trade practices that have been based on the short-term interests of particular states to the detriment of the world's poorest individuals. These policies have resulted in much food loss and ultimately require crisis intervention to prevent mass starvation. International trade policies need to be shaped by criteria that first ensure adequate food production and distribution.

13 The experience of the European Court of Human Rights provides an excellent example of how this can work in practice. Critics are likely to point out that this success has been built upon a common history and shared values. But this simply means that there may have to be multiple jurisdictions for such courts, with regional scope mapping onto shared histories and values. A supreme or 'world court' is of course a

more difficult institutional matter, as it would ultimately determine the areas inside and outside the federation's membership.

14 While I cannot deal with the relationship between a cosmopolitan federation and a 'rogue' state in this paper, I will state briefly that it is clear that such a federation is intended to be a 'defensive' league and to protect each member from possible aggression from 'rogues'. Once states have agreed to cease pursuing their internal disagreements through war, and also to defend one another, the situation of a 'state of nature' relationship no longer applies internally although it may reappear in the relations between the federation and dissociated states.

15 Pauline Kleingeld, 'Kant's arguments for a league of states', in L. Caranti (ed.), *Kant's Perpetual Peace: New Interpretative Essays* (Rome: LUISS University Press, 2006).

References

Anderson-Gold, S., *Cosmopolitanism and Human Rights* (Cardiff: University of Wales Press, 2001).

Flikschuh, K., *Kant and Modern Political Philosophy* (Cambridge: Cambridge University Press, 2000).

Franke, M., *Global Limits: Immanuel Kant, International Relations, and Critique of World Politics* (Albany: State University of New York Press, 2001).

Held, D., *Democracy and the Global Order* (Stanford, CA: Stanford University Press, 1995).

——, 'Cosmopolitan democracy and the global order: a new agenda', in J. Bohman and M. Lutz-Bachmann (eds), *Perpetual Peace: Essays on Kant's Cosmopolitan Ideal* (Cambridge, MA: The MIT Press, 1997).

Kleingeld, P., 'Kant's arguments for a league of states', in L. Caranti (ed.), *Kant's Perpetual Peace: New Interpretative Essays* (Rome: LUISS University Press, 2006).

Pogge, T., *World Poverty and Human Rights* (New York City: Polity Press, 2002).

13 • The Metaphysics of International Law: Kant's 'Unjust Enemy' and the Limitation of Self-Authorization

Oliver Eberl

Kant envisioned a scheme of international security that would help particularly small and weak nations to abandon the collective insecurity of the state of nature, where nations may fight one another just because they feel threatened or insulted. Instead, Kant sought to spell out the conditions for a perpetual peace among nations by introducing an epistemic authority. Such an authority would be an ordinary court. But in the absence of a regular court this authority could be substituted with an arbitrational court. Especially when the legal basis for the judgement is not positive law laid down by a united will but only contractual law from contract partners who come into conflict with each other, this form of neutral judgement becomes important. When the conflicting parties hold their respective claims to be just, they are allowed to go to war. Now, the argument for the epistemic impossibility of a just judgement of one's own case means that no war – no intervention – can be called just when a party to the conflict itself takes the decision about whether to go to war or not. It is epistemologically impossible for the invader to prove that its own war is just. This is Kant's argument against the tradition of the just war theory. If one follows this argument, the liberal interpretation has to be rejected that interventions in 'rogue states' can be justified by the intervener with Kantian theory, as these would be the 'unjust enemy' of today.[1] Interpreters usually assume that Kant changed his mind on the appropriate reaction to the 'unjust enemy' between his 'pacifistic' *Perpetual Peace* and his 'realistic' *Doctrine of Law*. An anti-revolutionist sentiment towards the French Revolution is considered as the main reason that Kant gave up the strict prohibition of intervention, which he had still defended in 1795, for an interventionist position in 1797–8.[2]

Kant did not really change his theory, however. Rather, he further developed his terminology by introducing the unjust enemy as a reaction to the export of revolution following the French Revolution. That said, it is commonly overlooked that Kant makes the case for interventions as early as *Perpetual Peace*. In pointing this out I do not want to allege that Kant had a bellicose tendency. Kant 'permits' war following the logic of right, or more concretely a differentiation of states of right. Kant makes no statement for war when he states in Preliminary Article 3 of *Perpetual Peace* that when standing armies are 'regarded by others as a threat of war, it would force them to undertake preventive attacks' (*ZeF* 8: 345).[3] With these words he merely describes the state of nature between states. In the Preliminary Articles Kant deals with international law in the classical Grotian sense: states have a right to go to war when they feel threatened. As a consequence, Kant prohibits standing armies – and not the right to go to war. On the level of the Preliminary Articles, states keep their lawless freedom. Only the international law of the federation of states as it is set out in the Second Definitive Article guarantees a law that preserves and secures 'the *freedom* of a state itself and of other states in league with it' (*ZeF* 8: 356). As long as this new law of the union or league is missing, an epistemic problem between states persists which may lead to war. 'The way in which states pursue their right can never be legal proceedings before an external court but can only be war; but right cannot be decided by war' (*ZeF* 8: 355). Without an authority, war 'cannot straightaway be declared wrong, since in this condition each is judge in his own case' (*ZeF* 8: 355). The aim of the league is to provide the states with an epistemic instance 'as if' they subordinated their rights to the decision of a judge. This is the function of the law of the league and its main achievement. Kant describes this problem even more explicitly in the *Doctrine of Right*: 'In the state of nature among states, *the right to go to war* (to engage in hostilities) is the way in which a state is permitted to prosecute its right against another state, namely by its own *force*, when it believes it has been wronged by the other state; for this cannot be done in the state of nature by a lawsuit (the only means by which disputes are settled in a rightful condition)' (*MS* 6: 346). Here, Kant describes the twofold – legal and epistemic – problem of actors in the state of nature: there is no law to rely on and therefore no judge above the actors. Kant does not pronounce a right to go to war. He claims only that *in the state of nature*, there is no way other than war for a state to seek its right. In the Preliminary Articles Kant therefore does not prohibit war in general but only certain causes and types of war, such as standing armies and punitive wars. This is the realist aspect of his 'philosophical sketch'. This argumentation reveals that the main problem of international law is an epistemic one. It will only be solved by establishing a judge among states, or an authority that acts 'as if' there were a judge.

Georg Cavallar has already convincingly explained that the concept of the unjust enemy belongs to the transitional phase from the natural to the legal condition, in which the majority serves as a substitute for the judicial and executive branches and erects horizontal law enforcement and, following that, public international law.[4] John MacMillan paves the way for the interpretation of the unjust enemy as something completely different from a liberal interventionist program when he states – in accordance with Cavallar – that Kant's unjust enemy 'is defined not by regime type but by behaviour. As such, Kant's notion of intervention holds similarities to the theory of collective security'.[5]

It is this similarity that I want to explore further. From here I will proceed in four steps: first, I want to discuss a proposal by Katrin Flikschuh that addresses Kant's metaphysics of cosmopolitan right in light of the unjust enemy. I will then criticize her idea that territory is the basis for the metaphysics of international law. Instead, I think that the judge, or the competent legal authority, should be the starting point of thinking about international law. Second, I will demonstrate how Kant rejected the balance-of-power system as a corollary of epistemic unilateralism. To this end, the unjust enemy will be compared with the second figure in Kant's *Doctrine of Rights* that allows for a preventive war: the *potentia tremenda*. Third, I will interpret Kant's unjust enemy with references to the concept of international law as 'primitive law' that Hans Kelsen develops in light of a missing central authority. Kelsen's interpretation of international law as a decentralized system of law enforcement is suitable because of this missing law enforcement monopoly in international law. In a last step I shall move over from interpreting the unjust enemy to more abstract questions of collective judgement and the metaphysics of international law.

1. The metaphysics of cosmopolitan right

When Kant describes the relation between states in the first lines of the Second Definitive Article he uses an argument that is well known to readers of his later *Doctrine of Rights*: 'Nations, as states, can be appraised as individuals, who in their natural condition (that is, in their independence from external laws) already wrong one another by being near one another; and each of them, for the sake of its security, can and ought to require the others to enter with it into a constitution similar to a civil constitution' (*ZeF* 8: 354). I want to bring to the reader's attention the idea that 'being near one another' causes the states' special problems in the state of nature. From the Second Preliminary Article of Kant's *Perpetual Peace* one can infer that Kant had in mind the endless disputes over territories that were 'exchanged' or 'purchased' together with their inhabitants. International law could thus be derived from the same motivation of securing 'mine and thine' that characterizes the internal right of states.

Consequently, Katrin Flikschuh interprets cosmopolitan right in line with this possessive view:

> On Kant's account, the move is from unilateral acquisition to *the idea* of original possession in common, and to the obligation to establish relations of Right with all peoples and individuals, wherever they happen to be on the earth's spherical surface. As an idea of reason, original possession in common of the earth's spherical surface – more specifically, *disjunctive* possession in common – represents a condition of cosmopolitan Right we ought to approach, not a pre-civil condition we decide to leave behind.[6]

According to Flikschuh, this line of argument establishes 'Kant's distinctive metaphysical perspective'.[7] For her, there is a strict parallel between cosmopolitan rights and internal state right: 'This means that the restriction of cosmopolitan Right to global mine-thine relations mirrors parallel restrictions at the level of mine-thine relations between individuals within states'.[8] Although I doubt that the parallel can be drawn this clearly between cosmopolitan and domestic right, because it omits the mentioned problem of the self-authorization of (first and foremost) foreign colonists,[9] my main concern here is to suggest that Flikschuh's reading of the metaphysics of cosmopolitan right is not valid for international law.

If we take Flikschuh's 'spherical surface of the earth' argument as a base for international law, it would not be a new public international law. It would still resemble the law that was codified by the 'sorry comforters' Grotius and Vattel, because it would only regulate the possession of land between monarchical rulers. Injustice in international law does not stem from the unjust possession of territory, but from the unjust possession of sovereignty, which is related to the conquest of this land. A more suitable argument for the metaphysics of international law should highlight the epistemic impossibility of being a fair judge in one's own case. International law therefore needs to be a neutral mode of solving disputes. The possession of land is only the root of the conflict, not the basis for solving it. However, when we take into account that states should be republics, as Kant states in the First Definitive article, we can draw a more detailed picture of how states resolve conflicts; the French nation thus solved the problem of territory for itself when it declared in its 1791 constitution that it would abstain from going to war to conquer territory.[10] This decision was motivated by the republican concern with the freedom of the people.

Kant is therefore convinced that a republican constitution will make a difference for decisions on warfare, as compared to despotic monarchies. The mine-thine problem can be stopped by states themselves, because a republic considers important the freedom of its people to give themselves a constitution, as Kant explains in the Second Preliminary Article of *Perpetual Peace*. Only because monarchs understand their land just as territory and not as the ground of a population having a right to self-determination does territory remain the major problem of international law. The injustice that is the object of international law is the wrongful acquisition of the people's sovereignty by monarchs. This sovereignty is not bound to a special territory; territory and the republican nation are different entities.[11]

Therefore, international law cannot be understood principally in terms of international mine-thine relations as Flikschuh's account suggests. Kantian international law does not simply focus on the transformation of provisional territorial possession into peremptory property. This would only perpetuate the doctrine of monarchical state possession. International law does not aim solely at distributive justice; its aim is also to secure peace as a precondition for security, and ultimately to allow states to transform into republics. In this perspective, it is not just the distribution of territory that international law needs to regulate, but also the democratic self-determination of peoples. The problem of the original acquisition of land takes second place to the problem of the original acquisition of the sovereignty that belongs to the people.

Of course there still remains the problem of judgement. It is the same problem that domestic law had to overcome. Without the metaphysical recognition that we have to accept a common authority no law is possible. So for Kant, international law should primarily overcome epistemic unilateralism. He also acknowledges that a unilateral decision to go to war cannot be equated with a unilateral acquisition of land, which can be retributively regulated. International law is in the state of nature as long as the problem of the unilateral decision to go to war to conquer territory is unresolved. This is the metaphysic of international law: reason irresistibly tells us that the condition of unilateral judgement in international law must have an end. This moral law 'can be *seen* to have an a priori basis and to be necessary' (*MS* 6: 215). In other words, it does not derive from observation; 'instead, reason commands how we are to act even though no example of this could be found, and it takes no account of the advantages we can thereby gain, which only experience could tell us' (*MS* 6: 216).

Careful readers of the *Doctrine of Rights* know that Kant brings up two cases for a possible preventive war: the *potentia tremenda* and the unjust enemy. The *potentia tremenda* is a state that disturbs the balance of power in the international state of nature. And the unjust enemy describes the case in which a state makes the foundation of international law impossible and threatens the freedom of all states. In the case of *potentia tremenda* one single state is entitled to fight against the strong power, but it may also seek out allies. Here, Kant does not speak of a right to change the constitution of the defeated *potentia tremenda*, neither does he mention the requirement that a majority of states be in danger, even though the disorganization of the balance of power affects all states. In the second case, that of the unjust enemy, Kant allows for the right to change the constitution of the state into a constitution favourable to peace. In neither of these two cases does Kant speak of the project of liberal regime change to build a federation out of republics. Kant equally does not mention such a right of 'regime change' in *Perpetual Peace*. Now, the question seems to be this: what are the function and the meaning of the unjust enemy in Kant's peace project? To offer an answer, I will compare the enemy of the territory-based balance of power – the *potentia tremenda* – with Kant's enemy of peace in a federation of states, the unjust enemy.

2. The *potentia tremenda* and the balance of power principle

The balance principle had been widely agreed upon in official European policy since the Peace of Utrecht in 1713. 'The treaty declared that its aim was "establishing and stabilizing the peace and tranquillity of the Christian World by a just equilibrium of power (which is the best and most solid basis of mutual friendship and permanence and concord)"'.[12] Until the end of the eighteenth century, it was a declared aim of the balance principle to 'safeguard the peace of Europe and the freedom and the existence of its smaller states'.[13] But the partitions of Poland in 1772, 1793 and 1795 gave the European public and all small states the horrifying example that weaker states are not protected by this principle when their stronger absolutist neighbours follow the idea of expansion.

Still, it was this principle that served for a judgement concerning wars and interventions. The preservation of the balance became the most important and most widely accepted legal reason for intervention. Under this condition, 'the difficult question for international law was to ascertain when a nation had the right to complain of another nation's growth and its threat to the general balance and, with that, to its own security'.[14] The answer is that nations have 'a right to conserve the balance' and 'to overthrow the growing power by armed force'.[15] A power was growing when it accumulated territory, because territory always meant the people on that territory also. People were immobile; they belonged to the territory, as Kant describes in the Second Preliminary Article: 'For a state is not (like the land on which it resides) a belonging (*patrimonium*). It is a society of human beings that no one other than itself can command or dispose of' (*ZeF* 8: 344). When Prussia, Russia and Austria partitioned Poland the first time in 1772 they were strongly interested in the population of the occupied territories. Russia took approximately 93,000 square kilometres and 1.3

million inhabitants, Prussia roughly 36,000 square kilometres and 340,000 inhabitants, and Austria about 82,000 square kilometres and 2.6 million inhabitants.

Long before the first partitioning of Poland, the balance principle and its consequence – the intervention in the internal affairs of a state – had been very strongly attacked by Johann Heinrich Gottlob von Justi. In his essay *Die Chimäre des Gleichgewichts von Europa* of 1758, Justi explains that the principle of equilibrium would allow for intervention in any state undertaking reforms, if these reforms were employed to strengthen this state. This would be a serious infringement of the principle of the freedom of every state which is to be protected by the equilibrium principle. Maurseth sums up Justi's argument: 'In its consequences, therefore, the balance-of-power doctrine will discourage human progress and greatly reduce the freedom of individual states which it claims to protect'.[16] Kant followed this argument. In *On the Common Saying* of 1793, Kant even uses the German term *Chimäre* to distance himself from the balance principle that he considered to be a *Hirngespinst*, a pipe dream. Kant states: '(E)in dauernder allgemeiner Friede durch die so genannte Balance der Mächte in Europa ist, wie Swifts Haus, welches von einem Baumeister so vollkommen nach allen Gesetzen des Gleichgewichts erbauet war, daß, als sich ein Sperling drauf setzte, es sofort einfiel, ein bloßes Hirngespinst' (*TP* 8: 312).[17]

In the *Doctrine of Right*, Kant speaks of a 'right of prevention (*ius praeventionis*)' ('Recht des Zuvorkommens') under Grotian international law (*MS* 6: 346) against the 'menacing increase in another state's power by its acquisition of territory (*potentia tremenda*)' (*MS* 6: 346). In the state of nature, a reason to go to war is found simply in another's wish to alter the status quo of the existing balance, even if this has occurred without any aggression. The disturbance of this balance is a legal cause for war. 'Accordingly, this is also the basis of the right to a balance of power among all states that are contiguous and could act on one another' (*MS* 6: 346). This means that the balance principle is, for Kant, only a principle of the international state of nature. This shows that it has nothing to do with public international law. The right of balance is from a legal point of view both useless and worthless. It is obvious that Kant rejects the balance principle as a basis for international law. At the same time, he also rejects the world state, the federation with supranational executive power. The third option he offers as something that provides for perpetual peace is collective security.[18] The federal peace union implements the first step towards a system of collective security because it takes the unilateral decision away from the single states and confers it on a collective body. The right of a balance of power is nothing more than a justification of the unilateral right to go to war. This concept of right based on the balance of power is the right of the 'sorry comforters' and has to be overcome. Kant does not 'allow' for war in the case of the *potentia tremenda*, but he describes the law of his era as one in the state of nature.

3. Constitutional change and the 'unjust enemy'

However, Kant deals with the balance in §56 of the *Doctrine of Right* as the right to go to war (*ius ad bellum*) and with the unjust enemy in §60. In between those paragraphs, he addresses the right during a war (*ius in bello*), the right after a war (right of the peace treaty), and the right to peace (right of neutrality). One might expect that Kant would then explain public international law. Before explaining the league of nations in §61, Kant determines the 'right of one state against the unjust enemy' in §60. But he points out in his question what an unjust enemy is that 'each state is judge in its own case', so all states are still in a state of nature (*MS* 6: 349). This is important because this remark reveals that the unjust enemy is a figure of the transformation phase between the state of nature and an enforceable public international law.[19] An 'unjust enemy' is

> an enemy whose publicly expressed will (whether by word or deed) reveals a maxim by which, if it were made a universal rule, any condition of peace among nations would be impossible and, instead, a state of nature would be perpetuated. Violation of public contract is an expression of this sort. Since this can be assumed to be a matter of concern to all nations whose freedom is threatened by it, they are called upon to unite against such misconduct in order to deprive the state of its power to do it. (*MS* 6: 349)

According to this argument, and going against the prohibition on forcible intervention in *Perpetual Peace*, it is permitted to let the defeated unjust enemy adopt a new constitution that is averse to the predisposition to war ('der Neigung zum Kriege ungünstig'). 'But they are not called upon *to divide its territory among themselves*' (*MS* 6: 349). The unjust enemy acts indirectly as the enemy of *all* states, as it concerns the peaceful condition among nations or the rightful order. An unjust enemy is supposed to act in accord with a maxim. To make a maxim visible, a state has to act 'repeatedly and constantly' according to it.[20] The Universal Principle of Right states: 'Any action is *right* if it can coexist with everyone's freedom in accordance with a universal law, or if on its maxim the freedom of choice of each can coexist with everyone's freedom in accordance with a universal law' (*MS* 6: 230). To have a maxim that is directed against law is unjust. Thus, the unjust enemy is the state against which all states together have a collective right of self-defence, if the pieces of evidence for the maxim of the suspected state threatening security and inhibiting the rightful condition- are acknowledged consistently. This may sound as though Kant has strong benchmarks in mind against a state that undercuts the federation and international law through its actions. But it would be false to claim that Kant permits the enforcement of a better – that is, republican – constitution with his notion of the unjust enemy. On the contrary, Kant rejects all assertions that the progress of law could be reached by force, as one can see in his critique of colonialism as a self-authorizing legitimation for conquest and war (*MS* 6: 352ff.). The unjust enemy theory provides no argument for a policy of regime change.

But it may still be unclear from this brief discussion what Kant allows and prohibits here, especially with regard to the new constitution. Here it seems to me that the translation is of greatest importance and a source of ambiguity. A comparison of the translations shows significant differences with the original wording. Kant originally wrote: '. . . sondern es eine neue Verfassung annehmen zu lassen, die, ihrer Natur nach, der Neigung zum Kriege ungünstig ist' (*ZeF* 8: 473). Nisbet translates this passage with 'they can only be made to accept a new constitution of a nature that is unlikely to encourage their warlike inclinations'.[21] Gregor translates differently: '. . . though it can be made to adopt a new constitution that by its nature will be unfavorable to the inclination of war'.[22] Again slightly differently, Colclasure puts it this way: 'Rather one does so in order to let it accept a new constitution, one which according to its nature is unfavourable to the inclination to wage war'.[23] Some interpreters take from Nisbet and Reiss's translation that the states may together give a new constitution to the defeated unjust enemy. In contrast, Colclasure is fully aware of the democratic problem of an imposed constitution and expresses the question whether the people is the only possible subject of the constitutional act. Indeed, Kant nowhere mentions that an external actor could give a people a constitution that contradicts their original contract. Nor does Kant say that the defeated unjust enemy must change its constitution. Only if there was a duty to adopt a certain constitution would it be possible to talk of a right of the victor to change the constitution of a different nation unilaterally. Since Gregor's translation is similar to Nisbet's, I hold Colclasure's version to be the most suitable. His translation alone leaves room for the original meaning of a constitution given by the people itself.

So what does the right to change a state's constitution really mean? To answer this question, we must keep two things in mind. First, in Kant's time there was only one republican state in Europe. This state followed the policy of collective security. France invited all peace-loving nations to build a federation with it; it declared the freedom and equality of all states, the principle of non-intervention, the right of states to choose their constitution and the illegality of any war except for (preventive) defence.[24] That is why conservative scholars find the idea of collective security a dangerous element in the French ideology.[25] Of course, the revolutionaries used the terminology of the tradition of Saint-Pierre and Rousseau. Robespierre declared on 24 April 1793: 'Whoever offends the freedom of a nation, is the enemy of all nations. He is more than an enemy. He is a rebel, a robber, a villain against mankind as such'.[26] That is why the counter-revolutionary monarchies appeared as such 'unjust enemies' for the revolutionaries. Indeed, in the years after 1793, the revolutionary wars developed the dynamics to intervene and change the constitution of defeated monarchical neighbours, first by plebiscite but soon without that. To clarify this point further I will give an historical example – other than Poland, which was also pressured to adopt a constitution by its neighbours – that illustrates what Kant had in mind when he explained the rights of states against an unjust enemy.

When the Anglo-Dutch army was defeated by the French Army of the North in January 1795, the Orangist Monarchy came to an end. Before that, it had been forcibly restored by an invasion of

Prussia and Great Britain in 1787 and fought an anti-revolutionary war against France. In February 1795, Dutch patriots immediately proclaimed a Batavian Republic. But for the Dutch, the 'gravest anxiety was whether the French would . . . impose a conqueror's peace complete with requisitions, assignates and perhaps territorial annexations'.[27] Officially, the French government declared – in accordance with Kant's views – that 'only the Batavian people, exercising its sovereignty, can change or modify its form of government'.[28] But a French faction wanted to annex Holland. General Sauviac, for example, argued that Holland 'has done nothing to avoid being classed among the general order of our conquests . . . It follows from this that there can be no reason to treat her any differently from a conquered country'.[29] In March the French government disclosed its conditions for peace: an indemnity of 100 million florins, a loan of another 100 million florins and the cession of a large territory.[30] The Dutch envoy Meijer wrote to the French Committee on 26 March 1795: '. . . it is with the most grievous indignation that we have learned of your desire to add to the French Republic a part of our territory, of which, *according to your own principles*, the Batavian Republic may not alienate without the freely expressed consent of the inhabitants of that part of the Republic'.[31] These words make clear how the old principle of territory and the new principle of self-determination collide.

Moreover, the spontaneously established meetings of 'Provisional Representatives' in the Batavian Republic were not able to formulate a constitution. The Assembly did not give its assent to a final version of the constitution (which proved to be very similar to the bourgeois French constitution of 1795) until 10 May 1797.[32] The Batavian constitution was the first constitution in modern Europe that was decided upon by its people. However, in the referendum on 8 August 1797 it was rejected because it could not win a majority in any of the nine provinces.[33] As a reaction, a group of Dutch revolutionaries purged the legislature on 22 January 1798. This *coup d'état* was directed by the French Ambassador Delacroix. The group arrested their opponents and erected a revolutionary executive.[34] A unitary government was erected and an 'Interim Executive Directory of Five' resembling the French Directory was set up. The French Ambassador wrote to his minister Talleyrand: 'An 18 Fructidor as wisely conceived and as happily executed as that which saved France has taken place this morning'.[35]

The French coup is an example of an unjust intervention in the constitution of a state. Now we see what it means when Kant writes about the unjust enemy 'to let *it* accept a new constitution' (emphasis added). According to Kant, the French ought to have waited for the people to accept a constitution, even though one had been rejected in 1797. They were neither allowed to decide on the constitution as an occupier nor to give the people a constitution by a coup. When Kant explains what measures the united states may and may not take against the unjust enemy he emphasizes the right of the people: 'But they are not called upon *to divide its territory among themselves* and to make the state, as it were, disappear from the earth, since that would be an injustice against its people, which cannot lose its original right to unite itself into a commonwealth, though it can be made to adopt a new constitution that by its nature will be unfavourable to the inclination of war' (*MS* 6: 349).

4. Overcoming self-authorization by collective judgement

Kant wants a federation of states, that is a congress 'to be established for deciding their disputes in a civil way, as if by a lawsuit, rather than in a barbaric way (the way of savages), namely by war' (*MS* 6: 351). The cooperation between states overcomes the balance principle and the connected self-authorization for war. Similarly, the league of nations was to attempt to decide disputes by a lawsuit and deny the right of each state to go to war: 'The principle of law which must remain dominant is the principle that the collective judgement of the community of nations must replace the right of each State to be the judge in its own case and the collective power of the community be substituted for the old right of the individual State to take the law into its own hands'.[36]

The theory of law developed by Hans Kelsen explores the link between collective measures and international law further. Kelsen answered the question of the fragility of international law with the idea of a decentralized sanctioning of legal violations.[37] For Kelsen as for Kant, a right must have the option to be enforced. However, as measured by the internal law of a state, international law appears to be 'primitive law'. It is – as in archaic societies – based on the principle of self-help. According to Kelsen, international law has decentralized possibilities of reprisal and war for sanctioning, even if it does not have a central monopoly of force at its disposal. This resembles the position that Kant holds: that a collective war is the sanctioning measure (not a punishment) against the unjust enemy, the judgement of all states being necessary to avoid unilateral self-authorization. The first way out of the primitive form is thus that of a collective enforcement action.[38] This action is decentralized when the international community acts through the individual state. Its centralization can take place based on the decision that only a central organ of the international community has the right to decide on the enforcement actions against members. The highest degree of centralization is reached – for Kelsen, not for Kant – when the members agree to their disarmament and when decision and the monopoly of force are central organs of the community. Under the United Nations Charter, the Security Council is the only organ of the UN competent as such to use force against its members as well as non-members.[39]

This is one of the major differences from the Covenant of The League of Nations.[40] This difference shows how big a step the Charter takes in the direction of a centralized collective security. 'The collective enforcement actions provided by the Covenant were almost completely decentralized. It was for the members, and not for a central organ of the League to decide whether a violation of the Covenant by illegal resort to war had occurred, and to decide what enforcement action had to be taken'.[41] This decentralized system of the Covenant is still very close to the one Kant proposed. All actions against the 'unjust enemy' are decided and taken on by the members themselves. Kelsen states therefore that 'under the Covenant, collective security, because of its decentralization, was indeed nothing else but a kind of collective self-defense'.[42] Hence this difference shows once again how close the Covenant is to Kant when conceived as a first step out of the primitive law. When the unjust enemy threatens the public treaties and the freedom of all states, they defend themselves collectively. This way one can understand Kant's idea of the collective actions against the unjust enemy as a form of collective self-defence. Recent scholars express this thought similarly, and it sounds like a summary of the results so far: 'Since the international community lacks a central authority for the enforcement of law and the maintenance of peace, it is necessary to provide a substitute solution for such central authority. This could be done by organizing the common defence of all States against the illegal use of force and at the same time by reducing to a minimum the right to and necessity of a State's individual law enforcement'.[43] Perhaps one can take as a result that with the notion of the unjust enemy, Kant brought us to the idea of collective security.

At the same time, Kant is very much concerned with the actions that should be taken against the unjust enemy: only certain weapons and means should be used and the respective state must be neither partitioned nor punished. While it seems to be clear that the right against the unjust enemy is a right of the community of states to collective self-defence, there still remains the question of Kant's addressees. Since he writes that the defeated unjust enemy should have the right to adopt a new constitution, I think that Kant spoke to his French friends and democratic readers. He explained to them that even their rights in the war against despotic regimes were limited. Even in the case of the unjust enemy – and here he followed the revolutionaries' terminology – any self-authorization shall be as limited as possible. He told the French revolutionaries that they could only decide that a state was an 'unjust enemy' when the majority of states shared the French judgement. The National Assembly in Paris could not decide upon this question alone. It has to be noted that Kant does not promote a liberal constitution, but he claims that the people of a defeated unjust enemy should be able to choose a new constitution. The function of the figure of an unjust enemy is the limitation of any self-authorization to declare war, occupy territory or manipulate constitutions – even on the part of the first European republic. Since self-authorization is inevitable without a judge, the step towards public international law is to leave behind classical great-power politics that focuses on territory and unilateral judgement. The first aim of international law must be to protect the people's right to adopt a constitution, not the redistribution and peremptory transformation of territory into secure property. The original right of citizens to self-determination is the basis of the metaphysics of Kant's international law.[44]

Notes

1 Susan Meld Shell, 'Reflections on a pleonasm: Kant on just war and "unjust enemies"', *Kantian Review*, 10/1 (2005), 82–111.

2 See as an example for the discussion Reinhard Hesse, 'Über Kants vermeintlichen Wandel vom Friedensutopisten zum Kriegsapologeten',

Kant-Studien, 98 (2007), 218–22, in reaction to the article by Heinz Kluss, 'Immanuel Kant und die Reichweite der Kanonen. Die Abkehr von der Illusion des ewigen Friedens', *Internationale Politik*, 11–12 (2004), 155–62.

3 Unless noted otherwise, all following quotations will refer to the Akademie edition while using the translation by Mary J. Gregor in Kant, *Practical Philosophy*, ed. and trans. M. J. Gregor (Cambridge: Cambridge University Press, 1999).

4 Georg Cavallar, 'Commentary: Susan Meld Shell, "Reflections on a pleonasm: Kant on just war and 'unjust enemies'"', *Kantian Review*, 11/1 (2006), 125–40.

5 John MacMillan, 'A Kantian protest against the peculiar discourse of inter-liberal state peace', *Millennium: Journal of International Studies*, 24/3 (1994), 549–62 (citation 559).

6 Katrin Flikschuh, *Kant and Modern Political Philosophy* (Cambridge: Cambridge University Press, 2000), p. 180.

7 Ibid., p. 180.

8 Ibid., p. 189.

9 For an account mixing Flikschuh's argument with an anti-colonialist impetus and the right of global communication see Peter Niesen, 'Colonialism and hospitality', *Politics and Ethics Review*, 3 (2007), 90–108.

10 Article VI of the constitution, see Günther Franz, *Staatsverfassungen*, 3rd edn (Darmstadt: Wissenschaftliche Buchgesellschaft, 1975), pp. 366–9.

11 Ingeborg Maus, 'Die Bedeutung nationalstaatlicher Grenzen. Oder: Die Transformation des Territorialstaates zur Demokratie', *Blätter für Deutsche und Internationale Politik*, 3 (2001), 313–23.

12 Alfred Vagts and Detlef F. Vagts, 'The balance of power in international law: a history of an idea', *The American Journal of International Law*, 73/4 (1979), 555–80 (citation 560).

13 M. S. Anderson, 'Eighteenth-century theories of the balance of power', in R. Hatton and M. S. Anderson (eds.), *Studies in Diplomatic Histories* (Harlow: Longman, 1970), p. 184.

14 Vagts and Vagts, 'The balance of power in international law', 565.

15 Ibid., 562.

16 Per Mauseth, 'Balance-of-power thinking from the Renaissance to the French Revolution', *Journal of Peace Research*, 1 (1964), 120–36.

17 Colclasure's translation: 'For an enduring general peace by means of the so called *balance of powers in Europe* is, like *Swift's* house, which was built so perfectly by a master builder according to all the laws of equilibrium that it immediately collapsed when a sparrow landed on it, is a mere fantasy' (Kant, *Toward Perpetual Peace and Other*

Writings on Politics, Peace, and History, ed. P. Kleingeld, trans. D. L. Colclasure (New Haven, CT: Yale University Press, 2006), p. 65; (original emphasis). Nisbet translates 'illusion': see Kant, *Political Writings*, ed. H. Reiss, trans. H. B. Nisbet (Cambridge: Cambridge University Press, 1991), p. 92.

18 For a more sceptical account that agrees on this point see Gabriel L. Negretto, 'Kant and the illusion of collective security', *Journal of International Affairs*, 46/2 (1993), 501–23.

19 Georg Cavallar, *Kant and the Theory and Practice of International Right* (Cardiff: University of Wales Press, 1999), pp. 103–12. Very critical on this point is Harald Müller, who states the term 'unjust enemy' would make no sense in the state of nature and must therefore belong to the phase of (forceful) transformation to the 'perpetual peace'. See Harald Müller, 'Kants Schurkenstaat. Der "ungerechte Feind" und die Selbstermächtigung zum Kriege', in A. Geis (ed.), *Den Krieg überdenken. Kriegsbegriffe und Kriegstheorien in der Kontroverse* (Baden-Baden: Nomos, 2006), p. 239. For discussion see Oliver Eberl and Peter Niesen, 'Kein Frieden mit dem "ungerechten Feind"? Erzwungene Verfassunggebung im Ausgang aus dem Naturzustand', in Oliver Eberl (ed.), *Transnationalisierung der Volkssouveränität. Radikale Demokratie diesseits und jenseits des Staates* (Stuttgart: Steiner, 2011), 219–49.

20 Cavallar, *Kant and the Theory and Practice of International Right*, p. 105.

21 Kant, *Political Writings*.

22 Kant, *Practical Philosophy*.

23 Kant, *Toward Perpetual Peace and Other Writings*.

24 Robert Redslob, 'Völkerrechtliche Ideen der französischen Revolution', in *Festgabe für Otto Mayer (1916)* (Aalen: Scientia Verlag, 1974).

25 Wilhelm Georg Grewe, *Epochen der Völkerrechtsgeschichte* (Baden-Baden: Nomos, 1984), pp. 490ff.

26 Redslob, 'Völkerrechtliche Ideen', 286. My translation.

27 Simon Schama, *Patriots and Liberators: Revolution in the Netherlands 1780–1813* (New York: Alfred A. Knopf, 1977), p. 195.

28 Ibid.

29 Ibid., p. 201.

30 In the Treaty of The Hague of May 1795 these conditions were more or less stipulated: France took Maastricht, Venlo and Dutch Flanders. See Schama 1977: 207.

31 Ibid., p. 203.

32 Ibid., pp. 265ff.

33 Ibid., p. 269.

34 Ibid., p. 274.

35 Ibid., p. 309.

36 Charles G. Fenwick, 'The "failure" of the League of Nations', *American Journal of International Law*, 30/3 (1936), 506–9.

37 Jochen von Bernstorff, *Der Glaube an das universale Recht. Zur Völkerrechtstheorie Hans Kelsens und seiner Schüler* (Baden-Baden: Nomos, 2001), pp. 74–9.

38 Hans Kelsen, 'Collective security and collective self-defense under the Charter of the United Nations', *The American Journal of International Law*, 42/4 (1948), 783–96 (citation 783).

39 Ibid., 785.

40 Jobst Delbrück, 'Collective security', in *Encyclopedia of Public International Law*, ed. Rudolf Bernhardt et al., vol. 1 (1992), pp. 646–56.

41 Kelsen, 'Collective security', 787.

42 Ibid., 793.

43 Delbrück, 'Collective security', 646ff.

44 I am grateful for comments by Tomas Baum, Jochen von Bernstorff, Charlotte Dany, Harald Müller, Howard Williams and Ilya Wynham. For a more elaborated interpretation of Kant's *Perpetual Peace* and the *Metaphysic of Morals* in terms of 'epistemic unilateralism', see Immanuel Kant, *Zum ewigen Frieden/Auszüge aus der Rechtslehre. Kommentar von Oliver Eberl und Peter Niesen* (Berlin: Suhrkamp, 2011).

References

Anderson, M. S., 'Eighteenth-century theories of the balance of power', in R. Hatton and M. S. Anderson (eds), *Studies in Diplomatic Histories* (Harlow: Longman, 1970).

Cavallar, G., *Kant and the Theory and Practice of International Right* (Cardiff: University of Wales Press, 1999).

——, 'Commentary: Susan Meld Shell, "Reflections on a pleonasm: Kant on just war and 'unjust enemies'"', *Kantian Review*, 11/1 (2006), 125–40.

Delbrück, J., 'Collective security', in *Encyclopedia of Public International Law*, ed. Rudolf Bernhardt et al., vol. 1 (1992), pp. 646–56.

Eberl, O. and Niesen, P., 'Kein Frieden mit dem "ungerechten Feind"? Erzwungene Verfassunggebung im Ausgang aus dem Naturzustand', in Oliver Eberl (ed.), *Transnationalisierung der Volkssouveränität. Radikale Demokratie diesseits und jenseits des Staates* (Stuttgart: Steiner, 2011), 219–49.

Fenwick, C. G., 'The "failure" of the League of Nations', *American Journal of International Law*, 30/3 (1936), 506–9.

Flikschuh, K., *Kant and Modern Political Philosophy* (Cambridge: Cambridge University Press, 2000).

Franz, G., *Staatsverfassungen*, third edn (Darmstadt: Wissenschaftliche Buchgesellschaft, 1975).

Grewe, W. G., *Epochen der Völkerrechtsgeschichte* (Baden-Baden: Nomos, 1984).

Hesse, R., 'Über Kants vermeintlichen Wandel vom Friedensutopisten zum Kriegsapologeten', *Kant-Studien*, 98 (2007), 218–22.

Kant, I., *Political Writings*, ed. H. Reiss, trans. H. B. Nisbet (Cambridge: Cambridge University Press, 1991).

——, *Practical Philosophy*, ed. and trans. M. J. Gregor (Cambridge: Cambridge University Press, 1999).

——, *Toward Perpetual Peace and Other Writings on Politics, Peace, and History*, ed. P. Kleingeld, trans. D. L. Colclasure (New Haven, CT: Yale University Press, 2006).

——, *Zum ewigen Frieden/Auszüge aus der Rechtslehre. Kommentar von Oliver Eberl und Peter Niesen* (Berlin: Suhrkamp, 2011).

Kelsen, H., 'Collective security and collective self-defense under the Charter of the United Nations', *The American Journal of International Law*, 42/4 (1948), 783–96.

Kluss, H., 'Immanuel Kant und die Reichweite der Kanonen. Die Abkehr von der Illusion des ewigen Friedens', *Internationale Politik*, 11–12 (2004), 155–62.

MacMillan, J., 'A Kantian protest against the peculiar discourse of interliberal state peace', *Millennium: Journal of International Studies*, 24/3 (1994), 549–62.

Maurseth, P., 'Balance-of-power thinking from the Renaissance to the French Revolution', *Journal of Peace Research*. 1 (1964): 120–36.

Maus, I., 'Die Bedeutung nationalstaatlicher Grenzen. Oder: Die Transformation des Territorialstaates zur Demokratie', *Blätter für Deutsche und Internationale Politik*, 3 (2001), 313–23.

Müller, H., 'Kants Schurkenstaat. Der "ungerechte Feind" und die Selbstermächtigung zum Kriege', in A. Geis (ed.), *Den Krieg überdenken. Kriegsbegriffe und Kriegstheorien in der Kontroverse* (Baden-Baden: Nomos, 2006), 229–49.

Negretto, G. L., 'Kant and the illusion of collective security', *Journal of International Affairs*, 46/2 (1993), 501–23.

Niesen, P., 'Colonialism and hospitality', *Politics and Ethics Review*, 3 (2007), 90–108.

Redslob, R., 'Völkerrechtliche Ideen der französischen Revolution', in *Festgabe für Otto Mayer (1916)* (Aalen: Scientia Verlag, 1974).

Schama, S., *Patriots and Liberators: Revolution in the Netherlands 1780–1813* (New York: Alfred A. Knopf, 1977).

Shell, S. M., 'Reflections on a pleonasm: Kant on just war and "unjust enemies"', *Kantian Review*, 10/1 (2005), 82–111.

Vagts, A. and Vagts, D. F., 'The balance of power in international law: a history of an idea', *The American Journal of International Law*, 73/4 (1979), 555–80.

Von Bernstorff, J., *Der Glaube an das universal Recht. Zur Völkerrechtstheorie Hans Kelsens und seiner Schüler* (Baden-Baden: Nomos, 2001).

Index